Music Teacher Education: Future Perspectives

Music Teacher Education: Future Perspectives

Edited by Kristyn Payne

www.larsen-keller.com

Music Teacher Education: Future Perspectives
Edited by Kristyn Payne
ISBN: 979-8-88836-010-1 (Hardback)

© 2023 Larsen & Keller

Published by Larsen and Keller Education,
5 Penn Plaza,
19th Floor,
New York, NY 10001, USA

Cataloging-in-Publication Data

Music teacher education : future perspectives / edited by Kristyn Payne.
   p. cm.
Includes bibliographical references and index.
ISBN 979-8-88836-010-1
1. Music teachers--Training of. 2. Music--Instruction and study. I. Payne, Kristyn.
MT1 .M87 2023
780.71--dc23

This book contains information obtained from authentic and highly regarded sources. Copyright for all individual chapters remain with the respective authors as indicated. All chapters are published with permission under the Creative Commons Attribution License or equivalent. A wide variety of references are listed. Permission and sources are indicated; for detailed attributions, please refer to the permissions page and list of contributors. Reasonable efforts have been made to publish reliable data and information, but the authors, editors and publisher cannot assume any responsibility for the validity of all materials or the consequences of their use.

Trademark Notice: Registered trademark of products or corporate names are used only for explanation and identification without intent to infringe.

For more information regarding Larsen and Keller Education and its products, please visit the publisher's website www.larsen-keller.com

Contents

Preface...VII

Chapter 1   **Intercultural Game in Music Teacher Education: Exploring El Sistema**...1
Eva Sæther

Chapter 2   **Intercultural Music Teacher Education in Israel: Re-imagining Religious Segregation through Culturally Responsive Teaching**.................................20
Amira Ehrlich and Belal Badarne

Chapter 3   **Engaging Practitioners as Inquirers: Co-Constructing Visions for Music Teacher Education**.................36
Danielle Shannon Treacy

Chapter 4   **Policy, Interculturality and the Potential of Core Practices in Music Teacher Education**.................56
Patrick Schmidt and Joseph Abramo

Chapter 5   **Structure and Fragmentation: The Current Tensions and Possible Transformation of Intercultural Music Teacher Education**...73
Albi Odendaal

Chapter 6   **The Discomfort of Intercultural Learning in Music Teacher Education**...86
Alexis A. Kallio and Heidi Westerlund

Chapter 7   **Assessing Intercultural Competence in Teacher Education: A Missing Link**.................................101
Sapna Thapa

Chapter 8   **Expanding Learning Frames in Music Teacher Education: Student Placement in a Palestinian Refugee Camp**...115
Brit Ågot Brøske

VI   Contents

Chapter 9   **Narrating Change, Voicing Values and Co-constructing Visions for Intercultural Music Teacher Education**.....................132
Laura Miettinen, Heidi Westerlund and Claudia Gluschankof

Chapter 10   **To Honor and Inform: Addressing Cultural Humility in Intercultural Music Teacher Education in Canada**.....................149
Lori-Anne Dolloff

Chapter 11   **The Reinvented Music Teacher-Researcher in the Making: Conducting Educational Development through Intercultural Collaboration**.....................163
Vilma Timonen, Anna Houmann and Eva Sæther

Chapter 12   **Bridging Musical Worlds: Musical Collaboration Between Student Musician-Educators and South Sudanese Australian Youth**.....................177
Kathryn Marsh, Catherine Ingram and Samantha Dieckmann

Permissions

List of Contributors

Index

Preface

Over the recent decade, advancements and applications have progressed exponentially. This has led to the increased interest in this field and projects are being conducted to enhance knowledge. The main objective of this book is to present some of the critical challenges and provide insights into possible solutions. This book will answer the varied questions that arise in the field and also provide an increased scope for furthering studies.

Music teacher education (or music education) is a field of practice that trains educators for careers as elementary or secondary music teachers, and school or music conservatory ensemble directors. It is also an area of research that deals with the ways of teaching and learning music. Music education encompasses various domains of learning, including the psychomotor domain (responsible for development of skills), the cognitive domain (responsible for acquisition of knowledge) and the affective domain (responsible for internalization of knowledge), along with music appreciation and sensitivity. Some of the major focus areas related to future research and practice in music teacher education include research education and research as intervention, reflexivity and professional learning in intercultural encounters, the capacity to aspire in music teacher education, and intercultural music education as political engagement. This book elucidates the concepts and innovative models around prospective developments with respect to music teacher education. It is appropriate for students seeking detailed information in this area of study as well as for music teachers.

I hope that this book, with its visionary approach, will be a valuable addition and will promote interest among readers. Each of the authors has provided their extraordinary competence in their specific fields by providing different perspectives as they come from diverse nations and regions. I thank them for their contributions.

Editor

Intercultural Game in Music Teacher Education: Exploring El Sistema in Sweden

Eva Sæther

Abstract El Sistema, the originally Venezuelan music teaching movement is spreading worldwide, suggesting Western classical music as a tool for counteracting poverty and segregation. In Sweden, this represents an interesting and perhaps provoking twist, as the hegemony of classical music in music teacher education has since long been replaced by the hegemony of popular music. Based on fieldwork during the implementation of El Sistema in Malmö, the most multicultural town in Sweden, this chapter analyses El Sistema through the concept of habitus crises, an important ingredient in the development of intercultural pedagogic competencies. Through the understanding of El Sistema as a glocal phenomenon, the potential of the El Sistema intervention is discussed. The discussion is framed by a mapping of the tension fields that El Sistema teachers are navigating. The experiences of the El Sistema teachers in Malmö point towards a music teacher training that actively prepares for teaching in segregated, multi-cultural and socio-economic vulnerable areas. The chapter concludes with suggestions for future music teacher training in interacting ethnospaces: stimulating habitus crises and promoting transformative learning.

Keywords Habitus crises · El Sistema · Intercultural competence

1 Introduction

The Europe of today might best be described as fluid *ethnospaces*, with migration and the conditions for integration as one of the greatest challenges. The concept of ethnospace, introduced by Arjun Appadurai (1992), takes into account that earlier socio-cultural "wholes," such as communities and villages, have been substituted by cosmopolitan and deterritorialized reproduction of group identity. The concept covers how "ethnospaces of today's world are profoundly interactive" (Appadurai

---

E. Sæther (✉)
Malmö Academy of Music, Lund University, Malmö, Sweden
e-mail: eva.saether@mhm.lu.se

1992, 48), and, furthermore, permits an understanding of modern belonging, beyond all national reference (Sloterdijk 2000), and of urban landscapes with "transnational dynamic and fluid occupancy" (Montilla 2014, 143). It is in these ethnospaces that the originally Venezuelan music-teaching movement El Sistema is rapidly spreading, suggesting a format for music education that promotes integration by using Western art music as one of the main tools for developing social cohesion. To music educators who have been questioning the relevance of Western art music as a viable model in a global world, this choice of genre might be surprising, or even provoking. Certainly, this was the case in Sweden, where already in the 1970s a national investigation on music education suggested that a wider range of genres and approaches to learning needed to be included in higher music education in order to address the needs of diverse societies (Olsson 1993). This investigation led to a reform, so successful that today the pendula has moved to the other side, placing pop-rock as the dominant genre in Swedish classrooms (Lindgren and Ericsson 2010).

This chapter takes the El Sistema in Malmö as a starting point for reflections on the 'intercultural game' (Pöllman 2016) in music education and the need for, and the development of, intercultural pedagogic competence in music education in today's interactive ethnospaces. After a section on intercultural pedagogic competence, the following two sections describe El Sistema as a *glocal* phenomenon, and give an overview of the competing discourses that have shaped music education in Sweden during the past decades. The term glocal, first introduced in social scientific discourse in the early 1990s by sociologist Roland Robertson, highlights the need to rethink the local and the global, not as opposites, but as two sides of the same coin (Roudometof 2015). Here the concept of glocalization is used to describe "how people relate linguistically, culturally and cognitively to one another and to the institutions they inhabit in times of change" (Sarroub 2008, 61). The third and fourth sections analyze the intercultural game within El Sistema and how established practices and the music teacher habitus might be challenged in the glocal context. In this way, the tension fields embedded in the El Sistema are approached as affordances for the development of intercultural skills in music teacher education. In the context of teaching an "alien" music genre to large groups of children in classrooms where Swedish is the minority language, it is in the daily efforts that teachers both need and develop intercultural pedagogic competence. As a whole, the chapter argues that in the Nordic context, El Sistema represents an interesting twist, since its implementation has the capacity to assist in developing a culturally sensitive music teacher education, based on theoretical awareness and practical experience.

2 Intercultural Pedagogic Competence

Despite the lack of reflexivity on intercultural competences in Swedish teacher education (Lorentz 2016), the idea of interculturality is not new in this context or in wider global policy. The term *intercultural* appeared 1974 in a UNESCO recommendation on education (UNESCO 1974). Under paragraph 22 it is stated that increased efforts to develop and mediate an international and intercultural approach are needed at all stages and in all forms of education. Both *intercultural* and *international* are used together with words such as *understanding* and *approach*. A historical overview of the discourse on intercultural education in Sweden shows how this vagueness in regard to the meaning of terms has continued in policy documents. However, a 1983 governmental document, referring to research and intercultural education (SOU 1983) suggests that this proposition never led to action or reform. In a 1985 parliamentary decision, intercultural education is described as an attitude, something that should permeate all school subjects (Lorentz 2016). This attitude, however, was never put into concrete action.

In the beginning of the 1990s, the Swedish government decided on a new curriculum, (Lpo 94 1994), in which multicultural society is mentioned and school is described as a cultural meeting place. The concept of *intercultural* has now disappeared from the national school documents and has been replaced by *internationalization* in which contact with schools and students in other countries is considered to be sufficient practice to develop the school as a cultural meeting place (Lorentz 2016). The same disappearance of the term *intercultural* applies to Swedish policy documents for teacher education. The report on new teacher-education (SOU 2008) problematically only mentions intercultural competence in the section on "Swedish for immigrants". In the current curricula for elementary school (Lgr 11 2011) and upper secondary school (Gy 11 2011), it is again internationalization that should contribute to increased understanding of multicultural society. A suggested (and very disappointing) interpretation of this disappearance of intercultural competence is articulated by Lorentz (2016): "Intercultural competence is good for Swedish students abroad, and might be good for immigrants in Sweden, it is not necessary for Swedish citizens" (Lorentz 2016, 70, my translation). It is therefore not surprising that intercultural teacher competence is not a topic of study in most Swedish teacher training (Lorenz 2016).

The tendency to diminish the value of intercultural competence contrasts what Touraine (2003) suggests is most important for democracy: an educational system that teaches intercultural communication. Expanding on what intercultural communication implies, Lorentz (2016) suggests that intercultural pedagogic competence is conceptualized and practiced as three different competences in interaction: communicative competence, social competence and civic competence. These three domains of intercultural pedagogic competence are related to what Illeris (2015) describes as the three areas that contribute to learning: functionality, sensitivity and sociality.

With the concept of *functionality*, Illeris (2015) shows that every learning process includes development of meaning, significance and skills. *Sensitivity* refers to the fact that learning processes benefit from mental and physical balance. *Sociality*, finally, points at how learning processes include our relation to and interplay with the surrounding world. Lorenz (2016) introduces five key phases in the process leading up to the goal – interculturally competent and aware teachers. The first phase, deconstruction, is to see or rather to choose to see actions, values and norms

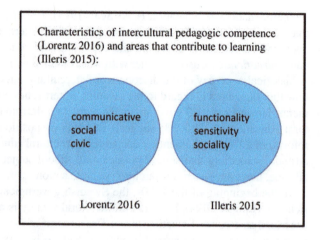

Fig. 1 The three characteristics of intercultural pedagogic competence (Lorentz 2016) and the three areas that contribute to learning (Illeris 2015) as tools for music teacher education in current ethnospaces

in one's own culture, and to be aware of one's own cultural identity/identities. This is to clarify one's own starting point and hopefully increasing one's understanding about the consequences of the actions of our own identity work. In the second phase, students learn to define and understand intercultural communication, for example, by their own hands-on experiences. The third phase, ethnorelative understanding, facilitates the motivation and capacity for accepting cultural differences, and understanding the concept of pluralism, for example, in relation to epistemological issues. The fourth phase involves cultural awareness, as students learn to see themselves as cultural products and as social creatures, and to understand intercultural sensitivity. Finally, the fifth phase on reflexivity aims at internalizing a reflective, intercultural approach towards the world, to acquire knowledge on cultural and social actions and norms. In music teacher education, the tool box (Fig. 1) might be used when guiding future music teachers through the five phases leading towards intercultural pedagogical competence.

Research shows that a content that creates integration and sociality is beneficial for learning (Illeris 2015; Lorentz and Bergstedt 2006; Lorentz 2016). In times where life conditions demand radical social readjustments, Illeris (2015) recommends *transformative learning,* in other words, a learning that fosters abilities to go beyond what is taken for granted. Transformative learning might also follow after what Pöllman (2016) describes as habitus crises (discussed below), or habitus dislocations as part of the intercultural game.

3 El Sistema as a Glocal Phenomenon

The outspoken ambition of El Sistema in Sweden is to contribute to the process of integration in multicultural societies is prompted by the fact that Sweden, as the EU at large, is faced with a need for strategies and actions for future social cohesion (see Pyrhönen et al. 2017). By 1 January 2015, the number of people living in the EU who were born outside of the EU was 34.3 million (Eurostat 2016). Since then, the Syrian crisis has added to the migration flows. In 2015 in Sweden, a total of 162,877 refugees applied for asylum, and around 35,000 of them were unaccompanied children (Migrationsinfo 2016), whose country of origin was most commonly Syria and Afghanistan. In Malmö, 32% of the inhabitants are immigrants, representing 186 countries (Malmö Stad 2019). This situation forms a challenge for all dimensions of society and not the least for the EU cultural sector responsible for handling the situation. A recent EU report (EU Voices of Culture 2016) on the role of cultural participation in promoting inclusion describes culture as the perfect arena for developing and maintaining democracy because culture "provides spaces for the articulation and dissemination of complex ideas, and facilitates broad participation in social space" (2016, 8). Hence, the cultural sector is "the perfect space from which to catalyse the development of polity and society as spaces in which refugees and other new citizens are afforded equal voice and status" (2016, 8). The Swedish El Sistema ambition emphasises social inclusion and democracy, thereby aligning to current trends in Swedish music education discourse, emphasizing the need for music schools and institutions to reach and involve all citizens and thereby contribute to a sustainable society.

The music education system El Sistema started initially in 1975 in Venezuela as a project designed to foster the training of Venezuelan musicians, and later as a tool for combatting poverty and to provide music education for children in the streets. The founder José Antonio Abreu introduced "The Foundation for the National Network of Youth and Children Orchestras of Venezuela" as a national project, but today El Sistema has spread to more than 60 countries and involves about one million children (Sistema Global 2016; Clausson and Thanner 2015).

In 1993, El Sistema received UNESCO's international music prize and since then its international success has grown alongside its list of awards, including the Swedish alternative Nobel Prize (the Right Livelihood Award) 2001, and the TED prize in 2009 (TED 2018a). It is clear, simply by looking at the prize list, that the expectations of El Sistema as a global "game changer" are high; for example, "The TED Prize is awarded annually to a leader with a creative bold wish to spark global change (…) solving some of the world's most pressing problems" (TED 2018b). The idea of classical music education as a means to save at-risk children, and the assumption that democracy can be promoted by giving all children the right to develop expressive tools, has given El Sistema many followers, but also raised critical concerns. We can ask, could it be, as Geoffrey Baker (2014) suggests, that El Sistema rather orchestrates youth to submission, and that Western art music is not the ultimate tool for music education in a society characterized by cultural diversity?

Given that it has substantially spread internationally and experienced varied reception, El Sistema takes on new local interpretations as it lands in different educational traditions. In Sweden, El Sistema is promoted not as a music education format that counteracts poverty but rather as a possibility for more integration in multicultural societies. In 2016, El Sistema started an orchestra (the Dream Orchestra) for newly arrived immigrants in Gothenburg. Music schools in 27

Swedish municipalities have started El Sistema activities, reaching out to 7000 children (El Sistema Sverige 2016). The El Sistema Sweden webpage states under the subheading "democracy and diversity" that the aim is to strengthen democratic values. Other ambitions are musical diversity, reaching out to both children and adults and involving local settings as well as established official contexts and institutions. The fact that formal institutions for music education and music performance are included has added value: "This contributes to the social mobilization that is crucial in places where segregation has hampered the possibilities for human growth. Together with music!" (El Sistema Sverige 2016, my translation). This ambition of democratic musical diversity is noteworthy, considering the original El Sistema's focus on Western art music.

Unlike in many other countries, the Swedish El Sistema challenges the established musical repertoire in schools (Lindgren and Bergman 2014) and simultaneously presents a countermovement to the general tendency to marginalize music as a subject in favor of the core subjects that are measured in the PISA tests, such as language and mathematics. The recent national report on the future of Swedish municipal music schools (SOU 2016) suggests a national policy that strengthens both the role and quality of the municipal music schools. It also states that these schools "can, want to, and should play an important role" (SOU 2016, 275) in the efforts to include new immigrants. El Sistema, with the outspoken aim to include 100 schools in the next few years (El Sistema Sverige 2016), has an interesting catalytic position in the ongoing change process of the municipal music schools in Sweden.

In Malmö, El Sistema started in 2013 at two comprehensive schools located in a part of the city where 85 different nationalities are represented and 33% of the inhabitants are born abroad. Malmö's El Sistema first started as a regular part of the municipal music school with the aim to protect "the cultural rights for all, and in the long run include more districts of Malmö" (Lorensson 2013). It would soon be obvious to the six carefully selected music teachers that they had been given the task to balance expectations of high artistic results with expectations of a music education that defeats segregation between privileged and socio-economically vulnerable parts of Malmö's population. The municipal music school that offers extracurricular music tuition within the region is financed by tax income. As such, the school should serve all citizens, a task that has been difficult, in spite of numerous projects to attract students from segregated areas (Hofvander Trulsson 2010). Based on research on how Malmö is growing into an increasingly segregated city (Salonen 2012; Stigendal 2007), the Malmö Commission recommended knowledge alliances to stimulate more democratic processes of governance, and an approach towards economic growth that includes culture (Stigendal and Östergren 2013). In Malmö, the Commission report paved the way for El Sistema, and influenced its practical interpretation. One thousand and two hundred children in Malmö are active in El Sistema. For nursery-school children, the program entails choir and eurythmics, and school children are offered violin, cello, trumpet, trombone, horn, percussion, eurythmics, choir, and orchestra. The children have lessons three times a week, plus concerts for parents once a month, and several external concerts each semester.

Thirteen music teachers are employed, and all of these teachers have a degree from the 5-year music teacher program at the Malmö Academy of Music. Members from the Malmö Symphony Orchestra regularly visit the El Sistema children as inspiring musicians – not as teachers – and the children regularly perform with the orchestra as part of their performing activities both in the local community and at the concert house.

4   Emerging Antagonistic Justifications

Research on the development of El Sistema in Gothenburg points at how current dominating discourses in Swedish music education are challenged by the teaching of classical orchestral instruments in music schools (Lindgren and Bergman 2014). It is symptomatic that the discursive field of Swedish music education can be examined through the growing body of research on issues of democracy and cultural diversity in music education. Concepts such as musical agency (Karlsen and Westerlund 2010; Karlsen 2012), educational reform (Drummond 2005; Schippers 2010), social mobility (Hofvander Trulsson 2010) and exotification (Sæther 2010) have been used to promote a quest for music educators and policy makers to reflect on music's communicative power, which can be used for good or bad. As Nettl already in 1985 stated, it is important to study the institutions where music is taught: "Our cultural values, too, ought to be discernible in our musical system. What kinds of values do we teach?" (1985, 73). What styles are regarded important or "good"? What teaching methods enhance individual or collective growth? What students are included? Nettl, who was skeptical towards the dominance of classical music in American music education, asked: "Does this perhaps mean that we like to think of our society, reflected in music, as a group of marionettes directed by a supreme puller of strings" (1985, 74). This skepticism can also be interpreted as a reminder that genre choices are value-laden, and that whatever choice is made, the music educators carry both responsibility and possibilities. Today, while there seems to be a consensus that music is an important part of cultural and identity negotiations, these aspects are not reflected in the general status of music as a subject in Swedish schools, or in higher music education.

5   Paradigm Shift

El Sistema can be positioned in relation to several competing discourses on music education in Swedish society. While international research in music education has in general welcomed a shift from the (globally) dominating teaching practices based on Western art music (Green 2006; Lebler 2008; Westerlund 2016), Swedish researchers also have had to problematize the use of the rock-band model as a dominant norm. Due to educational reforms in the 1970s and 1980s, the music teaching that takes place in Swedish schools has mostly been organized in the form of pop-rock bands, with the teacher serving as a facilitator to collaborative, student-centered learning. Initially, the intended impact was to stimulate active music making, and also to some extent to democratize the learning practices. However, as research has shown (Georgii-Hemming and Westvall 2010; Ericsson and Lindgren 2010; Bergman 2009) this stimulation and democritization has had limited impact on the students' opportunities to develop knowledge of music and develop instrumental skills – for instance, girls have often been given (or have taken) the role of the vocalist. The reforms have also led to a complete paradigm shift with one dominating musical genre (i.e. pop-rock), whereas other genres such as jazz, folk, world music and Western classical music have been marginalized.

6   Critical Practitioners

It is also possible to interpret El Sistema as a *community music* approach (Lindgren et al. 2016). Yet, as Kertz-Welzel argues, there has been a tendency in the research on community music to "oversimplify the complexity of musical activities" (2016, 118). In light of the rapid success in terms of the spreading of El Sistema, it might be useful to reconsider preconceptions of community music as completely separated from formal music education, and to look for mutual communication on shared problems. Music teaching in schools or community settings in current ethno-spaces demands skilled teachers: "Pedagogical heroism in terms of envisioning an elevated position of the community music facilitator, while at the same time offering the position to anybody who has the basic skills, is also a kind of *kitsch*" (Kertz-Welzel 2016, 121). Kertz-Welzel calls for "critical practitioners" (2016, 120) with professional training in order to avoid non-reflected activism. It is interesting to note that during the implementation phase of El Sistema in Malmö, the six employed music teachers were given scheduled weekly time for reflection to expand on their professional competence based on a 5-year, masters-level music teacher training. Many of the needed competences, like intercultural pedagogic competence, simply had to be developed in practice, since music teacher programs, with few exceptions, rarely prepare teachers for working with children in socio-economical vulnerable areas.

Moreover, the Swedish researchers Lindgren and Bergman (2014) use a critical-historical perspective to place El Sistema in a movement of on-going discussions on *Bildung*, legitimacy, aesthetics and identity. Both the general school system and the municipal music schools in Sweden rest on early nineteenth-century ideas of the value of education for the working class and socially vulnerable groups towards the development of both the individual and society. When it comes to extracurricular music teaching and learning in music schools, the discourse surrounding these historic ideas favors Western art music and strives for high musical quality through the master–apprenticeship model with its "traditional" instruction types. The opposite of this approach is the creative discourse – more prominent in educational practices – that highlights collaborative learning, group learning, peer assessment and hands-on music making. In the implementation of El Sistema in Malmö, there are traces of both of these approaches.

The instrumental teaching covers mainly instruments for the symphony orchestra, such as flute, violin and cello. However, the teaching methods include characteristics of the creative discourse, with the added ambition to enhance integration. In El Sistema Malmö, as in Gothenburg, music education is legitimized as being good for both social development and development of musical skills. This *double justification* is one of the major challenges for El Sistema music teachers. Another challenge for the teachers is the unusual (in a Swedish context) symphony-orchestra education that contradicts the "taken for granteds" with whom the music teachers have been raised and trained. To Bergman and Lindgren, "El Sistema in Sweden offers an aesthetic and ideological missions statement in which Babumba and Beethoven are equally possible in the repertoire of a symphony and choir performance" (2014, 55). "Babumba" is a song composed by El Sistema teachers Malin Aghed and Magnus Pettersson and its style refers to West African music. It is a typical example of the efforts of music teachers to expand the genre choices in El Sistema. Babumba has become a "hit" and is frequently included in El Sistema concerts. Another typical Swedish interpretation of El Sistema is the inclusion of repertoire from folk and world-music genres. Even if the children are trained for a possible future in a symphony orchestra, Western art music is not the one and only provided genre. The El Sistema teachers in Malmö put a lot of emphasis on the children's own musical creativity in order to move away from the genre issue. Thus, El Sistema can be understood as neither radical nor conservative, but more as a hybrid ingredient in glocal music-education contexts. It stirs up tension fields in late modern and postmodern societies.

7 Balancing in Tension Fields of El Sistema

Much in line with the idea of transformative learning, the German researcher Andreas Pöllman (2016) argues that schools and universities can and should facilitate intercultural learning because intercultural competence is increasingly important in culturally diverse societies. According to Pöllman, legal provision of formal equality – like Swedish society provides – is not enough to guarantee equal educational opportunities. Educational sites need to nurture a renewed feel for the intercultural game and involve students with ground-breaking interruptions of both "long-accustomed practical sense and taken-for-granted ways of being reflexive, possibly stimulating new forms of reflexive intercultural awareness" (2016, 6). One way of stimulating such interruptions would be to provide "direct in situ intercultural experiences" (Pöllman 2016, 6) by cross-cultural mobility that can provide strong and context-intensive opportunities for learning.

In the case of El Sistema in Malmö, the teachers were not exposed to other cultures "far away" but to the multiplicity of cultures and life conditions around them, in their own town and within the culture of their own profession. The intercultural game within their own location involved tension fields that can be understood as expressions of *habitus crisis*, which are an important ingredient in the development of intercultural pedagogic competencies. *Habitus* is a key concept in Pierre Bourdieu's social theory, used as a structured and structuring force to explain social action. People with similar living conditions tend to develop similar ways of acting – a structure of their habitus. In Bourdieu's thinking, these structures then generate structuring dispositions "that guide social practice" (Bourdieu 1990, 60). In the original form of this concept, habitus structures are so powerful that they counteract social mobility. The concept of habitus crisis is derived from Bourdieu's concept *habitus clivé*, discussed by Friedman (2016) as a tool to understand the emotional consequences and imprints of social mobility. In the context of education, Pöllman (2016) suggests a significant but yet unfulfilled potential of extending habitus crises to intercultural education. In Malmö's El Sistema, the teachers' habitus as music educators changed, in their reflexive practice in the collaborative development of the new, intense, music teaching format. Sometimes this change was smooth; sometimes the balancing of various tension fields resulted more in frustration.

7.1 Fieldwork in El Sistema Malmö

In my participant observation study at two schools during the first semester of El Sistema in Malmö, I further explored the tension fields present in the activities in which the teachers were involved. I interviewed local leaders and El Sistema music teachers, kept a fieldwork diary and received a reflective diary from one of the teachers. The data was analyzed through bricolage, and emerging categories identified, both theory driven and data driven, following Brinkmann and Kvale's (2015) guidelines for qualitative research. The use of participant observation was inspired by *radical empiricism*, a concept developed as a fieldwork approach by Stoller (1997) that invites the researcher to use sensory perception in order to understand the world. Radical empiricism in Stoller's version goes beyond participant observation in demanding that the researcher makes use of all senses in the field. In my own version of this approach, I used my fiddle in the fieldwork (Sæther 2015), and participated in the music-making with the teachers and the children.

The study shows that the tension fields can be thematized under four categories: (1) social worker versus the teacher, (2) the resource in the school, (3) exotification, and (4) creativity and the orchestra. Moreover, music teachers working with El Sistema constantly have to navigate their changing environments and represent a source for knowledge production in the underdeveloped field of intercultural pedagogic competence.

7.1.1 The Social Worker Versus the Teacher

According to my study, the music teachers of El Sistema found themselves torn between the double aims of El Sistema. On the one hand they needed to promote integration, on the other hand they were expected to train children towards high artistic achievements. Sometimes during the breaks between lessons, the teachers reflected on how to draw the line between working almost as a social worker and how to do simply the job of a music teacher. Since El Sistema prescribes meeting the children three times a week, there were a lot more chances for the children to develop musical skills than what the regular meeting with a music teacher would allow during one short weekly music school or school lesson. The frequent and intense learning activities (including concerts) also provided opportunities for building trust and friendship that contributed to relationships that were useful when the children or their families needed assistance. This new way of organizing the music activities in schools instead of the of music-school premises led to some habitus alterations – a milder form of crisis – for the music teachers, the children and their families. During the first semester, the teachers alternated between statements such as "this is what we have been trained for, but as ordinary music teachers we were never given the chance" and "we shouldn't be expected to solve all the problems of the school." Every Monday, the music teachers allocated a half day to reflect on results, challenges and developments, and to plan for the coming week according to these scheduled, future-oriented meetings. In these reflective conversations, the music teachers often worked with solutions for social problems as well as more pedagogical and musical tasks. Exemplifying their endeavors, the song "We want to build Malmö," composed by the teachers, indicates a willingness *to adapt to the task of being a social worker, a task that can be expressed in and through music-making*. Thus, the song is the creative result of the music teachers' willingness to negotiate towards the double aims of El Sistema amid the ambiguity of their circumstances.

> We want to build Malmö with music and songs
> We want to build Malmö with stone and concrete
> We want to build bridges
> Between all the people
> Between all the people in Malmö
> (Malmö Kulturskola 2013, my translation)

The leader of the municipal music school in Malmö has integrated El Sistema as one of the regular sub-departments, in order to be able to reach out to groups of citizens that have been difficult to attract. His argument is that: "Music is a cultural right for ALL, it belongs to all (…) there has always been a need for a catalyst, something that can break down the hindrances we tend to construct between ourselves, El Sistema can be that catalyst." Already during the first semester, the children and the teachers participated in numerous official concerts, positioning culture at the forefront in Malmö's development towards social sustainability. The music teachers were happy about the attention their work got in media: "this never happened before." But they were also troubled by some of the coverage as they did not want to belong to the discourse that describes immigrants as victims; as stated by one of the teachers: "It must not appear as if we pity these children. Our story is that we have an interesting and good activity." The tension between social and strictly musical goals was balanced by one of the teachers who pointed out that El Sistema could just as well have started in one of the privileged parts of Malmö, yet it just happened to start in one of the most segregated parts. This remark shows that the original policy goals of El Sistema in Malmö are difficult to combine with formal music education and that there is a tendency among the teachers to think of El Sistema as a tool for development of formal music education in elementary schools and municipal music schools. This was further developed in conversations between the teachers who also identified the possibilities for collective growth reconciled with the challenges of the twofold purpose of El Sistema:

Teacher 1: "It is not a new pedagogy."
Teacher 2: "Just nice that we are allowed to do it."
Teacher 3: "And that we can work together, as a group."

7.1.2   The Resource in the School

One of the important factors in the organization of El Sistema in Malmö is that it should be something that "fills the week (…) something to long for and think about" (leader of the music school), something that takes a big place in the life of the school. This ambition marks a big change for the music teachers. Most of them have years of experience as a marginalized teacher. Since music does not belong to the core subjects, the position of teachers in the schools' inner life may depend on the time of the year; for example, at Christmas and other festivities, music teachers are needed, while other times maybe they are not. Working with El Sistema has given these music teachers a much more visible position among their colleagues, and their mission has forced them to reflect on their duties as educators, beyond "just" being a music teacher – to accept habitus alterations. As one of the teachers expressed it: "We have to work with our value systems, and find a way to cooperate with the other players in the school system."

To the director of the cultural school, the hope is that El Sistema might change the reputation of the involved schools, thereby making them attractive to children from all parts of the city. At the start of El Sistema, the two selected schools in Malmö were of the category that socio-economically privileged families move away from or avoid. One way of strengthening the school culture is to involve the parents, therefore in El Sistema all families are invited to *vänstays*[1] once a week, for concerts

---

[1] *Vänstays* are evening concerts for and with the parents and other family members. In Swedish 'vän' means friend.

and musical activities. The *vänstays* during the first semester were quite challenging for all involved: for the parents because they normally did not come to school together with their children, certainly not after the end of the school day; for the children, because they were not used to performing for and with their parents; for the teachers because they had to arrange for safe transports to and from the *vänstays*, and make sure everyone was welcome; and for the invited musicians from the symphony orchestra because they rarely meet this kind of audience.

The music teachers working in El Sistema in Malmö develop new skills in this multifaceted work. They have to plan for new teaching methods, such as instrumental teaching for beginners in large groups, to re-think their professional roles and to cooperate at many levels with schools, parents, municipality and the symphony orchestra. This planning and cooperation leads to a sense of agency among the music teachers, as one of the teachers expressed: "This is what we were trained for, but earlier not given the chance to implement." Some of them, inspired by their experiences, have taken up their studies and are heading for a position where they can do research on their own practice. Even the aspiration to conduct research on their own, developing teaching methods, might be interpreted as a result of the habitus alterations.

7.1.3 Exotification and Creativity

During the first semester of El Sistema many journalists and politicians visited the schools. The children were invited to large gatherings, like kick-offs for teachers and civil servants. After only a few weeks of instrumental training on violin and flute, the children performed with the symphony orchestra. The song "We want to build Malmö" became one of the hits. Sometimes, the teachers also got tired of the official rhetoric on El Sistema about how good music is for integration. "We try to avoid talking about us and them," as one of the teachers said in one of the gatherings for reflection. The music teachers did not talk about immigrant children. Their students were just children from Malmö, and they thought El Sistema would be just as relevant to children in other parts of Malmö as to the segregated parts. During the first semester this insight grew stronger: "We are here to teach music – not to pity children."

This sensitivity towards exotification might be explained by some of the teachers' own experiences of working with children in refugee camps, and also from taking part in the intercultural projects at the Malmö Academy of Music during their teacher education. One way of solving the dilemmas of exotification and problematic genre choices in the fields of tension was to concentrate on the children's own music making. From the outset, the teachers involved the children in collaborative creations and asked them to compose their own music (See Fig. 2).

As mentioned above, the teachers also composed their own music for the children. At the end of the first semester, one of the teachers composed a song with lyrics that said nothing about integration or inclusion – instead it highlighted musi-

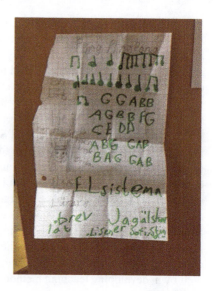

Fig. 2 First composition of one El Sistema pupil in Malmö that was played by the teachers and students in one of the music lessons

cal concepts: forte, piano, staccato and legato. Legato – softly connected – could be seen as a metaphor of how the teachers positioned themselves in relation to both the symphony orchestra and the official rhetoric of El Sistema as a tool for democracy. In this way, they showed a new understanding of the "intercultural game" as proposed by Pöllman (2016).

7.1.4 Habitus Crises in the Orchestra

In the first meeting between the Malmö Symphony Orchestra and the El Sistema children, the El Sistema teachers insisted on taking the initiative. They wanted the orchestra to come to the children – not the other way around. This first meeting was preceded by negotiations between the producers from the Symphony Orchestra and the El Sistema music teachers, who were not always in harmony with each other since the music teachers and the representatives from the symphony orchestra had different preconceptions of what a "children concert" could be. The final outcome was successful, however, the process involved strong, direct, context-intensive, in situ intercultural experiences, i.e. habitus crises. The first meeting in the children's sports hall interrupted the taken-for-granted ways of thinking and being of the children, their teachers and the professional musicians. In the first lesson after the concert in the sports hall, the children spoke of their strong experience of being allowed to sit in the orchestra next to the musicians. For the members of the orchestra, the concert in the sports hall forced them to leave their comfort zones to play for and with children who had never visited a concert hall.

8   Discussion and Conclusion

Four years after the start of El Sistema in Malmö the program has expanded to include four schools in Malmö. The growth has been deliberately slow, and has taken place within the economical frames of the municipal music school (El Sistema 2017). The initial group of six teachers has continued to develop their intercultural skills in collaboration with the newly employed colleagues. On the national level, El Sistema has intensified its efforts to develop new teaching methods, suitable for the learning contexts in which El Sistema lands, or creates generally in school environments. The recently launched El Sistema Academy serves as a center for education, research and cooperation for the music teachers and institutions concerned. In Gothenburg, the orchestra for refugees initiated in 2016, called the Dream Orchestra, was nominated to the prize "Music for all" (Årets musik för alla) with the motivation that it "encompasses integration as much as music." While it is evident that this orchestra is of importance to the involved members, the Dream Orchestra's[2] impact on structural integration remains to be validated. Although it is too early to say anything about the long-term impact of El Sistema in Malmö, by providing the pupils with expressive and musical tools, the children's agency may increase, both on macro- and micro levels.

For the future of music teacher education research, as well as for the professional education of music teachers, the El Sistema intervention in the Swedish educational landscape has already provided new perspectives by prompting reflexivity and active engagement with the intercultural game. The habitus dislocations, for the children, the teachers and the Symphony Orchestra members, are potentially important ingredients leading up to *transformative learning*, which Illeris (2015) identifies as central when social re-adjustments are necessary. These re-adjustments include the researcher, who, in practicing sensory scholarship, will naturally be involved in transformative or interactive research.

For the music teachers, El Sistema has offered a possibility to expand the frames of the music teacher profession, to develop collaborative teaching methods, and to reflect on the moral and political dimensions of being a music teacher, for example the potential dangers with exotification of immigrant children. The experiences from the implementation of El Sistema in Malmö show how teachers equipped with intercultural pedagogical competence – such as the El Sistema teachers develop in practice – might be able to stimulate in teaching what Illeris (2015) describes as transformative learning. Longitudinal studies, including the perspectives of the children, will show the implications of the transformations and habitus crises that the intervention of El Sistema in Malmö has offered.

Looking at El Sistema as a glocal phenomenon affords us to envision a future, intercultural music teacher education based on theoretical awareness and practical

---

[2] The Dream Orchestra started in April 2016 as a music activity for young refugees. The orchestra now has 30 members and rehearses three times a week. (See: http://www.elsistema.se/sa-gor-vi/dream-orchestra/).

experience. Through deliberate habitus crises, breaking with long-standing discourses and teaching methods, it is possible to stimulate reflection and to promote the agency of future music teachers. One way of provoking habitus crises is to include hands-on, intercultural teaching experiences in teacher training, and to combine this with time for reflection on the "taken for granteds" in music teacher education. Other possible strategies would be to strive towards transformative learning through curriculum developments. Including the five phases suggested by Lorentz (2016) in the curriculum would help music-teacher students to develop the intercultural pedagogic competence that is needed when teaching music in ethnospaces.

References

Appadurai, A. (1992). Global ethnoscapes. Notes and queries for a transnational anthropology. In R. G. Fox (Ed.), *Recapturing anthropology* (Working in the present) (pp. 48–65). Santa Fe: School of American Research Press.

Baker, G. (2014). *Orchestrating Venezuela's youth.* Oxford: Oxford University Press.

Bergman, Å. (2009). *Växa upp med musik - Ungdomars musikanvändande i skolan och på fritiden* [Growing up with music - Adolescents use of music in school and leisure time]. (PhD-thesis). Gothenburg: Gothenburg University.

Bergman, Å., & Lindgren, M. (2014). Social change through Babumba and Beethoven – musical educational ideas of El Sistema. *Svensk tidskrift för musikforskning – Swedish Journal of Music Research, 96*(2), 43–58.

Bourdieu, P. (1990). *The logic of practice.* Stanford: Stanford University Press.

Brinkmann, S., & Kvale, S. (2015). *InterViews. Learning the craft of qualitative research interviewing.* Los Angeles: Sage.

Clausson, M., & Thanner, L. (2015). *El Sistema. Svensk kulturskola i förändring.* Göteborg: B4press.

Drummond, John. 2005. Cultural diversity in music education: Why bother? Cultural diversity in music education: Directions and challenges for the 21st century, Patricia Shehan Campbell, John Drummond, Peter Dunbar-Hall, Keith Howard, Huib Schippers, Trevor Wiggins, 1–9. Brisbane: Australian Academic Press.

El Sistema. (2016). *El Sistema Malmö expands* [Online]. http://www.elsistema.se/?p=3952. Accessed 8 Jan 2017

El Sistema. (2017). *El Sistemas drömorkester nominerad till Faktumgalan* [El Sistema Dream Orchestra nominated to Faktumgalan] [Online]. http://www.mynewsdesk.com/se/stiftelsen-el-sistema/pressreleases/el-sistemas-droemorkester-nominerad-till-faktumgalan-1700286. Accessed 11 Jan 2017.

El Sistema Sverige. (2016). [Online]. http://www.elsistema.se/. Accessed 3 Jan 2017.

Ericsson, C., & Lindgren, M. (2010). *Musikklassrummet i blickfånget. Vardagskultur, identitet, styrning och kunskapsbildning. [The music classroom in focus. Everyday culture, identity, steering and knowledge production].* Halmstad: Högskolan i Halmstad.

EU Voices of Culture. (2016). *The role of culture in promoting inclusion in the context of migration* [Online]. http://www.goethe.de/ins/be/pro/voc/VoC_full%20report_Final_kleiner.pdf. Accessed 10 Apr 2018.

Eurostat. (2016). [Online]. http://ec.europa.eu/eurostat/statistics-explained/index.php/Migration_and_migrant_population_statistics. Accessed 5 Jan 2017.

Friedman, S. (2016). Habitus clivé and the emotional impact of social mobility. *The Sociological Review, 64*, 129–147.

Georgii-Hemming, E., & Westvall, M. (2010). Music education – a personal matter? Examining the current discourses of music education in Sweden. *British Journal of Music Education, 27*(1), 21–33.

Green, L. (2006). Popular music education in and for itself, and for 'other' music: Current research in the classroom. *International Journal of Music Education, 24*(2), 101–118.

Gy 11. (2011). *Läroplan, examensmål och gymnasiegemensamma ämnen för gymnasieskola 2011, Gy 11* [Curriculum for upper secondary school, Gy 11]. 2011. Stockholm: Skolverket. [Online]. http://www.skolverket.se/om-skolverket/publikationer/. Accessed 1 Jan 2017.

Hofvander Trulsson, Y. (2010). *Musikaliskt lärande som social rekonstruktion. Musikens och ursprungets betydelse för föräldrar med utländsk bakgrund* [Musical learning as social reconstruction. Music and origin in the eyes of immigrant parents]. Malmö: Malmö Academy of Music, Lund University.

Illeris, K. (2015). *Lärande* [Learning]. Lund: Studentlitteratur.

Karlsen, S. (2012). Multiple repertoires of ways of being and acting in music: Immigrant students' musical agency as an impetus for democracy. *Music Education Research, 14*(2), 131–148.

Karlsen, S., & Westerlund, H. (2010). Immigrant students' development of musical agency – Exploring democracy in music education. *British Journal of Music Education, 27*(3), 225–239.

Kertz-Welzel, A. (2016). Daring to question: A philosophical critique of community music. *Philosophy of Music Education Review, 24*(2), 113–130.

Lebler, D. (2008). Popular music pedagogy: Peer learning in practice. *Music Education Research, 10*(2), 193–213.

Lgr 11. (2011). *Läroplan för grundskolan, förskolan och fritidshemmet, Lgr 11* [National Curriculum for elementary school, preschool and youth recreation center, Lgr 11]. Stockholm: Skolverket. [Online]. http://www.skolverket.se/om-skolverket/publikationer/. Accessed 7 Jan 2017.

Lindgren, Monica, & Bergman, Åsa. (2014). El Sistema som överskridande verksamheter – konstruktioner av ett musikpedagogiskt forskningsprojekt. [El Sistema as border crossing activities – Constructions of a music education research project]. In Häikiö, T. K., Monica, L., & Johansson, M. (Eds.), *Texter om konstarter och lärande* [Texts on the arts and learning] (pp. 107–130). Göteborg: Göteborgs universitet, Konstnärliga fakulteten.

Lindgren, M., & Ericsson, C. (2010). The rock band context as discursive governance in music education in Swedish schools. *Action, Criticism and Theory for Music Education, 9*(3), 35–54.

Lindgren, M., Bergman, Å., & Sæther, E. (2016). Examining social inclusion through music education: Two Swedish case studies. *Nordic Research in Music Education, 17*, 65–81. Oslo: NMH-publikasjoner.

Lorensson, J. (2013). *Opublicerat måldokument från kulturskolan i Malmö* [Unpublished strategy document of municipal Art and Music School, Malmö.]

Lorentz, Hans. 2016. Interkulturell pedagogisk kompetens. Transformativ akademisk kunskap om integration i dagens skola. [Intercultural pedagogic competence. Transformative academic knowledge on integration in the school]. In Lorentz, H., & Bergstedt, B (Eds.), *Interkulturella perspektiv. Pedagogik i mångkulturella lärandemiljöer* [Intercultural perspectives. Pedagogy in multicultural learning contexts] (pp. 161–188). Lund: Studentlitteratur.

Lorentz, H., & Bergstedt, B. (2006). *Interkulturella perspektiv. Pedagogik i mångkulturella lärandemiljöer* [Intercultural perspectives. Pedagogy in multicultural learning contexts]. Lund: Studentlitteratur.

Lpo 94. (1994). *års läroplan för det obligatoriska skolväsendet* [National curriculum for the compulsory school] Stockholm: Skolverket. [Online]. http://www.skolverket.se/skolfs?id=100. Accessed 10 Apr 2018.

Malmö Kulturskola El Sistema. (2013). *Vi vill bygga Malmö.* [We want to build Malmö]. [Video file]. [Online]. https://www.youtube.com/watch?v=wWacDrP9iJ4. Accessed 8 Jan 2017.

Malmö Stad. (2019). [Online]. http://malmo.se/Service/Om-Malmö-stad/Demokrati-beslut-och-paverkan/Fakta-och-statistik/Befolkning/Befolkningsursprung.html. Accessed 1 June 2019.

Migrationsinfo. (2016). [Online]. http://www.migrationsinfo.se/migration/sverige/asylsokande-i-sverige/. Accessed 5 Jan 2017.

Montilla, A. (2014). Retracing propinquity and the ethno[flow]. *Civil Engineering and Architecture, 2*, 142–148. https://doi.org/10.13189/cea.2014.020305.

Nettl, B. (1985). Montana and Iran: Learning and teaching in the conception of music in two contrasting cultures. In M. E. N. C. I. Committee (Ed.), *Becoming human through music* (pp. 69–76). Reston: Music Educators National Conference.

Olsson, B. (1993). *SÄMUS en musikutbildning i kulturpolitikens tjänst? En studie om musikutbildning på 1970-talet* [SÄMUS – music education in the service of a cultural policy? A study of a teacher training programme during the 1970s] (Vol. 33). Göteborg: Musikhögskolan.

Pöllmann, A. (2016). Habitus, reflexivity, and the realization of intercultural capital: The (unfulfilled) potential of intercultural education. *Cogent Social Sciences.* https://doi.org/10.1080/23311886.2016.1149915.

Pyrhönen, N., Leinonen, J., & Martikainen, T. (2017). *Nordic migration and integration research: Overview and future prospects* (Policy paper 3/2017). Oslo: NordForsk.

Roudometof, V. (2015). Theorizing glocalization. *European Journal of Social Theory, 19*(3), 391–408.

Sæther, E. (2010). Music education and the other. *Finnish Journal of Music Education, 13*(1), 45–60.

Sæther, E. (2015). Exploring musical research sensibilities. In L. Bresler (Ed.), *Beyond methods. Lessons from the arts to qualitative research* (pp. 89–103). Malmö: Malmö Academy of Music, Lund University.

Salonen, T. (2012). *Befolkningsrörelser, försörjningsvillkor och bostadssegregation – en sociodynamisk analys av Malmö* [Population mobility, employment rates and housing segregation]. Retrieved from Malmö: [Online]. http://www.mah.se/Samverkan/Pagaende-samarbeten/Malmokommissionen-bidrar-till-ett-friskare-Malmo/. Accessed 19 Oct 2017.

Sarroub, L. K. (2008). Living "Glocally" with literacy success in the Midwest. *Theory into Practice.* https://doi.org/10.1080/00405840701764789.

Schippers, H. (2010). *Facing the music. Shaping music education from a global perspective.* New York: Oxford University Press.

Sistema Global. (2016). [Online]. http://sistemaglobal.org/about/. Accessed 3 Jan 2017.

Sloterdijk, P. (2000). From agrarian patriotism to theGlobal self. *New Perspectives Quarterly, 17*, 15–18. https://doi.org/10.1111/0893-7850.00231.

SOU. (1983). *Olika ursprung – gemenskap i Sverige: Utbildning för språklig och kulturell mångfald.* (SOU 1983:57). [Different origins – partnership in Sweden: Education for linguistic and cultural diversity]. (Huvudbetänkande av språk och kulturarvsutredningen [Published by the Commission on migrants' languages and culture in school and adult education in Sweden]). Stockholm: Liber Allmänna Förlaget.

SOU. (2008).Utredningen om en ny lärarutbildning. 2008. *En hållbar lärarutbildning.* (SOU 2008:109). [A sustainable teacher education]. Stockholm: Utbildningsdepartementet [Online]. http://www.regeringen.se/contentassets/d262d32331a54278b34861c44df8dbad/en-hallbar-lararutbildning-hela-dokumentet-sou-2008109. Accessed 7 Jan 2017.

SOU. (2016). *En inkluderande kulturskola på egen grund. Betänkande av Kulturskoleutredningen* (SOU 2016:69). [An including culture school on its own basis. National inquiry on the Swedish culture schools]. [Online]. .http://www.regeringen.se/contentassets/7037695d8c354057b9ece6fca046173f/en-inkluderande-kulturskola-pa-egen-grund-sou-201669. Accessed 19 Oct 2017.

Stigendal, M. (2007). *Allt som inte flyter. Fosies potentialer – Malmös problem* [Everything that doesn't float. The potentials of Fosie – the problems of Malmö]. Malmö: Malmö Högskola.

Stigendal, M., & Östergren, P-O. (2013). *Malmös väg mot en hållbar framtid: hälsa, välfärd och rättvisa* [Malmo towards a sustainable future: health, welfare and justice]. Malmö: Kommissionen för ett socialt hållbart Malmö.

Stoller, P. (1997). *Sensuous scholarship.* Philadelphia: University of Pennsylvania Press.

TED. (2018a). *Remembering José Antonio Abreu.* [Online]. https://blog.ted.com/remembering-maestro-jose-antonio-abreu/ Accessed 10 Apr 2018.

TED. (2018b). *TED Prize*. [Online]. https://www.ted.com/participate/ted-prize/ Accessed 10 Apr 2018.

Touraine, A. (2003). *Kan vi leva tillsammans?: Jämlika och olika* [Can we live together?: Equal and different]. Göteborg: Daidalos.

UNESCO. (1974). *Recommendation concering education for international understanding, cooperation and peace and education relating to human rights and fundamental freedom*. Paris: UNESCO [Online].. http://portal.unesco.org/en/ev.php-URL_ID=13088&URL_DO=DO_TOPIC&URL_SECTION=201.html. Accessed 7 Jan 2017.

Westerlund, H. (2016). Garage rock bands: A future model for developing musical expertise? *International Journal of Music Education, 24*(2), 119–125.

2

Intercultural Music Teacher Education in Israel: Re-imagining Religious Segregation Through Culturally Responsive Teaching

Amira Ehrlich and Belal Badarne

Abstract This chapter is a result of a rare effort of interreligious dialogue between two colleagues in Israeli music teacher education – an Orthodox Jew and a devout Muslim. In this act of collegial sharing, intercultural conversation is used as an instrument for research. The documented effort to communicate respective culturally grounded perspectives to one another illuminates taken-for-granted norms and habits and expands respective understandings of cultural assumptions that currently underlie structures of religious segregation in Israeli music teacher education. Working to reimagine such structures, the authors question the possibility of interculturalism in the context of segregation. Tracing the constraints of cultural diversity further, considering policy and music teacher education, the authors re-imagine socio-religious segregation in Israeli music teacher education as an opportunity for culturally responsive teaching. The analysis and the envisioning are grounded in the experiences of the two authors as lecturers in two specialized segregated programs of music teacher education geared towards Arabic speaking populations and the Jewish Ultraorthodox community. Conclusions aspire towards cultural specificity within each community as a platform for future intercultural sharing that the authors believe can enrich Israeli society at large.

Keywords Music teacher education · Cultural diversity · Culturally responsive pedagogy

---

A. Ehrlich (✉)
Faculty of Music Education, Levinsky College of Education, Tel Aviv, Israel
e-mail: amira.erlich@levinsky.ac.il

B. Badarne
Department of Education, Sakhnin College for Teacher Education, Sakhnin, Israel

1 Introduction: Exposing Cultural Assumptions Through Interreligious Dialogue

This chapter is a result of a rare effort of interreligious dialogue between two Israeli music teacher educators: Amira – an Orthodox Jew, and Belal – a devout Muslim. As colleagues working together in Levinsky College's Faculty of Music Education in Tel Aviv, we have chosen to engage in dialogue to share with each other cultural perspectives of our profession. In this act of collegial sharing, we use intercultural conversation as an instrument for research (Blommaert 2010; Scollon Scollon and Jones 2012). During the course of two academic years, we documented monthly conversations that were structured using the concepts of sharing, co-interpreting, and reflecting on each other's work. The current chapter represents one of the important frames of conversation that emerged, which we present including some quotations from our conversational recordings.

We believe that our documented effort to communicate respective, culturally grounded perspectives to one another forced us to clarify, question, and reflect upon our own cultural and professional premises. The resulting insights illuminate taken-for-granted norms and habits of ourselves and of our surroundings, even as they expand our respective understandings of our own and each other's cultural impacts on our work (Badarne and Ehrlich in print; Barret 2011).

In the current chapter, we use such insights to expose cultural assumptions that currently underlie structures of religious segregation in Israeli music teacher education. Working to reimagine such structures, we question the possibility of inter-culturalism in the context of segregation, advocating cultural responsivity (Gay 2010; Lind and McKoy 2016), as one possible starting point.

Our conversation acknowledges the vast tradition of sociological discourse on segregation and multiculturalism (e.g. Baumann 1999; Munroe 2000; Woodson 2016), the scope of which is way beyond the limits of our current endeavor. We engage in this on-going scholarly discussion in contributing perspectives from our own lived experience. We challenge this discourse in suggesting a reframing of our specific cases of segregation in education as opportunities for promoting the values of diversity and inclusion rather than acts of suppression.

1.1 Context

The two authors of this chapter – Amira and Belal – live and work in opposite socio-religious poles of Israeli society. They first met as graduate students in music education in Levinsky College, and later became faculty members at this same institution. Levinsky's Faculty of Music Education includes three main tracks of undergraduate music education: (1) a general program aimed at all local populations, (2) a segregated track created for Jewish Ultraorthodox women, and (3) a separate track mostly populated by Arabic speaking populations. At the time this study was conducted, Amira was teaching in all three Faculty tracks, and Belal was teaching in the separate track for Arabic speaking populations. The purpose of our collaborative study was to explore each of our experiences in teaching within culturally segregated programs of music teacher education. As a starting point, we acknowledge that such programs do not exist in a vacuum, but rather echo norms of socio-religious segregation evident in Israeli social structures, and in Israeli public education.

1.2 Israeli Norms of Socio-religious Segregation

Interreligious dialogue in contemporary Israel is both a daily reality and a framework for social activism. In a previous collaboration (Badarne and Ehrlich in print) we have described our shared conception of a gap between social structures and everyday interactions between Jews and Arabs in contemporary Israel. Many basic infrastructures of Israeli society enact religious segregation: neighborhoods, towns and even entire cities are characterized by categories and sub-categories of religious affiliation (Carter 2007; Semyonov and Tyree 1981). Public education in Israel is mandated through a paradigm of linguistic segregation that translates into overall separation between Jews and non-Jewish populations (Elazar 1997; Tzameret 2003). At the same time, daily interactions at public places of commerce and culture often entail close contact between Jews and Arabs of diverse religious and ethnic affiliations. The gap between small, everyday encounters and structural segregation is further evident in the abundance of non-government organizations (NGOs) active in facilitating meaningful interreligious dialogue between Jews and Arabs in Israel (Kronish 2015). This gap is evident in music education as well as in music teacher education.

1.3 Opening the Classroom Door

Although it would be less common for an NGO to invest in the cultivation of institutional dialogue within a college of education, in many ways our commitment to collegial dialogue is no less important than the interreligious factor of our work. The universal stereotype of the closed classroom door, with each teacher autonomous and independent within his/her institution – in this case – *is* actually an accurate description of our professional context. Therefore, the mutual sharing between two lecturers of music teacher education working within the same institution is an additional layer of interaction that enabled us to write this chapter.

1.4 (How) Can Segregation Promote Inter-culturalism?

In our current collaboration, this theme of opening the classroom door intersects with the interreligious effort, as we consider the challenges of Israeli music teacher education in relation to two segregated populations of contemporary Israeli society. Through the lens of intercultural frameworks, (Barrett 2011; Blommaert 2010; Gay 2010; Fitzpatrick 2012; Scollon et al. 2012; Talbot 2013), as researchers, we take interest in constraints and affordances that effect cultural contexts of music education. We believe that an explicit awareness of these cultural considerations is crucial for preparing pre-service teachers for the educational challenges that lie ahead. Such awareness is further required as a starting point to imagine a future of cultural enrichment working within each population that can subsequently act as a basis for intercultural sharing. Our current collaboration aims to outline cultural constraints and affordances of Israeli music teacher education as experienced in our respective practices.

We begin by outlining structures of socio-religious segregation in the Israeli education system. Interpreting Israeli music education policy as enforcing a standard of Western–Classical hegemony, we then trace the impact of this policy on institutional standards of music teacher education. The main focus of our conversation emerges as we explore the effects of these policy structures on our involvements in current institutional interventions of practice aimed at Arab and Jewish Ultraorthodox populations. Sharing our respective perspectives as active music teacher educators working within these specific cultures, we discuss future visions for a more culturally responsive music teacher education (Lind and McKoy 2016).

2 Structures and Policy of Israeli (Music) Education

Israeli public education is government mandated, and structured through a paradigm of socio-religious segregation. Four main streams of education exist as separate institutions, with separate inspectorates and curriculums for: (1) Jewish Secular, (2) Jewish Religious, (3) Jewish Ultraorthodox, and (4) Arabic speaking populations. While Jewish populations have been formally separated into sub-categories of religious affiliation, Arabic speaking populations including Muslim, Druze, Bedouin, and Christians all officially belong to one single, non-Jewish category. Several sub-categorizations and segregations of Arabic speaking groups exist de-facto in some areas of Israel as a result of specific community considerations and/or geographical constraints (Jabareen and Agbaria 2014; Tzameret 2003).

2.1 Segregation That Facilitates Social Cohesion

Elazar (1997) and Tzameret (2003) describe this sectarianism of Israeli State Education as a system based on civilizational and ideological principles, historically designed during the establishment of the State of Israel. Elazar (1997) interprets the irony entailed in such a system, by which the accommodation of sectarian differences in allowing different groups to pursue different visions resulted in creating a greater sense of social coherence, and even a sense of unity. Thus, in promoting segregated streams of education, historically, the Israel Ministry of Education has recognized the benefits of developing different curriculums for certain school subjects, as a catalyst for socio-religious and cultural diversity of Israeli society.

Historically speaking, the broadest example of this development is the 1953 legislation establishing the Jewish Religious stream of Israeli public education. Pre-State Jewish educational institutions existed in separate streams of education – separate schools for Zionist socialists, religious Zionists, and general Zionists (liberals); these later merged into the two basic streams of Israeli state education: a Jewish secular system and a Jewish religious State School system (Elazar 1997; Tzameret 2003). Tensions between the separate educational schools throughout the State's early history triggered political crises, the most dramatic case being the collapse of the Israeli government in 1951. At this time, a controversy over the division of new immigrants between secular and religious educational streams triggered a deep political divide that toppled the entire government (Tzameret 2003).

Ironically, the 1953 resolution legally recognized two segregated streams of public education – the secular and the religious. In this resolution, legislative segregation allowed the reestablishment and cohesion of a government that was impossible so long as the different visions of Israeli and Jewish education were conceptualized without it. The later educational reforms of Israel in the 1980s were similarly paradoxical, because they aimed at accommodating sectarian differences by allowing diverse groups to pursue different visions. In many subjects, such as history, literature, and civics, schools developed separate curriculums, teacher training, and textbooks to accommodate the difference between (1) secular Jewish schools, (2) religious Jewish schools, and (3) Arabic speaking populations. The more legitimacy government educational policy afforded to segregated difference, the greater the sense of social stability was (Elazar 1997).

Echoes of this seemingly paradoxical approach can be traced in current public discourse and debates on Israeli public education. Israeli President Rivlin's 2015 speech, which later came to be known as "The Speech of the Tribes,"[1] described Israeli social order as constructed of four segregated tribes living in conflict. President Rivlin named the four main sectors of society as secular, religious, ultra-orthodox, and Arab. Since 2015, this concept of conflicting "tribes" has become an explicit and dominant feature of Israeli public discourse. Indeed, Pew Research

---

[1] A Hebrew transcription of this speech can be read at: http://www.president.gov.il/ThePresident/Speeches/Pages/news_070615_01.aspx

Center's 2016 survey report on Israeli society proclaimed "deep divisions in Israeli society – not only between Israeli Jews and the country's Arab minority, but also among the religious subgroups that make up Israeli Jewry" (p. 5). The survey described Israeli Jewish identity as a "complex" entity (p. 6), constituted by a set of subcategories that function as "separate social worlds," and that are "reflected in starkly contrasting positions on many public policy questions" (p. 5).

Throughout 2017–2018 school year, Israeli media reported recurring allocations against religious foundations, allegedly infiltrating secular school systems as a form of religious coercion, as just another reminder of the ethos of separation that the Israeli government's status-quo agreements enforce and uphold (Ehrlich 2018). In 2017, the essence of President Rivlin's 2015 "tribes" speech, was translated into an activist initiative called "Israeli Hope."[2] The essence of its approach is evident in its double dedication to the fostering of internal cohesion within each sector, alongside a devotion to mutual respect of diversity, and acts of sharing. This Israeli approach to conflictual sectarianism thus deems the challenge of social cohesion no less important than the commitment to diversity, and conceptualizes segregation as an opportunity no less than as a challenge.

2.2 Common Core in Music as Hegemony

Notwithstanding the development of sectarian, differentiated curriculums in many school subjects, music and most arts subjects have been traditionally considered by the Israeli Ministry as "neutral enough" to be taught in a similar fashion, with similar standards within all sectors of Israeli society (Adler 2016). Within this context, music education is mandated through a single National Curriculum for all socio-religious sectors (Israel Ministry 2011). While allowing 30% of content to include specialized electives that can be developed in respect to a local culture, the Curriculum is based on a common core principle in which Western–Classical contents and pedagogies function as the main mandatory constituents. Although we embrace the recognition of additional musical cultures as possible electives, we interpret the hierarchy of core knowledge in relation to electives as testimony to an overall Western–Classical hegemony.

Indeed, Ehrlich (2016) has expounded on the hegemonic structure of the single Israeli National Music Curriculum. She has further described a "kind of imagined (or real) exclusive dependence on Western repertoires and pedagogies as a function of personal, social, and institutional conceptualizations of professionalism in music and music education" in Israel. Analyzing the aspect of music in Early Childhood Israeli Curriculum, Gluschankof similarly summated this sense of absurdity, describing the State of Israel, as manifested through such educational structures, as "what has become a Western-oriented country situated in the Middle East" (2008, p. 37).

---

[2] https://www.israeli-hope.gov.il/

2.3 Israeli Music Education Caught in a Double Bind

Interpreting the macro-structure of Israeli education alongside the micro-structure of Israeli *music* education, we perceive a double bind: the norm of socio-religious segregation in education at large, when combined with the Western–Classical hegemony of *music* education, seems to deny any prospect for cultural diversity. While the norms of segregation have been historically praised for allowing each sector to develop particular curriculums that cater to cultural specificity, the core of the National Curriculum of Music all but denies cultural specificity (Ehrlich 2016).

3 Experiences in Current Institutional Interventions

Working as Israeli music teacher educators, within this double bind, we have been taking part in current acts for social intervention towards diversity and inclusion. Levinsky College's Faculty of Music Education is active in the promotion of music teacher education in two socially segregated populations: Arabic speaking sectors and the Jewish Ultraorthodox sector. Over the past decade, the Faculty has developed specialized segregated tracks for music teacher education and accreditation.

As mentioned above, Levinsky's Faculty of Music Education currently includes three main tracks for undergraduate music education: (1) a general program aimed at all local populations, (2) a segregated track created for Jewish Ultraorthodox women, and (3) a separate track mostly populated by Arabic speaking populations. Currently, potential students of the Faculty can choose to study in the main socio-religiously-integrated programs, or choose the appropriate segregated parallel program.

As collaborating authors, we each have experience with the Arabic speaking classes: Amira as a cultural outsider, and Belal as an insider. Amira adds to this her experience in the Ultraorthodox program where she is somewhat of an insider.[3] Sharing respective experiences of teaching within these segregated programs allowed us to reflect on what is, and on what can be, beyond policy and curriculum.

3.1 Segregation That Enables Inclusion

Amira described her experiences teaching in the women-only Jerusalem campus for music teacher education. This unique self-segregated campus was established to cater to the special cultural needs of the Jewish Ultraorthodox community. Strict

---

[3] Elaboration on sub-sectors of Israeli Judaism is beyond the scope of the current chapter. Some additional notes on this can be found in Badarne and Ehrlich (in print).

social norms of complete sexual segregation, modest dress and behavior, and religious censorship of content, make it impossible for women of this sector to study in an integrated program. These norms affect program considerations of personnel, content, and pedagogies, and mandate that all must conform to cultural-religious dictates. Sharing her thoughts on this religiously and sexually segregated program, Amira recognized how segregation functions here as an enabling factor:

> Envisioning the future, I can see no real scope for change in terms of the Ultraorthodox segregated program. There is no way that religious leaders of this community will allow the women of their community to engage in studies that include musical performance in an integrated program. The segregated all-women's campus is an enabling factor, without which, I am afraid, women of this sector will not have access to this type of professional and academic study and accreditation.

Belal described the history of an additional effort to expand Levinsky's Music Education Faculty, through a partnership with the Safed Academic College, that lead to the establishment of a music teacher accreditation program, oriented towards Arab populations (including Muslims, Druze, and Christians) of the Northern Districts:

> You know the title of this program is not 'Arab.' At first it seemed almost circumstantial that 99% of the students enrolled in this program were Arab. Perhaps that is why no real thought was given to the details of the program – there was no thought or effort to culturally adapt, because, at first, the idea was that this was a geographically distinct program aimed at students from the North of the country. This has changed, and today – about ten years since its establishment – there is an effort to recognize and incorporate more Arab-based content and faculty members.

The initial motivation of this second segregated program was based on a geographical outreach, allowing students from the Northern districts of the country to complete their accreditation with minimal travel. Only as the program developed, did the cultural aspect of the student population became salient. The challenge of this program became manifested in the language gap between Arabic speaking students and a Hebrew speaking institution and staff. Belal and Amira agreed that this gap is not only linguistic, as it entails other cultural discrepancies, mainly between an aural-oriented tradition (Arab) and the centrality of music literacy and academia (Hebrew):

> Amira: "I feel that the problems Jewish, Hebrew-speaking faculty have teaching in this program are not limited to language."
> Belal: "Language is also culture, yes. But you have to understand where these students are coming from – it is not necessarily only the difference of Arab cultures, it is also a difference in the type of academic culture that they experienced at other institutions."
> Amira: "Yes, I see. But even that has something to do also with the Arabic cultures and their epistemologies and educational practices."
> Belal: "and – don't forget – the academic norms of more geographically peripheral institutions that are more lenient and less active in establishing academic standards of reading and writing."

Formal standards for acceptance and program curriculums are the same for all three of Levinsky's music education undergraduate programs. Nevertheless, as active faculty members of these programs both Belal and Amira attest to efforts towards inclusion of students whose cultural backgrounds differ from standard Western benchmarks. In collegial conversations with them, program directors and Faculty heads have expressed their perception of these segregated tracks as acts of social intervention, and described their work to expand potential student inclusion. During conversation, Amira recalled a Faculty meeting that she and Belal had attended, where one program director admitted to the group:

> Efforts for inclusion sometimes entail creativity, for example, in investing in a wider perspective of in-depth interviewing, and in observing applicants within their own fields of practice, rather than depending solely on standardized institutional entrance exams.

Other specific examples of this came up in our dialogue:

> Amira: "Actually, some of the women who are accepted to the Ultraorthodox music education program begin their music studies for the first time – they come in with no real musical background. Little to zero demand for previous knowledge is required – it is mostly a future-oriented approach, women who show some previous acquaintance with music, usually some high school music education, alongside a commitment to develop themselves professionally can be accepted. Some of these women choose vocal training as their lead instrument because they think it will be easier than starting an instrument so late in life."

> Belal: "The same is true of some of the Arabic speaking populations. But also, there are several prominent and talented musicians from Arab communities who have no formal music education and have no chance of passing written exams, but when they perform, it is like 'wow'! Some of them are really great performing musicians, but they have no experience in reading Western notation, or understanding the basics of Western music theory, and so they cannot easily pass the exams. In my experience, I think all musicians should have Western music literacy as part of their training because I think this contributes to developing international professionalism. But if we accept only those students who already have this knowledge and skills we will be limiting the potential of the program."

3.2 Constraining Musical Knowledge

Even though acceptance standards are sometimes compromised for the benefit of broader inclusion, once students are accepted to either of the segregated programs, they must prove themselves in the same Western-oriented studies as those enrolled in the college's main integrated program. This often turns out to be no less challenging for the faculty teaching them, than for the students who have been accepted to learn. For the most part, the same faculty members teach in all three programs, with only minimum matching of a few, culturally affiliated faculty members within respective segregated programs. Belal explains:

> Since the program is inclined towards Arabic speaking populations, you would think more could be done to accommodate these students. Most of them lack in-depth musical knowledge of Arabic musical traditions, and this is something they should be getting through the program and are not. Also, as far as language is concerned, there should be more space and preference for Arabic speaking teachers.

Amira agrees:

> In both segregated programs it often seems that all efforts are aimed at bringing the students to the content and level of the 'regular,' non-segregated program – as if that is the base, the standard. And I often wonder if more can be done to affirm and develop students' own culturally affiliated musical worlds. I have no doubt that the more they can interact with teachers from inside their own cultural worlds, this can happen more.

So, although the first important step has been taken towards broader inclusion and flexibility of the gateways into music teacher education, curriculums, course contents, and pedagogies have yet to undergo any major reconsideration. In many ways, Levinsky's Faculty of Music Education now echoes broader structures of Israeli music education where socio-religiously segregated groups of students share a single, hegemonic standard of teaching and learning. Even though public elementary and high school in Israel are socio-religiously segregated, all share the same Western, classically dominated, core music curriculum. At the same time, the college Faculty boasts two culturally segregated programs, but has done little work towards developing the cultural specificity of these programs' curriculums.

4   Translation Instead of Transformation

Levinsky's segregated music teacher education programs are based on a copy and paste of the curriculum that was previously established in the Faculty's integrated program. We interpret this approach as an act of translation rather than transformation. In a similar but broader gesture of intervention in Israeli music education, the Music Subject Committee of the Israel Ministry of Education commissioned a special task force in 2015 to create an Arabic version of the State Music Curriculum that was published in Hebrew in 2011. Again, this act was taken as an outward effort to recognize diversity and cater to culturally segregated populations. To date, however, we have witnessed most efforts being applied in the literal translation of existing policy documents from Hebrew into Arabic, rather than an overall reconsideration of the needs at hand.

4.1   The Mystery of the Missing High-School Music Programs

Our questioning of the effectiveness of such efforts is grounded in some lacunae that we have experienced in our respective fields of practice. In the Israeli public education system, there are currently over 130 registered high-school music-major programs dispersed throughout the country. All of these programs exist within the jurisdiction of Jewish school sectors. While several of these programs take place within schools that are open to non-Jewish populations, no high school music program exists in any school *within* the segregated Arab sector. The percentage of Jewish Ultraorthodox schools within this realm is also almost non-existent. Similar proportions exist in the realm of elementary school music, where over 80% of Jewish secular and Jewish religious schools teach music as a school subject, compared to almost non-existent percentages in Arab and Jewish Ultraorthodox schools (National Inspectorate of Music 2016).

This situation may not be surprising, considering that, in the most general terms that go far beyond music in education, both Arab and Jewish Ultraorthodox education systems have been repeatedly interpreted as lagging behind the Israeli public-education systems standards evident implemented in other sectors (e.g. Jabareen and Agbaria 2014; Perry-Hazan 2013). Socio-cultural constraints in Islamic decrees identify music as Harram (unholy), and both Islamic and Jewish conservative traditions associate music with licentious behavior (see e.g.: Badarne and Ehrlich in print; Dalal 2016; Shiloah 1992, 1997). These constraints may be effecting a low priority for music education within both religious contexts.

4.2 Policy and Music Teacher Education: Who's the Chicken and Who's the Egg?

Nevertheless, addressing this extensive lack of formal music education in Arab and Jewish Ultraorthodox schools, we believe that both policy and music teacher education have been instrumental in creating and perpetuating this situation. In terms of policy, for example, it is imperative to note that Israeli high-school music-matriculation exams focus almost absolutely on Western–Classical traditions and literacy (Ehrlich 2016). These same traditions and literacy act as gatekeepers to most music programs in Israeli institutions of higher education, where potential music teachers receive state certification. Music teacher education for both the elementary and high-school levels is structured through this same hegemonic approach that shapes the high-school music-matriculation exam.

Indeed, describing the constraints of Arab music education in Israel, Dalal (2016) implicated Western musical literacy as distracting Arab youngsters from their native musical literacies – those that are predominately oral by nature, and include aural sensitivity to quarter tones that elude Western, well-tempered tuning. Dalal notes a positive shift that occurred in the mid 1990s with the opening of several non-Western, undergraduate music programs that include dedicated training tracks for music teacher certification.

For the purpose of this current study, we have conducted an internet-based search of Isreali higher- education in music. Searching course descriptions and syllabi of such programs to-date within two Israeli accredited institutions of higher education that are leading this non-Western trend. Our findings reveal a persistent gap between non-Western content of music credits versus Western-dominated *music education* courses that comprise such programs. Perhaps, so long as Music Education policy stagnates within its Western–Classical paradigm, music teacher education must comply, while other undergraduate degrees are freer to pursue change.

4.3 "How Can I Teach What I Don't Know?"

During our daily encounters with Israeli music teachers and music education students in college courses and Professional Development seminars, we have asked current and future music teachers from Arabic speaking and Jewish Ultraorthodox communities to respond to the idea of a more multicultural curriculum. Belal and Amira have each conducted several classroom discussion groups on this topic, as an integral part of the music pedagogy classes and professional development courses that they teach. These discussions with students were part of their routine classroom interaction, and Belal and Amira retrospectively summarized sentiments from such encounters and shared this data with each other. Both researchers found that during such discussion it was quite common for respondents to implicate music teacher education as responsible for their own lack of knowledge of "other" musics. Teachers often remarked: "how can I teach what I don't know". Such responses indicate patterns of exclusion, if interpreted as proof of the dominance Western–Classical knowledge.

Another interpretation of this response can point to gaps between teachers' perception of formal knowledge as the basis of classroom teaching, negating other informal or cultural knowledge that they may have. Indeed, both Arab and Jewish religious communities incorporate music in their community religious practices (Shiloah 1992, 1997). Be it the cantillation call to prayer of the Mosque, or the prayer-song within the synagogue, or the impressive musicianship of wedding ensembles, religiously-oriented communities of both faiths boast rich musical traditions. Many of these community-based practices rely on aural traditions and include unique musical expertise that cannot be represented using Western–Classical notation.

5 Re-imaging Change

We interpret Israeli music education as existing within a predicament of a double bind, with the socio-religious segregation of the Israeli school system on the one hand, and the hegemonic implications of a single National Curriculum of Music, on the other. Addressing the challenges of music *teacher* education within this system, we would like to envision possibilities of expanding repertoires and pedagogies in ways that may connect school music practices with the musical lives of our students. Like Gay (2010), we feel a need for more second-order change, one that can effect deep structures, and underlying assumptions, rather than allowing the incorporation of culturally specific musical practices as additional knowledge and secondary techniques.

5.1 Segregation as Opportunity

Our experience has taught us that socio-religious segregation is sometimes crucial to allow for safe spaces and the existence of music teacher education where otherwise impossible (in terms of religious observances, language, and even geographical distances). Jewish Ultraorthdox women will never be allowed to engage in musical performance in the presence of any men or women beyond their own religious denomination. Arabic speaking populations were always a small minority in Levinsky's undergraduate music education programs before the separate program for Northern populations existed. Having a full class of Arabic-speaking future teachers encouraged discussion about the development of a culturally specific music curriculum – something that previously was overlooked or ignored.

Given the social segregation characteristic of the Israeli school system, we can imagine the possibilities of culturally responsive teaching (Gay 2010; Gaztambide-Fernández 2011; Lind and McKoy 2016); and we imagine that *segregation can become an opportunity to incorporate culturally specific musical expressions as legitimate and formal bodies of knowledge.*

Lind and McKoy defined culturally responsive teaching as "a mindset that requires careful thought in regards to content, context, and instruction" (2016, p. 97). In a recent Faculty gathering, Belal presented an outline of musical knowledge relevant to Arabic speaking populations. This outline included central concepts of Arabic music theory (maqamat and rhythms) and of Arabic music history (genres, composers, and performers). Around the same time, in an exercise of curriculum planning, Amira challenged students of the Arabic-speaking program to suggest a potential high-school music curriculum that would be relevant to the youth of their own communities. Student efforts echoed Belal's outline, incorporating listening examples of artists such as Fairuz and Om Kalthoum, and composers such as Fared el Atrash and Mohamed Abdel Wahab. Students demonstrated how to use such examples to practice identification and replication of rhythmic patterns and maqamat improvisational techniques.

Throughout this exercise, Amira noticed that most of the Arabic students' lesson planning intuitively tended towards a more holistic approach, with theory, history, and repertoire intertwined in a way that Western pedagogies can only aspire to:

> No matter what the starting point of any proposed lesson or unit was, the students always took care to move between listening, performing, and improvisational creativity, creating methodological and content-based links between these diverse learning activities.

Belal responded to Amira's experience:

> Indeed, when you study an Eastern instrument in an Eastern tradition, your teacher will take responsibility for your theoretical knowledge in the most practical way. While you are studying performance, you are obviously gaining knowledge of the structures and functions of maqamat and rhythms, that allow improvisation and composition. I am not sure that this is how it works with a Western instrumental teacher.

Thus, while both students and Faculty members are thus capable of envisioning a culturally relevant curriculum for Arabic-speaking populations, such a curriculum is not being systematically developed or implemented in teacher education or within schools. Amira expressed further criticism in the automatic adaptation of knowledge into Western formats, noting the tendency to perpetuate the Western split between music theory and music history rather than letting go of this dichotomy.

Amira expressed additional frustration toward the Ultraorthodox program, in what she experiences as a kind of ignorance of Christian, pagan, and secular underpinnings of Western repertoire and music history.

> The Ultraorthodox suspicion of modernity has qualified anything 'classical' as *kosher*. Thus, as long as the music historically belongs to the Western classical tradition it is deemed as 'proper'. I often witness women singing or performing music taken from contexts quite opposite to Ultraorthodox standards of cultural purity, but the women are completely oblivious. Mozart's Aria 'Voi Che Sapete', for example, is a standard for beginning voice students. This aria is all about passion and desire that are forbidden for Ultraorthodox women to express so explicitly in public. I listen to them singing and wonder what their teacher has told them that the song is about.

Amira imagines that deep thought and awareness of such gaps between local cultural norms and cultural implications of the music involved could facilitate a music education that is much more aligned with the actual cultural values of this community. In her work, Amira has, for example, suggested incorporation of prayer song and even joyous dance tunes that are part of community life.

6   Conclusions

As music teacher educators acting for change, we negotiate possibilities within our classrooms and lecture halls, even as we lobby for policy reform. In doing so, we are opening up a space between policy and institutional dictates, and between dictates and practice. Such action begins even in a simple acknowledgement of Gaztambide-Fernández' assertion that "*the lives of all students are already filled with meaningful musical practices*" (2011, p. 32). By encouraging students to bring such musics to class (via recording and/or live performance) we act to affirm the conceptualization of all musics as legitimate academic knowledge.

Engaging music education students from Arab and Jewish populations, we are guided by Gay's question: "How would teaching attitudes and behaviors differ if they emphasized talent, potential, and strengths of culturally diverse students, families, and communities instead of their problems and pathologies" (2010, p. 144). Rather than addressing Western notation as a mandatory, core departure point, we invite students to share and to explore their own musical lives, just as they live them. In doing so, we act to promote the musical agency of student–teachers, and invite them to be creative about repertoires and pedagogies that they are designing for future classrooms.

For now, our work is limited to those individuals who *have* passed the gatekeepers of higher music education. Our hope is that such work may prove the value and necessity of expanding the cadre of music education students, even as it challenges policy frameworks.

We believe that social coherence may be promoted through local development of diverse musical practices that are more culturally aligned with their own specific Jewish and Arab communities than Western–Classical literacy. We imagine future efforts could then include frameworks for intercultural sharing based on cultural specificity rather than solely on the common core Western hegemonies. Finally, we suspect that Israeli society as a whole can benefit from the investment in such enriching diversity.

Culturally specific music education that balances internal community needs with intercommunity sharing can serve as an example of social activism that works to affirm cultural and religious diversity as a source of social vitality. In this way, Israeli music teacher educators can join in efforts to contribute to the complex matrix of socio-religious tensions, explicitly addressing the challenge affirm diversity, while exploring possibilities cohesion that do not undermine such affirmations. Such a professional standard can turn the field of music education into a social laboratory committed to experimenting with balances of diversity, inclusion, sharing, and cohesion: the core challenges of Israeli society and of all other multicultural societies.

References

Adler, S. (2016). *National Religious State Education.* Presentation at Mandel Institute of Educational Leadership, Jerusalem.

Badarne, B., & Ehrlich, A. (in print). Dancing on the limits: An interreligious dialogue exploring the lived experience of two religiously observant music educators in Israel. In A. Kallio, P. Alperson & H. Westerlund (Eds.), *Perspectives on music, education and religion: A critical inquiry.* Bloomington: Indiana University Press.

Barrett, M. S. (2011). *A cultural psychology of music education.* Oxford: Oxford University Press.

Baumann, G. (1999). *The multicultural riddle: Rethinking national, ethnic, and religious identities (Zones of religion).* New York: Routledge.

Blommaert, J. (2010). *The sociolinguistics of globalization.* Cambridge: Cambridge University Press.

Carter, G. R. (2007). Learning together, living together. *Educational Leadership, 65*(2), 82–84.

Dalal, I. (2016). *HaChinuch hamusicali ba'migzar ha'Aravi* [Music education in the Arab sector]. Presentation at Israeli Musicological Society Winter Conference, Tel Aviv.

Ehrlich, A. (2016). Dictating "diversity": A case of how language constructs policy in Israeli music education. *Finnish Journal of Music Education, 19*(2), 30–47.

Ehrlich, A. (2018). *Pray, play, teach: Conversations with three Jewish Israeli music educators.* Unpublished doctoral dissertation, Boston University.

Elazar, D. (1997). Education in a society at a crossroads: An historical perspective on Israeli schooling. *Israel Studies, 2*(2), 40–65.

Fitzpatrick, K. R. (2012). Cultural diversity and the formation of identity: Our role as music teachers. *Music Educators Journal, 98*(4), 53–59.

Gay, G. (2010). Acting on beliefs in teacher education for cultural diversity. *Journal of Teacher Education, 61*(1–2), 143–152.

Gaztambide-Fernández, R. A. (2011). Musicking in the city: Reconceptualizing urban music education as cultural practice. *Action, Criticism, and Theory for Music Education, 10*(1), 15–46.

Gluschankof, C. (2008). Music everywhere: Overt and covert, official and unofficial early childhood music education policies and practices in Israel. *Arts Education Policy Review, 109*(3), 37–46.

Israel Ministry of Education. (2011). *Musica: Tochnit limudim* [Music: A curriculum]. Tel-Aviv: Ma'alot.

Jabareen, Y., & Agbaria, A. K. (2014). Otonomiya LaHinuch HaAravi BiIsrael [Autonomy for Arab education in Israel]. *Giluyi Daat, 5*, 13–40.

Kronish, R. (2015). *Coexistence & reconciliation in Israel: Voices for interreligious dialogue.* Mahwah: Paulist Press.

Lind, V. R., & McKoy, C. L. (2016). *Culturally responsive teaching in music education.* New York City: Routledge.

Munroe, M. E. R. (2000). Unamerican tail: Of segregation and multicultural education. *Albany Law Review, 64*(1), 241–308.

National Inspectorate of Music. (2016). *Presentation at the Dostrovsky forum for music and dance education.* Jerusalem: Van Leer Institute.

Perry-Hazan, L. (2013). *Hahinuch haharedi biIsrael* [The ultraorthodox education in Israel]. Jerusalem: Hebrew University.

Semyonov, M. & Andrea, T. (1981). Community segregation and the costs of ethnic subordination. *Social Forces, 59*(3), 649–666.

Scollon, R., Scollon, S. W., & Jones, R. H. (2012). *Intercultural communication a discourse approach* (3rd ed.). Chichester: Wiley-Blackwell.

Shiloah, A. (1992). *Jewish musical traditions.* Detroit: Wayne State University Press.

Shiloah, A. (1997). Music and religion in Islam. *Acta Musicologica, 69*(2), 143–155.

Talbot, B. C. (2013). Discourse analysis as potential for re-visioning music education. *Action, Criticism, and Theory for Music Education, 12*(1), 47–63.

Tzameret, T. (2003). *Hahinuch baasor harishon* [Education in the first decade]. Tel Aviv: Open University.

Woodson, K. (2016). Diversity without integration. *Penn State Law Review, 120*(3), 807–866.

3

Engaging Practitioners as Inquirers: Co-constructing Visions for Music Teacher Education in Nepal

Danielle Shannon Treacy

Abstract This chapter explores how co-constructing visions might engage teachers as inquirers in a 'majority world' context by reflecting on a series of 16 Appreciative Inquiry workshops involving over 50 musician-teachers in the Kathmandu Valley, Nepal in 2016. It extends the concept of teachers' visions (Hammerness, Teach Educ Q 31(Fall):33–43, 2004) through socio-cultural anthropologist Arjun Appadurai's notions of the imagination (Modernity at large: Cultural dimensions of globalization. University of Minnesota Press, Minneapolis, 1996) and the social and cultural capacity to aspire (Culture and public action. Stanford University Press, Stanford, 2004). The chapter reflects on the processes that took place when co-constructing visions, including the ways co-constructing visions may have been the fuel for action, and analyzes the implications of the resulting co-constructed visions. The findings highlight the importance of developing and supporting collaborative learning for the development of both preservice and inservice music teacher education.

Keywords Teachers' visions · Co-constructed visions · Imagination · Capacity to aspire · Appreciative inquiry · Majority world · Nepal

Music teacher education today is faced with the challenge of preparing professionals for an uncertain future; teachers who are capable of ethically engaging in intercultural settings, and continuously and systematically inquiring to increase their professional knowledge (see e.g. Cochran-Smith and Lytle 2009; Holgersen and Burnard 2013). One possible way of engaging with such an uncertain future is through envisioning. In the field of education, Karen Hammerness defines teachers' visions as the

---

D. S. Treacy (✉)
Sibelius Academy, University of the Arts Helsinki, Helsinki, Finland
e-mail: danielle.treacy@uniarts.fi

images that teachers hold of "ideal classroom practices" and that reveal their "hopes and dreams" (2004, 34). She describes how visions represent a teacher's aspirations, a reach beyond their current practice, and she connects them to teacher motivation both to change teaching practice and curriculum, and in relation to teacher identity and feelings of success (Hammerness 2015). Visions have also been found to have implications for teacher education. It has been proposed, for example, that effective teacher education programs are designed around and promote a clear and shared vision of good teaching, are coherent, and offer opportunities to learn that are aligned with the vision and grounded in teaching practice (Darling-Hammond 2006; Hammerness 2013; Klette and Hammerness 2016). Furthermore, the relationship between a teacher's vision and the teacher education program vision has been found to either help or hinder new teachers' development (Hammerness 2015).

In music teacher education, visions have been recognized as a possible tool "for critical examination of music teaching traditions and beliefs that so often (unconsciously) shape ideas and practices" and for "assessing music teaching and learning" (Ferm Thorgersen et al. 2016, 60). Similarly, Talbot and Mantie describe the "truly reflective practice required for visioning" (2015, 176) which they highlight as an important way of questioning and resisting a "passive acceptance of the legitimate order" (2015, 177) in the music teaching profession. Talbot and Mantie stress that "the failure to analyze and imagine how things could be different, however – to imagine different rationalities – almost certainly guarantees that things will not change" (2015, 176). This said, Conkling has recognized the complex and interrelated influences of both compliance and utopian thinking on teachers' visions. She uses examples of the myths of prediction and control, teacher as expert, and the ability to teach as a natural talent, to illustrate that "compliance is a powerful force in shaping teachers' visions" (2015, 191) and therefore "might be difficult for preservice teachers to avoid" (2015, 191). Thus, she argues that music teacher educators have a responsibility to preservice teachers to acknowledge the policies and practices that may constrain them as future music teachers, while designing meaningful and transformative experiences and teaching "envisioning greater equity, inclusion, creativity, and joy for the children who will be in our preservice teachers' future classrooms" (Conkling 2015, 191).

These understandings of teachers' visions may be insufficient, however, in a research study that involves co-constructing visions for the development of music teacher education in Nepal. First, because visions have been found to be individual and not necessarily shared by all colleagues, other educators, or other institutions (Ferm Thorgersen et al. 2016; Hammerness 2013; Juntunen 2014). Second, because the research on teacher visions and program visions has so far been limited to western contexts and countries with established teacher education programs. In a 'majority world'[1] context, such as Nepal, where music teacher education is only beginning to be developed, the situation may be radically different.

Due to these limitations, this chapter extends the concept of teachers' visions through the case of music teacher education in Nepal and socio-cultural

---

[1] The 'majority world' is a concept offered by Dasen and Akkari (2008) to challenge western ethnocentrism and to acknowledge that, in terms of global population, the rich, industrialized nations of the West and North actually comprise the minority.

anthropologist Arjun Appadurai's notions of the *imagination* (1996) and the social and cultural *capacity to aspire* (2004). Although a music education curriculum was adopted by the Nepalese Ministry of Education in 2010, there is currently no formal, government-recognized music teacher education. Consequently, the Nepal Music Center (NMC)[2] contacted the Sibelius Academy, University of the Arts Helsinki in 2012, which led to collaborative developmental work and research on music teacher education between the two institutions. As its name suggests, the resulting research project, *Global Visions Through Mobilizing Networks: Co-Developing Intercultural Music Teacher Education in Finland, Israel and Nepal*, has an overall objective to explore the negotiation of visions for co-developing intercultural music teacher education globally through partnerships and collaboration. As Nepal is a country characterized by extraordinary diversity, currently recognizing 126 caste/ethnic groups, 123 languages spoken as mother tongue and ten religions (Government of Nepal 2012), and as it is experiencing an intensified rate of societal change and globalization, the development of intercultural music teacher education in Nepal may be seen to play an important role in positioning diversity and difference as opportunities, rather than problems to be overcome.

In the absence of music teacher education, musicians in the Kathmandu Valley are employed to teach music in private schools, music institutions, and private homes, usually on the basis of artistic merit; thus, I use the term musician-teachers. As part of the Global Visions project, I facilitated a series of Appreciative Inquiry[3] workshops with musician-teachers to co-construct visions for music education in Nepal over an 11-week period between April and June 2016. The workshops were conceived as one possible way to address some of the aims of the Global Visions project, including promoting music teacher agency, creating a network of practitioners, and having a practical impact on the development of music teacher education by including practitioners in the process of knowledge building.

My work in the Global Visions project begins with a presupposition of equality (Ranciere 1991), as I aim to adopt an anti-colonial stance (Patel 2014) in order to ethically undertake a research project immersed in the complexities of western ethnocentrism (e.g. Dasen and Akkari 2008). I am a first-generation Canadian (Canada being a settler colony), of parents who emigrated from both colonized and colonizing European countries, and I now live in Finland as an immigrant. In Nepal, my whiteness and university-researcher status carry privilege and power, positioning me as a 'foreign expert.' I am simultaneously answerable to the Nepali participants, to the research project leaders, and to the Sibelius Academy and Academy of Finland who fund my work. My personal investment in this research project is linked to the successful completion of my doctoral studies and to my future career, which made me dependent upon Nepali musician-teachers attending and participating in the

---

[2] The Nepal Music Center (NMC) was established in 2005 and is home to "Nepal Sangeet Vidhyalaya" (NSV) the first music school in Nepal established with due permission from the Ministry of Education, Government of Nepal. Representatives from NMC were included in the national panel that collaborated with the Ministry of Education to develop the national music curricula.

[3] For more on Appreciative Inquiry (AI), see e.g. Cooperrider, Whitney and Stavros (2005) and Watkins, Mohr and Kelly (2011); the workshops will be described in detail below.

workshops, not only for the co-construction of knowledge but also for my own professional gain (Patel 2014).

Although a primary aim of the workshops was to co-construct visions for music education in Nepal, I was conscious of the limited availability of professional development opportunities or active music teacher associations in Nepal. Consequently, I envisioned the workshops as a community of inquirers in which participants could develop their teaching through learning from and with each other, and that this community might support the building of a music teacher network and thus have value beyond its research beginnings. As such, this chapter addresses the following research question and sub-questions:

- How might the process of co-constructing visions engage practitioners as inquirers in a majority world context?

  - What are the characteristics of the processes that take place when co-constructing visions?
  - In what ways might co-constructing visions be the fuel for action in a majority world context?

1 Imagination and the Capacity to Aspire

To push towards an understanding of co-constructed visions, and move beyond the sphere of North America and Europe, I draw upon the work of Arjun Appadurai, particularly his notions of the imagination (1996) and the social and cultural capacity to aspire (2004). Appadurai identifies the imagination, especially when collective, as a potential "fuel for action" (1996, 7) and thus "central to all forms of agency" (1996, 31). He describes it as,

> An organized field of social practices, a form of work (in the sense of both labor and culturally organized practice), and a form of negotiation between sites of agency (individuals) and globally defined fields of possibility. (Appadurai 1996, 31)

The imagination informs the daily lives of ordinary people in numerous ways. It is used both to discipline and control citizens, and for collective dissent and redesigning ways of being together (Appadurai 2000).

Appadurai's ideas of imagination flow into what he describes as the capacity to aspire, "the social and cultural capacity to plan, hope, desire, and achieve socially valuable goals" (Appadurai 2006, 176). He describes aspirations as being related to "wants, preferences, choices, and calculations" (Appadurai 2004, 67) and being formed through social interaction and located "in a larger map of local ideas and beliefs" (2004, 68). As such, co-constructing visions with Nepali musician-teachers could be understood as engaging their collective imagination in aspiring towards what they deem to be *socially valuable goals*.

According to Appadurai (2004), however, the capacity to aspire is unevenly distributed in society. As a navigational capacity, it is the better off or more privileged in any society who "have used the map of its norms to explore the future more frequently and more realistically, and to share this knowledge with one another more routinely than their poorer and weaker neighbors" (Appadurai 2004, 69). This uneven distribution may also be linked to opportunities to practice the capacity to aspire, for instance in educational development globally where practitioner expertise and participation is often overlooked. This has also been the case with the Nepali musician-teachers who have so far not been included by the government in the planning of music teacher education. Appadurai (2006) argues that the uneven distribution of the capacity to aspire is both a sign and gauge of poverty, but something that can be changed by politics and policy.

Intimately connected to the capacity to aspire is what Appadurai (2006) calls the right to research, which he defines as the capacity to systematically increase one's current knowledge relative to a task, goal, or aspiration (176). The capacity to aspire and the right to research are intimately connected because "without aspiration, there is no pressure to know more. And without systematic tools for gaining relevant new knowledge, aspiration degenerates into fantasy or despair" (Appadurai 2006, 176–177). Appadurai further argues that the right to research is essential to "claims for democratic citizenship" (2006, 167), as one needs to be informed in order to participate in democratic society especially in a world of rapid change and global flows (2006, 177). Hence, aspiring together may also motivate Nepali musician-teachers to learn both from and with each other and towards increased democratic participation.

2 Co-constructing Visions for Music Education in Nepal

In order to address the first research sub-question, I here introduce Appreciative Inquiry and provide a detailed description of how the visions were co-constructed.

2.1 *Appreciative Inquiry*

An early challenge in this study was to find a method of co-constructing visions for music education in Nepal that would avoid ethnocentrism and coloniality. I chose to apply Appreciative Inquiry (AI, see e.g. Cooperrider et al. 2005; Watkins et al. 2011), which comes from the field of organization development and the practice of change management, and is grounded in social constructionist theory (e.g. Gergen 1978, 2009). AI appeared to be particularly well suited to this study, as envisioning together is built into the four phases of its 4D cycle of Discover, Dream, Design and Destiny. Reminiscent of Appadurai's notion of imagination, AI strongly connects envisioning to action, as Cooperrider and Whitney explain that "human systems are forever projecting ahead of themselves a horizon of expectation (...) that brings the future powerfully into the present as a mobilizing agent" (2001, 624). Although the participants were musician-teachers, the workshops were predominantly discussion-based. While we did make music together at the beginning of most workshops, it was the discussion, not the music-making, that aimed specifically at co-constructing visions.

Throughout the inquiry, I applied AI critically, remembering that it was developed in the United States of America and that most of the references that informed my workshop planning were North American (e.g. Cooperrider et al. 2005; Watkins et al. 2011). AI, however, is not new to Nepal (see e.g. Messerschmidt 2008; Odell and Mohr 2008). It has been used since 1994 (NAINN n.d.), including Imagine Nepal (IN), which was launched in 2002. According to the Imagine Nepal website

> AI practitioners in Nepal incepted IN to contribute to restore peace and harmony in Nepal by using their talent and skills in managing conflicts and fostering equitable development through the process of Appreciative Inquiry.... as a movement for peace and prosperity in Nepal. (Imagine Nepal, About Us, par. 2)

Cooperrider and colleagues describe this as having involved the mobilization of "more than 1,000 appreciative leaders throughout Nepal" (Cooperrider et al. 2005, vii).

In addition to an awareness of possible ethnocentrism, applying AI critically also meant that I was engaged in ongoing ethical deliberations related to issues of power, cross-cultural (Liamputtong 2010) and anticolonial (Patel 2014) research, and informed by a reach for collaborative ethnography (Lassiter 2005) and ongoing dialogue with my Nepali co-facilitator. In addition, prior to facilitating these workshops in 2016, I visited the Kathmandu Valley on two different occasions for 3 weeks each in 2014. The music lessons I observed during school visits, interviews with seven musician-teachers and seven administrators from six different schools, and two pilot AI workshops in a music institution during 2014 served to inform the planning of the 2016 workshops, both in terms of the questions asked as well as ethical, methodological and practical considerations. For example, although the Global Visions project aims to envision music teacher education, these workshops focused on music education in general with a goal of producing knowledge for the development of Nepali music teacher education. This focus was a result of my interviews with musician-teachers in 2014 because when I asked questions related to their wishes for music teacher education the responses were rather limited. In 2016, while planning and facilitating the workshops I continued to visit schools and music lessons, this time also sometimes teaching.

2.2 Building a Network

In the planning stages, the workshops were targeted to musician-teachers teaching in Kathmandu Valley's private schools as many of these schools offer music as an extracurricular activity or school subject. As an outsider, it seemed to make sense to focus on school-based musician-teachers if music was a new subject in the national curriculum, and the Nepal Music Center did not have any knowledge of musician-teachers in government schools. However, I came to learn that many musician-teachers teach in combinations of private schools, music institutions, and homes. Additionally, if a major aim of the study was to build a network of music teachers then limiting participation to certain teachers would begin the network from a position of exclusion rather than inclusion. Thus, I chose to open participation to all musician-teachers.

Invitations were sent via telephone, email and Facebook to the musician-teachers who had participated in the pilot workshops I offered in 2014, administrators from schools I had visited in 2014, and teachers from the Nepal Music Center's network and one other music institution's network. Those invited directly were informed that they could invite others. The workshops took place with three different groups of musician-teachers. For clarity and anonymity, they are here named Group A and B, which took place in two different music institutions, and Group C, which took place at a private school. Group C's workshops began the same week as Group B's with the goal of bringing them together, thus the same materials were used in both. In addition, a separate workshop titled, *Encouraging girls' participation in music in Nepal*, was organized as gender issues, namely the increased challenges females face in studying music or pursuing a career in music, arose as an important topic during the other workshops, and I wanted to provide a female-only space for discussion. For the sake of brevity, this workshop is presented elsewhere (Treacy 2019).

Participation in the workshops and the study as a whole was voluntary and informed consent was given by all participants. The first workshops were bilingual, with all written materials in both English and Nepali, and an effort to ensure that all speech was translated between English and Nepali. As the participating musician-teachers were comfortable participating in English, however, workshop materials from the second workshops onward were only in English. A translator continued to be present at all times and participants were encouraged to express themselves both verbally and in written responses using the language of their choice. While acknowledging that "backstories are as limited as all the data excerpts that appear" (Jackson and Mazzei 2012, xii), I offer Table 1 as a brief introduction to the musician-teachers to provide context for the reader.

2.3 Co-constructing with Nepali Musician-Teachers

For the purposes of this chapter, the empirical material can be divided into three types. First are the audio recordings from all 16 workshops, transcribed in part and translated as needed. Second are participant written responses, both individual and group. Third are the handouts that I created for the workshops, the notes that I took during the workshops, my personal researcher diary, and what I have called a *dialogic researcher diary*. In September 2016, with the musician-teacher who acted as the co-facilitator and translator for the workshops, I initiated this dialogic researcher diary, in which we took turns writing and responding to each other's reflections, as a space for ongoing dialogue.

Throughout the process, meaning developed "within relations" (Kuntz 2015, 69). Following each workshop, I used the written response sheets completed by the participants and my own notes from the workshops, combined with carefully listening to the recordings, to compile and thematize the participants' responses and create a plan and handouts for the following workshop. An effort was made to preserve

Engaging Practitioners as Inquirers: Co-constructing Visions for Music...   43

Table 1 Overview of the musician-teachers involved in the workshops

Number of participants[a]	53 musician-teachers participated in at least one of the workshops:
	Group A total 16, each workshop 3–9
	Group B total 29, each workshop 16–23, including 2 non-Nepali
	Group C total 8, each workshop 5–7
Number of workshops	Group A: 8 3-h workshops (the first two of which were repeated with different groups of teachers for a total of ten meetings[b])
	Group B: 4 2-h workshops
	Group C: 2 workshops ranging from 1 to 1.5 h each
Gender	9 women:
	Group A total 2, 1 participated throughout
	Group B total 7, 5 participated throughout
	No female musician-teachers worked at Group C's school
Where they teach	Private schools, music institutions, homes
	Some teach in as many as five different places
Types of lessons	Private, small and large groups, mixed ensembles
Teaching experience	Ranged from a few months to decades
How they learned	Formally: private and group lessons in music institutions and universities
	Informally: self-teaching, learning with or from a friend or family member, making use of the internet, video lessons and reference books
	In India: one in a university brass band, and one had 5 years of formal music studies

[a]Numbers do not include me or my Nepali co-facilitator who is also a musician-teacher
[b]In the beginning, Group A workshops were offered on 2 different days of the week as finding a single time that suited many musician-teachers was challenging

the musician-teachers' own words as much as possible. We then began each workshop with dialogic reflection on my interpretations in group discussions, in which I also asked questions to clarify comments or ideas about which I was uncertain, for example, the social stigma regarding music and musicians, the prevalence of creating or composing in music lessons, or the 'right' music to teach in schools. Drafts of this chapter were also shared with workshop participants prior to publication, and the ongoing findings of the project as a whole continue to be regularly shared "so that they may serve and be interrogated by [the] community" (Patel 2014, 369). In the text below, all quotes from the participants appear in their original English.

2.4 Developing the Capacity to Aspire Through the 4D Cycle

2.4.1 Discovering the Potential for Learning from and with Each Other

The **Discovery** phase of AI aims to appreciate what the participants deem to be "the best of what is" (Cooperrider et al. 2005, 5). To do so, the musician-teachers began by interviewing a partner, following an interview guide that I had created. One of the core principles underlying AI is that "the questions we ask set the stage for what we 'find'" (Watkins et al. 2011, 73) and that "even the most innocent question evokes change" (Cooperrider and Whitney 2001, 623). Indeed, Cooperrider and Whitney maintain that "inquiry and change are a simultaneous moment" (Cooperrider and Whitney 2001, 623). Thus, I present the initial questions in Table 2 to allow the reader to reflect upon how they may have shaped the resulting co-constructed visions. The questions were different for the different groups because Group A was based at the same music institution as the 2014 pilot workshops and I wanted to respect the time and discussions of the pilot workshop participants. I did so by using the three themes they had identified as being the most important to pursue as a starting point: Making teaching and learning fun, encouraging students' self-expression, and teaching with limited resources (see Table 2 Group A questions 3, 4 and 5). With Group B and C, however, we started from the very beginning and I adapted the generic Appreciative Inquiry questions (Cooperrider et al. 2005, 25; Watkins et al. 2011, 155–156; see Table 2 Group B and C questions 1, 2 and 7), but also added questions based on my developing understandings from earlier interviews, workshops, and school visits (see Table 2 Group B and C questions 4 and 5). Upon reflection, the number of questions were too many for the time available, however they served their important role of stimulating dialogue and thus discovery with fellow musician-teachers.

Following the partner interviews the musician-teachers formed groups of approximately six teachers to reflect on the interviews by sharing a story or highlight. The small groups were then asked to decide on three to five topics or themes they wished to pursue during the next session. The process of interviewing a peer, listening carefully to their answers, taking notes, and then introducing their partner to a group took some explanation as to why the teachers should not simply write down their own answers. This, however, was the beginning of a process aimed at developing a community for learning from and with each other:

> I thought I was the only one who faces problems teaching students but there are other teachers with the same problems and so we can together overcome these problems. (Musician-teacher)

At the same time, it provided an opportunity for the musician-teachers themselves to be inquirers, practice the research skills of interviewing, and impact the direction of our workshops.

My role in the workshops was that of planner and facilitator. As a facilitator, I aimed to be for the participants "a means of knowledge – without transmitting any knowledge" (Rancière 2010, 2), instead highlighting the already existing local expertise as well as the potential for learning from and with each other. This challenged the musician-teachers' expectations for a workshop led by a 'foreign expert.' In the anonymous feedback, for example, 3 of the 18 returned response sheets mentioned the "visiting teacher" or "foreign trainer" "from [an] international university" as part of their motivation for first coming. One of the musician-teachers elaborated:

> it was very surprising and some of [the teachers] were confused [about] what is going on in the workshops. Because, you were supposed to talk all the time. They thought that you know all the things and will tell to the others.... This is because also they never had that type of experience and their school also never asked how school can be made better. (Musician-teacher)

Table 2 Questions used for partner interviews during the first workshops

Group A discovery interview questions
1. Think about a time when you were really engaged in and excited about your work. Please tell me a story about that time.
2. Think about a time when you learned something that helped make your teaching even better. Please tell me a story about that time.
3. Think about a time when students were really motivated and engaged. Please tell me a story about that time.
4. Think about a time that promoted student self-expression. Please tell me a story about that time.
5. Think about a time when you experienced great music teaching even though there were limited resources available. Please tell me a story about that time.
Group B and C discovery interview questions
1. *Best Experience:* Think about a highpoint in your experience as a music teacher. Please share a story about that time. When and where did it occur? What happened? Who was involved? Why do you consider it a high point? What made it exciting or engaging?
2. *Values: A value is something you consider to be of worth, excellence, usefulness, or importance; something you regard highly.* What do you especially value:
(a) About being a music teacher?
(b) About your strengths as a music teacher?
(c) About the school(s) you teach in?
3. People learn in different ways and experience the joy of learning in a variety of settings, both in and out of the classroom.
(a) Describe a learning or mentoring experience that was particularly meaningful for you. When and where did it occur? Who was involved? Why was this experience so effective and memorable?
(b) In your experience, what are one or two of your most effective tools or techniques for enhancing student learning and success?
4. In your experience, what are the best ways of engaging students when they are at different levels of ability but in the same class or lesson?
5. What have you found to be the most useful resources or approaches for structuring student learning throughout the school year?
6. What do you consider to be the most important factor contributing to excellent music education in your school(s)?
7. *Three wishes*: What three wishes do you have for enhancing music teaching and learning in Kathmandu?

2.4.2 Navigating the Capacity to Aspire

The **Dream** phase calls for participants to imagine "what might be" (Cooperrider et al. 2005, 5) if the best moments and experiences discovered in the previous phase were to occur more regularly. My uncertainty about how the process would unravel was frequently mentioned in my researcher diary:

> I have a hard time imagining how the next session will go. It is an experiment for me too. (Researcher diary)

In all three groups, we began the second workshop by reviewing the summary of themes that I had compiled and thematized based on the participants' written response sheets, my own notes taken during the first workshop, and my listening to the audio recordings. This was followed by a full group discussion of both the themes and my interpretations.

In Group A, the first Dream activity involved a group discussion guided by questions to imagine what outstanding music education, including their own teaching, could be like 3 years from now. This proved challenging, so for the third workshop I approached the dream by building upon a comment from one of the musician-teachers in the previous session, "If we want to change anything then we need to start from ourselves." Again, we tried partner interviews, but this time with five questions related to what they wished to accomplish or what they imagined success would look like for them this academic year.[4] Based upon these interviews they brainstormed opportunities to improve music teaching and learning in Kathmandu. This brainstorming continued in workshop four when we also experimented with having 10 min of freewriting to stimulate the discussion.

My ongoing search for different approaches to Dreaming in the workshops with Group A informed my planning of the second workshops with Groups B and C. Group B was asked to form small groups and, from the summary of themes, agree upon three that could have the greatest impact towards excellent music education. For each theme, they were asked to brainstorm an action plan and aspiration statement (ex. By May 2017 what we most aspire to in terms of X is Y). In Group C our workshop started 30 min late but had to end on time since we met before their music lessons. As a result, we only got as far as each teacher selecting their personal three, and missed the opportunity to then engage in discussion to agree upon a shared three.

For the fifth workshop with Group A, I prepared a handout that combined the summary of themes from Group B and C's first workshops with the themes that had been brainstormed during Group A's third and fourth workshops to stimulate further discussion and reflection for the creation of their own dreams. From this, each teacher selected three themes that they believed could have the greatest impact towards excellent music education, and during the following workshop Group A agreed on three shared themes.

2.4.3 Design and Destiny

In the **Design** phase participants co-construct a future "grounded in the realities of what has worked in the past combined with what new ideas are envisioned for the future" (Cooperrider et al. 2005, 7). In both Group A and Group B, brainstorming around the selected themes led to the formation of the co-constructed visions. In Group A, for each of the three agreed upon themes, the musician-teachers brainstormed the key elements of their ideal version of it and ideas about specific things that could occur now or in the near future for its realization. In Group B, each musician-teacher was asked to first independently select the theme s/he found most

---

[4] The academic year started around April 20, with some variation by school.

compelling to work with and then form a small group with others who selected the same theme. In these small groups they then brainstormed to create a provocative proposition, meaning "a statement that bridges the best of 'what is' and 'what might be'" to convey positive images of the ideal future (Cooperrider et al. 2005, 168), and an action plan. Time was given at the end of this workshop to report back to the larger group to get feedback before refining their ideas and sharing them with me so that I could type them for the final workshop handout. This kind of brainstorming was received quite positively:

> For me it was really wonderful to have a brainstorming session on various issues, which I'd never thought of before. (Musician-teacher)

The **Destiny** phase is about finding "innovative ways to help move the organization closer to the ideal" (Cooperrider et al. 2005, 7). During the final workshop with Group B we read and reflected upon each of the co-constructed visions with a focus on refining them. The musician-teachers were given time after we read the draft of each vision to reflect on and independently write feedback guided by questions provided on the response sheets. This was followed by a full group discussion. The process was repeated for each of the co-constructed visions. Allowing time for written response prior to the group discussion was an attempt to capture plurality and what might remain unsaid. Throughout the AI 4D cycle, I was highly aware that its focus on co-constructing, and thus consensus, resulted in a loss of multiple perspectives. Time restraints, however, influenced both the number of questions for which teachers wrote responses and how much discussion could be had.

With Group A we took the opportunity to have a group discussion based on the drafts of Group B's co-constructed visions as a way of sharing and stimulating ideas, and because the two groups had some overlapping themes. The group discussion was guided by the same questions as Group B. Group A's final workshop then began with reviewing, reflecting upon and refining their own co-constructed visions.

As a final activity in both groups, we created and shared Individual Actions based on the parts of the visions each musician-teacher wanted to bring to life. The Individual Actions were either in the form of a simple commitment (e.g. an action that could easily be taken within the next few weeks), an offer (e.g. sharing a resource or expertise, giving a workshop, helping another teacher, collaborating with someone), or a request (e.g. something needed from another person or group to contribute to one of these dreams) (see Watkins et al. 2011, 241–242). I chose this as a final activity because I noticed that as we became better at imagining an ideal future, the challenge became pinpointing *how* to realize it. Individual Actions appeared to be a way for each person to find some step that they could take. The result was that we ended the workshops "on an uplifting note" (Researcher diary).

My researcher diary from these last days in Kathmandu reminds me how exhausting and emotional this process was, and how my uncertainties continued until the end. Referring to our penultimate workshop with Group A, I wrote:

> Monday's workshop was nice. Maybe it's because I've been feeling tired that I feel a bit like the momentum is down. Why did [Musician-teacher] stop coming? Did we go beyond our natural life span? Though, when I said that the following Monday would be our last it felt sad to me as well. (Researcher diary)

Having spent so much time together, our final Group A workshop had an unexpected festive feel. In addition to the snacks that I usually provided, the musician-teachers surprised me by bringing special foods to share with the group that they wanted me to try.

3 The Co-constructed Visions

To address the second research sub-question, here the co-constructed visions are presented, followed by a focus on how the visions led to both envisioning continued collaboration and action in the form of an all-female gig and a community of musician-teachers.

3.1 The Visions

The visions that resulted from the 4D cycle are summarized in Table 3, organized from macro to micro levels. I understand these visions to be "temporally located" (Patel 2014). In another time or with other teachers, the resulting visions may have been different. These visions are also important for what they do *not* include, or their silences. For example, despite gender issues being highlighted in workshop discussions and even inspiring a female-only workshop, they did not find their way into the visions (Treacy 2019). It is also crucial to contemplate the degree to which my questions and presence influenced the resulting visions. For instance, in retrospect the leading nature of Group B and C's third question, which began with the statement "People learn in different ways and experience the joy of learning in a variety of settings, both in and out of the classroom" (see Table 2), may have led to the seventh vision, *"That music teachers would use a variety of teaching and learning techniques in the classroom to make learning easier for students because no one method will work for every teacher or every student"* (see Table 3). Finally, these visions should be viewed not as a final product, but as the beginning of a process, and not only for the musician-teachers who co-constructed them. The visions have been shared with decision makers currently involved in the development of Nepal's first government-recognized music teacher education program, for example in March 2017 and November 2018 when I presented my ongoing research project and preliminary findings to representatives from the Ministry of Education, Tribhuvan University, and the Nepal Music Center.

Table 3 Summary of the co-constructed visions (organized from macro to micro levels)

Society
To live in a society where music is valued, including where people recognize that music is vital, where the social stigma has been overcome and where music is for all
Profession
To create a music community that brings all music lovers to work together and create professionalism
To develop unity between the major music institutions in Nepal so that activities become more controlled, efficient
Institutions
To develop an internationally recognized music and music education (music teacher training) course in Nepal through affiliations with an outside university for Nepali, eastern and western musics
That music would be an included (and valued) subject in schools
To have properly designed music organizations with enough instruments, proper classes, etc.
Individuals
That music teachers would use a variety of teaching and learning techniques in the classroom to make learning easier for students because no one method will work for every teacher or every student

3.2 *Imagining Continued Collaboration*

As can be seen from the co-constructed visions, the experiences in the workshops led to the musician-teachers envisioning continued collaboration. This is reflected in the vision to *"Create a music community that brings all music lovers to work together and create professionalism."* Although collaborating to reflect on their teaching practice and learn from and with each other was a new experience, musician-teachers overwhelmingly felt that this kind of community building was "necessary." Such a lack of professional collaboration is common not only for Nepali musician-teachers, but music teachers globally who often work in relative isolation (see e.g. Bates 2011; Burnard 2013; Sindberg 2011; Schmidt and Robbins 2011).

This vision was elaborated through discussions and written responses. One group's response captures some of the details:

> Build a community so that skills are divided among many and the community becomes the 'voice of the voiceless,' networking is created with other music lovers (teachers, students and aficionados), and lobbying with the government for various things. The community is a bridge between the government and professionalism. The community works as an advocate to the government regarding music education policy; a creator of awareness among parents and students; provides opportunities to students and teachers; regulation/standard maintenance or monitoring is also what a community for music could do. (Group written response to dream activity, parenthesis original)

Through engaging their capacity to aspire, the musician-teachers envisioned the music community exercising voice, for example through "lobbying with the government" and creating "awareness among parents and students." This capacity to exercise voice is crucial to inclusion and participation in democracy (Appadurai 2004). Appadurai considers voice to be a cultural capacity,

> because for voice to take effect, it must engage social, political, and economic issues in terms of ideologies, doctrines, and norms which are widely shared and credible, even by the rich and powerful. Furthermore, voice must be expressed in terms of actions and performances which have local cultural force. (2004, 66–67)

In the case of the imagined music community, musician-teachers recognized context-specific challenges. One of the groups raised a concern:

> even if a community is formed, there will be fractures or factions based on nepotism, favouritism, difference in customs or ethnicity, or religion, or groupism (these are all the ill effects of politics and its infection on professionalism and community). (Group written response to design brainstorming, parenthesis original)

There was general consensus that "this prevails in our society" and "that's how it has always been." In imagining how it might be avoided, the majority of ideas were connected to appreciating and learning through difference,

> difference in community and ideas should be used to enhance education instead of making it an issue for ex. instrument, ideas, ethnic music. (Musician-teacher)

Appreciating difference involved getting to know others from different backgrounds for example through shared activities like workshops, and accepting and learning "all forms of music":

> This can be avoided when learning music from other cultures/ethnicities is encouraged (sarangi and sanai are instruments played by 'low caste people', but if a movement starts where people accept folk instruments/music regardless of 'social stigma' then it's a positive change). (Musician-teacher, parenthesis original)

At the same time, however, in this context it appears that not all differences are welcome, as ideas including keeping the community "free of politics" and even excluding "politically affiliated people" were offered, echoing the group response above. A musician-teacher explained:

> we were talking about creating an open community where we can include everyone from society because this is the only way of creating sustainable social development.... In this context, teachers fear that if they allowed any political party in the community then they would certainly... use [it] for political purpose. Politicians are always concerned with their party agenda not the teacher's benefit. It is good to have politicians so that they can help us raise the music teacher's agenda to national policy makers. But, they only do so if they are getting power and position. (Musician-teacher)

Teachers also stressed ideas related to providing equal opportunities in a society that is very stratified along ethnic and caste lines. Musician-teachers envisioned a music community in which "each person should be valued equally, treated equally and for example if we favour someone then there should be a specific reason" (Musician-teacher). It was also recognized how these attitudes need to start from within:

> Unless music teachers, music learners, and music researchers view one another with equal respect, we cannot expect the society to view music positively as a whole & community building isn't possible. (Musician-teacher)

3.3 Fuel for Action

Although we ended the workshops by sharing Individual Actions, my intention was never to follow up on these. Rather, I saw them as an opportunity for the teachers to envision small ways that they could create change. This was particularly important, because as it became easier to envision what the future could look like for music education in Nepal, it continued to be challenging to envision how and who could help the visions be realized. Feelings of agency, however, were evident in the musician-teachers' final responses, for example, to the question about what they had valued about participating in the workshops one teacher wrote:

> Having a common dream and working for it, making it possible (changing the society). (Musician-teacher, parenthesis original)

At the time of writing, the women who attended the *Encouraging girls' participation in music in Nepal* workshop initiated a Facebook conversation of over 40 members, which turned into a closed Facebook group with over 30 members. They held meetings and rehearsals to plan and organize an all-female gig to raise awareness and enhance female participation in music in Nepal. The gig was held in January 2017 with six acts and over 20 performers, including performances of new compositions created specifically for the event. In addition, in November 2016 a group of 25 people met, including head teachers and musician-teachers, for an event they titled 'Strategic Planning for the Future of Music Education in Nepal' that made use of the co-constructed visions as a starting point for future work. This group met again in December 2016 for 'Planning for Action' and carefully planned a series of 5 monthly workshops to be held from February to June 2017. Despite this, attendance continued to drop so significantly that not all of these meetings took place and, as of this writing, a small group of committed and enthusiastic musician-teachers are reconsidering their approach. Their experience highlights the extremely fragile nature of teacher communities.

The original enthusiasm for their meetings may have been attributed to their initiation by a foreign teacher who participated in the workshops and taught at the prestigious international private school where the meetings took place. Because of this, the community could be seen as continuing to be organized in cooperation with a 'foreign expert' and therefore possibly related to feelings of "success in a globalised world" (Appadurai 2006, 172). However, it may be that this foreign teacher has access to resources, in terms of time and financial stability for example, that the local teachers do not necessarily have. Additionally, it was also suggested that the diminishing attendance may have been related to the current lack of collaboration between institutions – a lack of collaboration countered in the vision "*To develop unity between the major music institutions in Nepal so that activities become more controlled, efficient.*"

Thus, for workshops or meetings such as these to survive, it is not enough that they are valued by, for example, the musician-teachers. More importantly, they need to be valued and supported by the educational institutions "as vital sources of knowledge and action" (Cochran-Smith and Lytle 2009, 154), so that participating in and organizing workshops is not merely something left to the responsibility of teachers and relegated to their limited free time. Rather, institutions should consider what is essential to "create and sustain the conditions for critical inquiry communities within and across settings," for example by making "inviolable the necessary time for substantive collaboration" (Cochran-Smith and Lytle 2009, 154), perhaps by including such meetings as part of the paid work of a teacher. Such actions would open the right to research to a wider community. Indeed, Schmidt and Robbins argue that "success will be more likely if the work of such communities is systematically structured as part of a school- or district-wide educational mission" (2011, 99; see also Cochran-Smith and Lytle 2009).

4 Intercultural Learnings

The overarching research question of this chapter sought to consider how the process of co-constructing visions might engage teachers as inquirers in a majority world context, by reflecting upon the 16 Appreciative Inquiry workshops I facilitated with Nepali musician-teachers during an 11-week period. This reflection suggests that as Nepal works to develop its first music teacher education program, a program that needs to educate interculturally competent teachers capable of guiding teaching and learning for students from 126 caste/ethnic groups in 77 national districts in a rapidly changing and globalizing society, decision makers now need to envision the kind of music teacher education program they wish to develop. Do they merely wish to provide teachers with "vocational credentials" (Appadurai 2006, 175), or do they wish to nurture music teachers' capacities "to make independent inquiries about their own lives and worlds" (Appadurai 2006, 173) and thus the teaching and learning taking place in their communities in the face of increasing diversity and an uncertain future? In other words, teachers who have the capacity to imagine, aspire, inquire and take action, and who adopt "inquiry as stance" (Cochran-Smith and Lylte 2009).

The process of co-constructing visions presented in this chapter is one example of potential professional development through engaging in group inquiry. Although some musician-teachers originally participated in the workshops because of the certificate, participating led, for some at least, to an appreciation for both learning from and with each other, and for the already existing knowledge and expertise within their community. At the same time, it fueled a desire to know more and to take action. As can be seen in the co-constructed visions, the process was also "a valuable mode of critique of the inequities in schools and society and of knowledge hierarchies, which have implications within as well as beyond the local context" (Cochran-Smith and Lytle 2009, ix; see also Treacy et al. in press). Recalling Appadurai (2006), however, for other musician-teachers, participation in the workshops may have been the 'cost' of gaining some kind of vocational credential to potentially increase their employability in a country where the current availability of professional development for musician-teachers is extremely limited.

Reflecting on facilitating this process also highlights my own learning through this, my first experience using AI. My readings of the literature on teachers' visions (see e.g. Hammerness 2004, 2015) suggested that visions are something that teachers *have* and just need to be asked about, while my readings of the AI literature suggested that images of an ideal future naturally emerge out of the positive examples shared in the Discovery phase. My experience in Kathmandu, however, was characterized by an ongoing search for different angles from which to approach the Dreaming or envisioning, because it turned out to be a rather challenging process. This strongly resonates with Appadurai when he identifies the imagination as "a form of work" (2006, 31) and states that "the capacity to aspire, like any complex cultural capacity, thrives and survives on practice, repetition, exploration, conjecture, and refutation" (2004, 69). Thus, these workshops were sites for practicing navigating the capacity to aspire with other musician-teachers. Still, working with musician-teachers I frequently wondered how the workshops, the resulting visions, and our overall experiences may have been different if, rather than spoken discussions, we had used music as our primary tool for navigating the capacity to aspire.

Thus, my biggest intercultural learning did not come from the co-constructed visions and their related discussions. Rather, it came from the challenges of the process itself, highlighting the need for intercultural music teacher educators to remain reflexive and flexible. My work required an ongoing willingness to be open to redesigning my plans and finding alternatives, to try again, and again (and again) when needed, and to acknowledge and embrace the ever present and often uncomfortable or unsettling uncertainties of the process, for both participants and facilitators. Throughout, I needed to allow myself to be guided by ongoing dialogue, especially focused on listening, with my co-facilitator and the musician-teachers. This dialogue, whether in person or online, spoken or written, continues to serve an important role in our ongoing reflection and interpretation.

Acknowledgements This publication has been undertaken as part of the project *Global Visions through Mobilizing Networks: Co-developing Intercultural Music Teacher Education in Nepal, Finland, and Israel* (2015–2020, https://sites.uniarts.fi/web/globalvisions) funded by the Academy of Finland (project no. 286162).

The author would like to thank her co-facilitator Prem Gurung, the musician-teachers who participated in the workshops and shared their perspectives and experiences as part of this research, and the music institutions and private schools who supported the project, *dhanyabaad!* She would also like to thank the doctoral community at the Sibelius Academy, University of the Arts Helsinki for comments and guidance in refining this text.

References

Appadurai, A. (1996). *Modernity at large: Cultural dimensions of globalization*. Minneapolis: University of Minnesota Press.

Appadurai, A. (2000). Grassroots globalization and the research imagination. *Public Culture, 12*(1), 1–19. https://doi.org/10.1215/08992363-12-1-1.

Appadurai, A. (2004). The capacity to aspire: Culture and the terms of recognition. In V. Rao & M. Walton (Eds.), *Culture and public action* (pp. 59–84). Stanford: Stanford University Press.

Appadurai, A. (2006). The right to research. *Globalisation, Societies and Education, 4*(2), 167–177. https://doi.org/10.1080/14767720600750696.

Bates, V. C. (2011). Preparing rural music teachers: Reflecting on "shared visions". *Journal of Music Teacher Education, 20*(2), 89–98. https://doi.org/10.1177/1057083710377722.

Burnard, P. (2013). Introduction. In E. Georgii-Hemming, P. Burnard, & S.-E. Holgersen (Eds.), *Professional knowledge in music teacher education* (pp. 189–201). Surrey: Ashgate.

Cochran-Smith, M., & Lytle, S. L. (2009). *Inquiry as stance: Practitioner research for the next generation.* New York: Teachers College Press.

Conkling, S. W. (2015). Utopian thinking, compliance, and visions of wonderful transformation. In S. W. Conkling (Ed.), *Envisioning music teacher education* (pp. 181–194). Lanham: Rowman & Littlefield Education.

Cooperrider, D. L., & Whitney, D. (2001). A positive revolution in change: Appreciative inquiry. *Public Administration and Public Policy, 87,* 611–630.

Cooperrider, D. L., Whitney, D., & Stavros, J. M. (2005). *Appreciative inquiry handbook: For leaders of change* (2nd ed.). Brunswick: Crown Custom Pub.

Darling-Hammond, L. (2006). *Powerful teacher education: Lessons from exemplary programs.* San Francisco: Jossey-Bass.

Dasen, P. R., & Akkari, A. (2008). Introduction: Ethnocentrism in education and how to overcome it. In P. R. Dasen & A. Akkari (Eds.), *Educational theories and practices from the majority world* (pp. 7–23). New Delhi: Sage.

Ferm Thorgersen, C., Johansen, G., & Juntunen, M.-L. (2016). Music teacher educators' visions of music teacher preparation in Finland, Norway and Sweden. *International Journal of Music Education, 34*(1), 49–63. https://doi.org/10.1177/0255761415584300.

Gergen, K. J. (1978). Toward generative theory. *Journal of Personality and Social Psychology, 36*(11), 1344–1360.

Gergen, K. J. (2009). *An invitation to social construction* (2nd ed.). Thousand Oaks: Sage.

Government of Nepal. (2012). *National population and housing census 2011 (National report)* (Vol. 1). Kathmandu: National Planning Commission Secretariat Central Bureau of Statistics. [Online] http://unstats.un.org/unsd/demographic/sources/census/wphc/Nepal/Nepal-Census-2011-Vol1.pdf. Accessed 15 Jan 2018.

Hammerness, K. (2004). Teaching with vision: How one teacher negotiates the tension between high ideals and standardized testing. *Teacher Education Quarterly.,* Fall, *31,* 33–43.

Hammerness, K. (2013). Examining features of teacher education in Norway. *Scandinavian Journal of Educational Research, 57*(4), 400–419. https://doi.org/10.1080/00313831.2012.6 56285.

Hammerness, K. (2015). Visions of good teaching in teacher education. In S. W. Conkling (Ed.), *Envisioning music teacher education* (pp. 1–20). Lanham: Rowman & Littlefield Education.

Holgersen, S.-E., & Burnard, P. (2013). Different types of knowledges forming professionalism: A vision of post-millennial music teacher education. In E. Georgii-Hemming, P. Burnard, & S.-E. Holgersen (Eds.), *Professional knowledge in music teacher education* (pp. 189–201). Surrey: Ashgate.

Imagine Nepal (n.d.). About us. [Online] http://www.imaginenepal.org.np/index.php/about-us. Accessed 17 Feb 2017.

Jackson, A. Y., & Mazzei, L. A. (2012). *Thinking with theory in qualitative research: Viewing data across multiple perspectives.* London: Routledge.

Juntunen, M.-L. (2014). Teacher educators' visions of pedagogical training within instrumental higher music education. A case in Finland. *British Journal of Music Education, 31*(2), 157–177. https://doi.org/10.1017/s0265051714000102.

Klette, K., & Hammerness, K. (2016). Conceptual framework for analyzing qualities in teacher education: Looking at features of teacher education from an international perspective. *Acta Didactica Norge, 10*(26), 26–52.

Kuntz, A. M. (2015). *The responsible methodologist: Inquiry, truth-telling, and social justice.* London: Routledge.

Lassiter, L. E. (2005). *The Chicago guide to collaborative ethnography.* Chicago: The University of Chicago Press.

Liamputtong, P. (2010). *Performing qualitative cross-cultural research.* Cambridge, UK: Cambridge University Press.

Messerschmidt, D. (2008). Evaluating appreciative inquiry as an organizational transformation tool: An assessment from Nepal. *Human Organization, 67*(4), 454–468. https://doi.org/10.17730/humo.67.4.xp341p168m141641.

Nepal Appreciative Inquiry National Network (NAINN) (n.d.). *Six years' 4 D planning 2005 Sept. – 2010 Oct.* [Online] https://appreciativeinquiry.case.edu/uploads/NAINN%204D%20 PLAN.doc. Accessed 17 Feb 2017.

Odell, M. J., & Mohr, B. J. (2008). The power of a positive lens in peace building and development. In M. Avital, R. J. Boland, & D. L. Cooperrider (Eds.), *Designing information and organizations with a positive lens* (pp. 307–327). Oxford: JAI Press.

Patel, L. (2014). Counting coloniality in educational research: From ownership to answerability. *Educational Studies, 50*(4), 357–377.

Rancière, J. (1991). *The ignorant schoolmaster: Five lessons in intellectual emancipation.* Stanford: Stanford University Press.

Rancière, J. (2010). On ignorant schoolmasters. In C. Bingham, G. Biesta, & J. Rancière (Eds.), *Jacques Rancière: Education, truth, emancipation* (pp. 1–16). New York: Continuum.

Schmidt, P., & Robbins, J. (2011). Looking backwards to reach forward: A strategic architecture for professional development in music education. *Arts Education Policy Review, 112*, 95–103. https://doi.org/10.1080/10632913.2011.546702.

Sindberg, L. (2011). Alone all together- the conundrum of music teacher isolation and connectedness. *Bulletin of the Council for Research in Music Education, 189*, 7–22. https://doi.org/10.5406/bulcouresmusedu.189.0007.

Talbot, B. C., & Mantie, R. (2015). Visions and the legitimate order: Theorizing today to imagine tomorrow. In S. W. Conkling (Ed.), *Envisioning music teacher education* (pp. 155–180). Lanham: Rowman & Littlefield Education.

Treacy, D. S. (2019). "Because I'm a girl": Troubling shared visions for music education. *Research Studies in Music Education.* Advance online publication. https://doi.org/10.1177/13211 03X19845145.

Treacy, D. S., Thapa S., & Neupane S. K. (in press). "Where the social stigma has been overcome": The politics of professional legitimation in Nepali music education. In A. A. Kallio, S. Karlsen, K. Marsh, E. Saether, H. Westerlund (Eds.), *The politics of diversity in music education.*

Watkins, J. M., Mohr, B. J., & Kelly, R. (2011). *Appreciative inquiry: Change at the speed of imagination* (2nd ed.). San Francisco: Pfeiffer/Wiley.

4

Policy, Interculturality and the Potential of Core Practices in Music Teacher Education

Patrick Schmidt and Joseph Abramo

Abstract This chapter provides examples of current and promising practices in intercultural music teacher education, while highlighting how policy thinking can help construct empowering conditions and experiences. In contrast to current policy environments, where music educators are seen as the target of policy, we situate music educators as *teacher-as-policy-maker* as a guiding image for teacher preparation that need not and should not mean a distancing from practice. In this conception, music teachers are the generators of policies with others. In this chapter, we address how research in teacher-education core practices can be aligned with and facilitate learning about policy enactment in preservice music education. We demonstrate how core practices, as a pedagogical approach, identify learning how to teach as a "high leverage" practice to be developed. We end the chapter by articulating some core practices in intercultural teaching and policy that music teacher educators might implement to help preservice teachers develop, practice, and enact their own practices.

Keywords Policy · Interculturality · Core-practices · Music education

1 Introduction

The role and impact that music and arts educators can exert on policy thinking and practice remains significantly underexplored. This presents an important gap globally – particularly in light of growing and challenging policy initiatives – that places educators of all stripes, and specially music educators, as targets of policy issues, such as teacher accountability and autonomy, work intensification, curricular streamlining,

---

P. Schmidt (✉)
Don Wright Faculty of Music, Western University, London, ON, Canada
e-mail: patrick.schmidt@uwo.ca

J. Abramo
Neag School of Education, University of Connecticut, Mansfield, CT, USA
e-mail: joseph.abramo@uconn.edu

and assessment. Just as significantly, active policy participation remains underexplored in the arts fields regardless of evidence that policy thinking and activism can shape educational action and directly affect the nature, extent, and impact of our programs (Fulcher 1999).

Consequently, this chapter provides examples of current and promising practices in teacher education, while highlighting how policy thinking can help construct empowering conditions and experiences. To do so we use the notion of *teacher-as-policy-maker* as a guiding image for teacher preparation that need not and should not imply a distancing from practice. On the contrary, we argue, grounding practice in policy thinking is another way to acknowledge that critical dispositions – which can facilitate thoughtful, creative and engaged curricular work – are embedded in (and renewed by) a recognition of agency (by oneself and by others). Put in different terms, subaltern actors are also often non-innovative, non-participative actors. This is a logic of empowerment, one that ought to be inimical to any teacher education program, globally. Yet, its absence is easily uncovered.

Unfortunately – and counterproductively, in our opinion – a complexity surrounding teachers' effects on school polity and its policies is generally absent from teacher education, and specifically absent from discussions over the development of "core practices." In this chapter, we explore policy, music teacher education and power, as well as tensions between various policy-level demands. What might be the "core practices" of music teacher policy? How can music teacher educators help preservice and inservice music educators develop the necessary practices to effect changes in policy in music education and, more broadly, in education and their communities? How might discussion of teachers' actions in relation to policy keep teacher practices "complex"?

Central to these questions of preparing educators for the profession of teaching, including policy action, is a tension between developing core practices while naming the limits and conditions that make those core practices possible. Addressing the complex tension between limits and possibilities is ultimately a process of discovering the discourses that drive policy within schools and examining how power drives these discourses. Raising awareness of the capacity that individuals have to respond to policies and policymaking decisions is one way to provide music education stakeholders with the needed confidence to interact with the policy process and thus more aptly impact their own professional conditions and re-establish the participative power of those at the center of the production of educational aims and ideals, that is, educators (Kos 2010; Schmidt and Robbins 2011; Schmidt 2017). This same capacity and process can also be extended to challenging issues such as interculturality and the demands it places within music education environs today (Westerlund et al. 2015). We argue, consequently, that if music educators can influence policy work they can also advance interculturality by means of including it in their own core practices.

This chapter proposes that, if teacher educators can navigate this tension between providing preservice teachers the capacity to develop 'practical' teacher practices and the necessary dispositions and abilities to question and affect policy, while naming the conditions and discourses embedded within policies (e.g. interculturality), then the payoff, can be rather strong. With successful navigation, teacher educators can bridge the divide between the demands that educational reform and its policies place on teachers; while working to reverse the narrowing space deemed *appropriate* for teacher action and practice.

2 Policy(ing), Core Practices and Interculturality

There is nascent evidence that discourses aimed at decoupling teachers from curricular, managerial and political power can indeed be assuaged. The 2013 Center for American Progress report focuses on the educator's voice. It evidences in clear terms the capacity of the *teacher-as-policy-maker*:

> Teacher leaders are capable of far more than feedback…we are capable of even more than closing the 'implementation gap' between a policy's intended outcome and its actual impact on students in the classroom. We are capable of helping to design the kinds of systems our students need. (NNSTOY 2015, 10)

Acknowledging such capacity as existing and available, teacher educators are pushing back, with some challenging and exploring so-called "core practices." Core practices are teacher practices that "occur with high frequency in teaching, are enacted across different curricula or instructional approaches, preserve the integrity and complexity of teaching, are research based, and have the potential to improve student achievement" (Whitcomb et al. 2009, 209). Core practices are ways to conceptualize the key abilities and skills that educators should develop. In addition to enacting practices, core practices might be a way for teacher educators and teachers to enact policies in the practice of teaching.

Core practices have limitations as well as potentials. Enacted without care, they can become part of the problem despite them being aimed to *solve* teacher accountability; core practices can be named, ossified, measured, and applied *to* teachers. However, enacted correctly – e.g. constructively, critically, openly – these practices are rendered sufficiently "complex" (Lampert et al. 2013). And, teacher educators, using the categories they use to construct "core," "high-leverage" practices, can help teachers to become agents in the writing and developing of their core practices (Dutro and Cartun 2016). Such 'writing up' of one's practices stands as a signpost for a more complex, educational and professional foundation, which could be seen as the formation of the *teacher-as-policy-maker*. This notion metaphorically represents a new parameter, or set of goals, for teacher education and professional development that are also in line with the general aims of this book and in particular the notion of interculturality.

According to UNESCO's 2015 *Guidelines on Intercultural Education*, intercultural education goes beyond traditional aims of respecting and valuing diversity – while upholding them as a necessary baseline – as it needs to concern itself with "the learning environment as a whole, as well as other dimensions of educational processes, such as school life and decision making" (2015, 19). This concern for intercultural work framed as part of school life is a component of what we call below an engagement with *policy networking* and in alignment with how we situate our conception of the *teacher-as-policy-maker*. We do so by placing it within Weaver-Hightower's ecological conceptualization of policy as "an extremely complex, often contradictory process that defies the commonly held image of singular purpose and open, effective planning" (2008, 153). By aligning diversity needs and teacher work with progressive understandings of policy (Ball 2009; Fischer 2003; Sabatier 2007), we place teachers within the 'epistemic community' (Haas 1992), appropriately having rights and claims over the curricular, but also, the political, structural and organizational aspects of schooling; that is, the territories within which power is exerted in educational settings. This view is critical of teacher-education policies that assume (or pretend to assume) value-neutral decision-making and those that ignore issues of power, arguing that such models (and teacher education programs that fail to challenge them) are not only ineffective but also regularly misleading, *de facto* facilitating the alienation of teachers from their own work.

Teachers have the *framing capacity* (Schmidt and Morrow 2015) to interact mindfully with policy thinking, engaging in what Bolman and Deal have called "mapping the political terrain" (2008, 2016). This is critical today as central challenges to intercultural education, such as higher mobility, forced migration, challenges to diversity, and growing cooptation of cultural forms, present themselves front and center in any responsible and equity-directed educational environment. Skills that would shape such capacity, however, need to be fostered and supported, and teacher education, at both undergraduate and graduate levels, is central to that enterprise. The educational leadership literature shows us how we can use *policy as tactics*, employing ideas, such as: controlling meeting agendas and decision-making processes; practicing cooptation, buffering, listening, diplomacy, humor, and strategic application of data; and using rewards and sanctions as well as avoidance (Blase and Blase 2002; Crow and Weindling 2010). Again, teacher education should dedicate time and efforts toward, "how teachers can learn policy tactics such as employing strategies for persuading others, circulating information, provoking and guiding discussions, asking critical questions, preaching, using language carefully, and employing government language." But, we are also interested in a broader understanding of *policy savvy* that "expands policy into an alternative conceptualization of influence, change, and use of discursive practices, facilitating spaces for coalition work, framing and strategically organizing change, and developing the capacity to read political environs" (Schmidt 2017, 18). This disposition can be facilitated by the notion of core practices and can have meaningful impact on the enactment of educational aims based on intercultural understandings.

Before we get there however, we need to challenge the ways that policy is still traditionally seen. Our aim is to present policy as a more accessible, pragmatic and critical aspect of the education of teachers.

3 Reconsidering Policy and Political Membership

Writing at the edge of a historical shift in the way policy work was to be viewed, Aaron Wildavsky's 1979 classic book *Speaking Truth to Power* challenges the rational choice and scientific rhetoric of policy thinking and the formalistic objectivism of its methodological approaches. In his own words:

> This is my quarrel with the present paradigm of rationality: it accepts as immutable the very order of preference it is our purpose to change, and it regards as perfectly plastic the recalcitrant resources that always limit their realization. (Wildavsky 1979, 404)

His point is that policy is a political and thus a socio-cultural artifact. People and their preferences make policy. Objectivity and rationality have as much (or as little) to do with policy as rationalization and ideology. And this means that the hierarchizing of policy work is a construction of a particular, power-laden worldview, where the logic is as follows: some individuals ought to be the purveyors of policy, otherwise decision-making becomes inviable. *Or,* some individuals ought to be the purveyors of policy analysis, otherwise decision-making becomes unreliable. He set out to change the arena, arguing that challenging such a worldview is a matter of education, agency, and, naturally, hard work.

From Wildavsky and a subsequent line of *policy thought* (Ball 2009; Sabatier 2007; Schneider and Ingram 1997; Stone 2011) we learn that there is nothing *wrong* in equating policy with participatory engagement, even with activism. Indeed, Wildavsky argues that "when it becomes clear that people (re)make their social structure much like they (re)make their policies, the next stage in the study of public policy analysis as a social process will have begun" (1979, 405). This is in alignment with the notion of core practices we articulate here. For teacher educators, helping novice teachers enact *policy thought* in their teaching can be challenging (Schmidt 2017). Learning the ability to think globally, or on the "macro" level, while realizing results in the "micro" work of teaching is a messy process. What are the key skills and knowledge that teachers need to engage and enact policy? Even more difficult, how do teacher educators help novice teachers learn these skills and knowledge in ways that do not reduce the learning of teaching to a simplistic list that does not accurately prepare students for the complexity of professional teaching? The pedagogical approach to teacher education, known as core practices (Ball and Forzani 2009; Grossman and McDonald 2008; Lampert et al. 2013), attempts this challenging work of retaining complexity while designating and rehearsing those key practices. Core practices, then, are a promising arena where teachers can develop this agent-oriented, practice-based conception of policy, moving away from a removed view of policy as imposed by administrators or legislators on teachers.

Thus, these notions of policy as enacted and core practices as a way of developing this enactment are important for our discussion in three ways: First, by clarifying that all of us have a stake, and thus a responsibility, when it comes to policy. This means that in the context of schooling, teachers are both entitled to engage and responsible for engaging in policy thinking and policy work. To think of the *teacher-as-policy-maker*, then, is not to invent a utopian paradigm, but rather to unearth (or simply underscore) socio-political concerns such as those associated with interculturality, claiming space to enact them. Second, by clarifying that policies are not designed to act as their own causes. This means that, problematically, we have come to see policies as closed systems, working to sustain their own *original* intents and nothing else; today this is particularly compounded by the fact that economists (or economic thinking) are mostly leading the way on policy design and analysis (Fischer 2003). Finally, teacher educators can purposefully help novice teachers develop and rehearse the ability to create, shape and enact policy in practice.

The challenge, as the reader can already see, is that in the absence of the first element (e.g. individual and/or community agency/participation/understanding), the second element (e.g. the notion of policy as a closed system serving its own cause) becomes common sense. The logic is: experts spent a lot of time designing this policy, now the role of those who are subject to the policy is to follow its directives, without interference. Further, and completing the vicious cycle, the perpetration of the idea of policy as a closed system creates its own authority, where interference or mismanagement are presented as capable of unraveling the policy; and thus, engaged actors (seen as a form of disturbance) can be presented as likely culprits for policy failure. In this problematic model, policy is to be *administered*, with groups identified and variables (particularly human variables) controlled, as in an experimental research design.

Traditional, or what we are calling here *closed policy design and understanding* is then the ideological stance that conceives and values policy as designed to "act as its own cause." Wildavsky, on the other hand, was the first to suggest that we should *value* policy (as a concept) and policies (as distinct enactments of that concept) in more open terms. As the founding Dean of University of California at Berkeley's Graduate School of Public Policy, his work is informed by educative parameters. The school of thought he established at Berkeley proposes that a critic or analyst should "value policies by the extent to which they (1) permit learning, or (2) the ease by which errors are identified, as well as (3) the motivation produced by organizational incentives to correct error" (1979, 392). The impact of policy is thus not simply the *solution* of identified problems (as problems are always present and always changing), but programs of actions that foster iterative and contextual efforts, which amplify original aims and link problem-solving to local initiative. Policy thus is no longer just a thing (the text, directive, legislation, and implementation design) but a process (the potentially creative problem solving that policy triggers). This opens up the possibility of other considerations, for instance, the notion of *policy networks* (see Sörensen and Torfing 2007) where interdependence is considered; those Etzioni (1968/1992) explores, studying how *policy participation*, as well as manipulation, involves psychological states or emotions; or the *democratic* models for policy practice as articulated by Schneider and Ingram (1997). As a space for research in the field of music teacher education the role of networks in "linking actors from different countries, levels and spheres in transnational, multi-level and multi-cultural networks" (Sörensen and Torfing 2007, 311) clearly aligns with intercultural interests, has great potential, and yet has been widely neglected.

Following Sabatier (2007) our position is that a *valuable* policy is one which affords the space for multiple communities to enter, to join in, and, in that process, to learn. From learning and from incentives (which can be economic or external, but also contextual or intrinsic), adaptation and new action ensues. The notion of networks of interaction are then crucial here and particularly significant to our argument in this chapter, as teacher input – qualified, thoughtful, and as a regular and systematic occurrence – is essential to a fully functioning educational environment.

4 Policy Participation and Framing Skills

It is not harsh to say, then, that views of and dispositions toward policy that continue to disregard Wildavsky's notions, operate, knowingly or not, within assumptions that aid in the *colonization* of the policy subject. Paternalistically and patronizingly, much of the educational apparatus in a growing number of places have kept and continue to keep teachers from exerting their policy responsibilities and rights. Unfortunately, teacher education has not been a sufficiently positive contributor either.

The challenge is not simply with teachers. Given the nature of labor within schools today, leadership remains a central problem. Winton and Pollock (2012), for example, highlight that critical leadership and policy learning are largely absent from the education of principals. Indeed, curricular analyses of principalship programs in North America show wide emphasis on managerial development; in line with a shift in the role of the principal in the last 15 years from curricular leader and vision-setter to structural manager. If one looks at the over-representation of outside unidirectional policies (the impositions of NCLB, for example), the narrowing of how leadership is conceptualized in schools, the intensification of teachers' labor, and professional formation that gives strong preference to content expertise and behavioral management, the strengthening of schools as highly hierarchical spaces should come as a surprise to no one. Regardless of the effect of political or policy savvy (Laes and Schmidt 2016), research shows that educators acquire leadership and political skills on the job, often through mistakes. Teacher education by-and-large does not consider *policy-directed core practices*. This shows how few studies explore the ways that school leaders gain political skills, pointing out that the literature is even more scant when it comes to the formation of teachers' political (policy) skills. It seems critical then that a participative vision for/of policy be rekindled.

Given all of the above, we stand with Schmidt: "policy cannot be *farmed out* to others nor relegated as outside the purview of teachers. Given that the policy enter-

Policy, Interculturality and the Potential of Core Practices in Music... 63

prise is a process requiring constant adjustment, only our [teachers] active participation can engender intelligent and integrative decision making" (Schmidt 2017, 17). Schmidt's views on policy are in line with a 2013 report by the Center for American Progress, in which Elizabeth Evans, founder of VIVA Teachers (Voice, Ideas, Vision, Action), writes:

> We have seen over and over again this kind of light-bulb moment that management and union leadership alike have when they listen to ordinary classroom teachers talking about policy and they actually hear substance that's both reinforcing and adding nuance and depth to what they've already been thinking. (2013, 14)

Without a critical education in policy thinking, teacher education and professional development structures prevent what the literature calls *policy learning;* that is, the capacity to learn from contextual experiences and understand how to navigate and influence spaces. The capacity to *learn policy* then seems to be a *core practice* that teacher education ought to develop. This overriding core practice could provide the framework for other, more specific and directed critical capacities which work to "keep learning to teach complex" (Lampert et al. 2013). Complex teacher training would address, for example, intercultural action within musicianship or pedagogical and curricular parameters.

Now that we have outlined a macro reconfiguration of the impact that policy thinking can have on teacher practice, the next sections emphasize the development of other significant and specific *core practices* within teacher education. We now return, in more depth, to the literature of "core practices" as originating from teacher education in the US. We describe it within current debates about teacher accountability, the rationale of core practices as a pedagogy, and its limitations. Finally, we provide some core practices of intercultural teaching in regards to policy.

5 Rationale for Practice-Based Teacher Education

The recent shifts in teacher accountability and policy towards managerial aspects where teachers are the targets of policy rather than their locus (outlined above) have affected how some teacher educators conceive the pedagogies they employ to educate teachers. In response to these closed systems of policy, for better or worse, some teacher educators have shifted toward "practice-based" development of so-called "core practices." Advocates of core practices suggest that core practices are a response to teacher education over the last 30 years, which has focused on development of dispositions of teachers. Ball and Forzani argue that "the focus in teacher education can slip easily into an exclusively cognitive domain, emphasizing beliefs and ideas over the actual skills and judgment required in enactment" (2009, 503). Grossman and McDonald elaborate:

> Much of the research on teaching in the past two decades has focused on teachers' knowledge – of specific subject matter, of learners and learning, of ways to teach specific content – and teachers' beliefs. And while we would be the first to agree that these are critically

important aspects of teaching, teaching, at its core, is an interactive, clinical practice, one that requires not just knowledge but craft and skill. (2008, 189)

Core practice advocates suggest that teacher education has focused on dispositions, or the necessary habits of mind in order to teach, as well as content knowledge and knowledge of pedagogy. While these are of importance, focus on these areas has failed to help preservice teachers apply and rehearse those dispositions and knowledge.

In embedding these dispositions and knowledge and practices in craft and skill, advocates further argue that educators need to delineate the essential or core practices of teaching. These core practices are "high-leverage practices" (Grossman et al. 2009), which are applicable to various educational settings. In conceiving these broadly applicable, high-leverage practices, advocates argue that these practices are "kept complex" (Lampert et al. 2013). In other words, in developing core practices, there can be a tendency to atomize the process, turning practices into series of competencies or unreflective behaviors, for example, waiting 5 s after asking a question for students to respond. In contrast, advocates suggest core practices that teachers will understand and be able to execute in all the different ways that the core practices might be enacted in different contexts.

6 The Potentials and Limitations of Core Practices

This critique of teacher education and shift in conception towards core practices of teaching is potentially fruitful. It has the capacity to embed learning the craft of teaching within action. This aspect has much in common with constructivist aspects of teaching because learning to teach is embedded within action. However, in relation to intercultural teaching, the concept of core practices has some limitations, and the idea of developing intercultural teaching may provide further critique of a core-practices approach to teacher education. By addressing these critiques, core practices may become a way to engage teachers thoroughly and systematically in intercultural teaching.

To begin a critique, core practices must be historicized within the current trends in the US that we outlined earlier. Teacher "accountability" in the US – and increasingly in other countries – has worked to de-professionalize teacher education. "Accountability" advocates have instituted teacher evaluation systems that make causational links between teaching and effects on students but ignore the variability within different teaching contexts. They have also called for limiting teaching education to mere training through alternative routes to teacher licensure. Core practices in teacher education are potentially a capitulation to these moves to de-professionalize teacher education in the name of "accountability." Core practices might exacerbate these aims, which consider teachers as targets of policy in a closed system – as mere workers who enact policy in a direct, de-professionalized way, rather than the generators and adapters of policy who constitute the professionalism of teaching. De-professionalization is befitting of, and embedded within, the move towards more managerial conceptions of administration in schools. Core practices, conceived as a set of non-negotiable essential practices, would serve these aims.

This aim to de-professionalize the profession is also potentially anti-democratic. As critics have noted, recent policies by organizations like NCTQ (2013) that promote *free choice* and *accountability* and a critique of traditional teacher education programs housed in universities are aimed to dismantle public education, with particularly negative consequences for urban schools, communities lacking resources, and students of color (Ravitch 2013). As teacher educators adopt these core practices, the potential arises to shift emphasis away from issues of diversity and equity. As Zeichner notes,

> [An] element that is not typically included in discussions of preparing teachers to enact high-leverage teaching practices is the development of teachers' cultural competence and ability to teach in culturally responsive ways…. Not discussing this aspect of teaching in culturally diverse settings implies that the successful implementation of core teaching practices alone will result in better learning outcomes for students who are now underserved by the public schools. The evidence does not support this assumption. (2012, 380)

The emphasis of *core* practices that work in all educational contexts has the potential to wash away differences in pedagogy required for different cultural contexts. This is at the detriment of students of color. Issues of power are necessarily embedded with any notion of *core*. As Dutro and Cartun note, "[c]ore always already signifies an outside that surrounds it. Core and surround – one term cannot hold meaning without the other. Thus, as a metaphor, it cannot but construct boundaries of what is in and what is out, what is in the center and what is not" (2016, 120). As a result, they suggest that *whom* we teach, and *who* we are, give rise to what is considered "core." Who "we" are is structured around "bodies," or the race, of teachers and students. As a result, Dutro and Cartun explain:

> bodies pose questions. Those questions embedded in bodies and their very different locations, we argue, must be explicitly part of the field's conversations about aspects of teaching identified as central and how to take them up with novice teachers. In other words, language positioning some teaching practices at the center can be an invitation to consider how language works to create binaries and prompt processes that complicate what is explicitly or implicitly named as what counts most in moments of teaching. (2016, 120)

These critiques urge educators aiming to employ core practices to consider weighing them carefully with concerns about intercultural teaching that might become absent in their application. Core practices, as measured and determined by practice as it currently stands, potentially support any racist (and classist, sexist, able-bodied, etc.) educational systems that marginalize people of color and could construct them as bodies that do not respond to the effective strategies that core practices purport to articulate.

These critiques suggest that for core practices to remain creative they must question the concept of "core," looking to how core evolves and is enacted in different teaching contexts. This is particularly important around the concept of "intercultural," including race, nationality, and other traditionally marginalized identities. Core practices – rather than relying on a conception of core as 'what just works' –

requires a theoretical foundation. In other words, to use a term borrowed from Marx, core practices might lack a robust interaction with theory in 'praxis.' As Marx and Engels note, "[d]ivision of labor becomes truly such only from the moment when a division of material and mental labor appears.... From this moment onward, consciousness *can* really flatter itself that it is something other than consciousness of existing practice, that it *really* represents something without representing something real" (1970, 51–52). The 'thinking' of policy and the 'labor' of teaching must be melded in the activity of praxis, in the sense Marx intended it. In this way, we might be calling for 'core praxis' with particular emphasis on thinking of practice in relation to theory, policy, and institutional and systemic structures. In this sense, the melding of policy as 'abstract' (or removed rules that govern and guide practice) with the actual practice of teaching, a mutually beneficial union, informs the professional practice of teachers.

7 Core Practices of Intercultural Music Teaching

We have highlighted the potential and the limits of core practices in reference to intercultural music teaching. Within the tension between the potential and limits, we ask, what might be some core practices of intercultural music teaching? In asking this question, it is important to find a balance between some of the areas we have covered by embedding all inquiry in practice. Policy, or the macro, might not be learned in discussion, but embedded within practice, or the micro. In learning about and through practice, there is the question of "grain size;" teacher educators might "keep practice complex" by not overly prescribing practice, and creating lists of competencies and discrete behaviors. However, in the quest of "keeping it complex," teacher educators must not easily slip into a "cognitive domain" where dispositions are secured without embedding the enactment of those dispositions in practice. Finally, they must also balance the micro of local concerns and the macro of global and universal ideals. They must balance generalities of "good teaching" regardless of context, with the adaptability and specificity of teaching in various contexts. This balancing of policy, theory and practice to find the key or essential aspects of teaching might be a form of what we are calling "core praxis." In particular, attention to issues of diversity, equity, and even alterity must become central to this task, which is not easy. However, we provide a starting point for how teacher educators might enact core policies and practices in intercultural teaching.

The following constitutes a potential initial list of "core practices" in intercultural teaching in music education. These become a starting point to begin thinking about the practices that music teacher educators might focus on as they help preservice teachers prepare for teaching in the continually evolving, contemporary intercultural landscape. Key to these core practices of intercultural teaching is, to reiterate Schmidt's words, the ability to "learn policy tactics such as employing strategies for persuading others, circulating information, provoking and guiding discussions, asking critical questions, preaching, using language carefully, and employing government language" (2017, 18). Music educators might implement these strategies towards the core practices listed below. While this is an incomplete, precursory list of only three practices, no list of core practices could ever totally encompass the diversity of teaching; core practices are complex, intercultural practices, melding theory with practice.

7.1 Core Practice 1: Represent Diversity in Music and Curricula

It has been noted many times that music is a universal cultural practice. For example, Blacking (1974) notes that every culture has some form of music making. These musics are conceived as "art," cultural artifacts, objects, a social process, or in other forms. Music educators have called for an engagement with and learning about these diverse cultural practices; and an "intercultural" approach, as articulated in this book, necessarily calls for a "multicultural" engagement that engages, teaches, and facilitates a variety of musical cultural practices. This is an area that has traditionally received attention within music education through areas including praxial education, popular music and informal practices, and multiculturalism.

However, a less discussed topic within music education regards an understanding of how discourses define the "multi" in multiculturalism. Concomitant with this engagement with different cultures is the concept of "alterity" or otherness. As teachers engage in "other" cultures, they might become cognizant of how this concept of otherness is constructed and represented by discourses on race, gender, nationality, and other forms of identity. As Baumann (2006) suggests, the lines between identity and otherness are continually drawn and redrawn. This suggests that otherness is not based on inherent differences between different groups of people, but are, instead, socially constructed. For example, the lines of "Western civilization" is constructed around a host of discourses on, for example, race, and religion. Drawing these lines ignores similarities along other lines. As music educators engage in intercultural teaching, they might work to interrogate the discourses that create otherness. Teacher educators might embed this in practice by requiring teachers to create and teach within the musics of a variety of cultures, understanding how they are similar and different, and most importantly, under what assumptions and discourses those similarities might be created.

In light of "intercultural" (in the sense that "inter" describes the mixing of these different cultures), music teacher educators might think about multiculturalism not as comprised of discrete practices where music educators adhere to "authentic" practices, but look at cultural and musical intersections and the changing nature of musical practices. Musical instruments might be an example of this complexity: Teacher might learn to play instruments associated with particular practices, but also how one adapts musical instruments to work within and contribute to those practices. Importantly, then, how teachers might inform policies towards issues of multiculturalism is key to this practice including issues of representation in curricula on the local, regional, and even national levels.

7.2 Core Practice 2: Reflect on Practice in Reference to Diversity and Equity

As schools become increasingly diverse throughout the world, as with growing populations in the US and immigration in Europe, among other places, teachers are required to attend to issues of diversity, inclusion, and equity. They may begin to understand how particular well-established practices in music education might create access barriers in music education. For example, curricula focusing on the music of particular demographics might discourage students of color. Focus on Western classical music, and recent engagement of popular music construed as American and Anglo rock might not encourage students of color to participate. Practices where students must pay for their own materials might discourage participation of students with economic needs.

Part of understanding schools' practices in reference to diversity is understanding how students interact with one another. Recent changes in politics and governance in the USA and parts of Europe have shifted towards populist sentiments and have given rise to racist and xenophobic actions by certain parts of these populations. Students and schools are not immune to these shifts. Managing these interactions with the aims of diversity and inclusion could be a practice that music teachers might develop. In understanding how students interact with one another, music teachers might become aware of microaggressions, which Sue defines as "the everyday verbal, nonverbal, and environmental slights, snubs, or insults, whether intentional or unintentional, that communicate hostile, derogatory, or negative messages to target persons based solely upon their marginalized group membership" (2010, 3). Understanding how students may enact microaggressions through social interactions, and particularly the ways they are enacted through music, is a potential focus. Teacher educators might gear this for practice by engaging students in teaching and framing issues through curriculum and policy.

7.3 Core Practice 3: Invite Students to Engage in Praxis

If the practice aspect of core practices is to be taken seriously, then practice might be extended to work with the preservice teachers' students. As preservice teachers begin to think about issues of diversity and inclusion and how to apply relevant, supportive practices, they might also turn their attention towards engaging their students in those same aims. Preservice educators might begin to help their students understand how social, political, and economic forces influence individuals. They might focus on how music becomes a representation, product, and tool of these systems of inequality, including helping students to develop a critical vocabulary and to understand the ethical, political, and musical aspects and results of institutional inequality. Addressing inequality might also include identifying microaggressions in music. How is a dominant group's (mis)appropriation of music, dance, and other cultural forms from marginalized populations a part of students' creation and consumption of music? What are the economic inequalities that influence and shape musical practices? How will we engage with our community in light of what we learn from answering these questions? These are some questions teachers can ask of students to engaging them in approaching issues of inequality.

However, because core practices are embedded within practice it is important to focus these questions and actions in the process of teaching. These are difficult topics to address with students. They and their families may have strong opinions on these topics. The delicateness of addressing such sensitive issues may be particularly difficult for early career teachers who do not have the experience, community trust, or the job security that more veteran teachers might enjoy. Therefore, it is important for teacher educators to introduce preservice teachers to strategies that engage students in social practice. A commitment to core practices would also require teacher educators to give preservice teachers the opportunity to practice these strategies in scaffolded, "safe" contexts. Drawing upon literature in multicultural education (Banks 2014), social justice-oriented teaching and action (Picower 2012), and dialogic education (Freire 2000) may serve as theoretical frames to generate and practice social praxis with students.

8 Conclusion

Within these core practices of intercultural teaching, music teacher educators might begin to help preservice teachers navigate the terrain and tension of intercultural teaching, practice, and policy. With this aim, teacher educators might *keep it complex*. This complexity requires that they embed learning to teach in practice, while melding it with theory to create praxis. They might aim to make teachers the creators rather than simply the targets of policy, merging the 'macro' of policy with the local or 'micro' of teaching (Schmidt and Colwell 2017). In cultivating these core practices, there is the seemingly contrary practice of questioning and de-centering these core practices. The concept of 'core' has the potential to ossify practice, ignore difference, and, as a result, potentially become 'anti-intercultural' or at least 'un-intercultural.'

As we see it then, these could be initial steps to create core practice of intercultural teaching in music, while also considering the need to examine *core practices* in terms of curriculum and policy. In curricular or pedagogical terms, core practices, such as those we articulated, might include teachers paying attention to representation of diversity in music and curricula, reflecting on their practice in reference to diversity and equity, and inviting their students also to engage in intercultural praxis. In policy terms, looking at our teacher education and teachers' *core practices* might mean to further focus on the fact that policy enterprise is a process requiring constant adjustment, and thus only our active participation can engender intelligent and integrative decision making. A *core practice* here then might be a modicum of focus on the development of *policy savvy* where music educators come to own policy as an alternative conceptualization of influence, and in the process, learn how to use to their advantage curricular, organizational, and political discursive practices, facilitating spaces for coalition work, framing and strategically organizing change, and developing the capacity to read their political environs. We believe a combined approach can prove capacious and create an avenue for powerful, positive change in the teaching profession.

References

Ball, S. J. (2009). *The education debate*. Bristol: Policy Press.

Ball, D. L., & Forzani, F. M. (2009). The work of teaching and the challenge for teacher education. *Journal of Teacher Education, 60*, 497–511. https://doi.org/10.1177/0022487109348479.

Banks, J. A. (2014). *An introduction to multicultural education* (5th ed.). Boston: Pearson, Allyn & Bacon.

Baumann, G. (2006). Grammars of identity/alterity: A structural approach. In G. Baumann & A. Gingrich (Eds.), *Grammars of identity/alterity: A structural approach* (pp. 18–50). New York: Berghahn.

Blacking, J. (1974). *How musical is man*. Seattle: University of Washington Press.

Blase, J., & Blase, J. (2002). The micropolitics of instructional supervision: A call for research. *Educational Administration Quarterly, 38*(1), 6–44.

Bolman, L. G., & Deal, T. E. (2008). *Reframing organizations: Artistry, choice and leadership*. San Francisco: Jossey-Bass.

Bolman, L. G., & Deal, T. E. (2016). *Reframing organizations: Artistry, choice, and leadership* (6th ed.). San Francisco: Jossey-Bass.

Crow, G. M., & Weindling, D. (2010). Learning to be political: New English headteachers' roles. *Educational Policy, 24*(1), 137–158.

Dutro, E., & Cartun, A. (2016). Cut to the core practices: Toward visceral disruptions of binaries in PRACTICE-based teacher education. *Teaching and Teacher Education, 58*, 119–128. https://doi.org/10.1016/j.tate.2016.05.001.

Etzioni, A. (1968/1992). *The active society: A theory of societal and political processes*. New York: Free Press.

Fischer, F. (2003). *Reframing public policy: Discursive politics and deliberative practices*. New York: Oxford University press.

Freire, P. (2000). *Pedagogy of the oppressed*. New York: Continuum.

Fulcher, G. (1999). *Disabling policies? A comparative approach to education policy and disability*. London: The Falmer Press.

Grossman, P., & McDonald, M. (2008). Back to the future: Directions for research in teaching and teacher education. *American Educational Research Journal, 45*, 184–205. https://doi.org/10.3102/0002831207312906.

Grossman, P., Hammerness, K., & McDonald, M. (2009). Redefining teaching, reimagining teacher education. *Teachers and Teaching: Theory and Practice, 15*, 273–289. https://doi.org/10.1080/13540600902875340.

Haas, P. (1992). Epistemic communities and international policy coordination. *International Organization, 46*(1), 1–35.

Kos, R. (2010). Developing capacity for change: A policy analysis for the music education profession. *Arts Education Policy Review, 111*(3), 97–104.

Laes, T., & Schmidt, P. (2016). Activism within music education: Working towards inclusion and policy change in the Finnish music school context. *British Journal of Music Education, 33*(1), 5–23.

Lampert, M., Franke, M. L., Kazemi, E., Ghousseini, H., Turrou, A. C., Beasley, H., & Crowe, K. (2013). Keeping it complex using rehearsals to support novice teacher learning of ambitious teaching. *Journal of Teacher Education, 64*, 226–243. https://doi.org/10.1177/0022487112473837.

Marx, K., & Friedrich Engels, F. (1970). *The German ideology* (Vol. 1). New York: International Publishers Co.

National Council on Teacher Quality. (2013). *Teacher prep review.* Washington, DC: National Council on Teacher Quality.

Picower, B. (2012). *Practice what you teach: Social justice education in the classroom and the streets* (Vol. 13). New York: Routledge.

Ravitch, D. (2013). *Reign of error: The hoax of the privatization movement and the danger to America's public schools.* New York: Alfred K. Knopf.

Sabatier, P. (2007). *Theories of the policy process.* Boulder: Westview Press.

Schmidt, P. (2017). Why policy matters: Developing a policy vocabulary within music education. In P. Schmidt & R. Colwell (Eds.), *Policy and the political life of music education* (pp. 11–36). New York: Oxford University Press.

Schmidt, P., & Colwell, R. (Eds.). (2017). *Policy and the political life of music education.* New York: Oxford University Press.

Schmidt, P., & Morrow, S. (2015). Hoarse with no name: Chronic voice problems, policy & music teacher marginalization. *Music Education Research, 18*(1), 1–18.

Schmidt, P., & Robbins, J. (2011). Looking backwards to reach forward: A strategic architecture for professional development in music education. *Arts Education Policy Review, 112*(2), 95–103.

Schneider, A., & Ingram, H. (1997). *Policy design for democracy.* Lawrence: University Press of Kansas.

Sörensen, E., & Torfing, J. (Eds.). (2007). *Theories of democratic network governance.* Basingstoke: Palgrave Macmillan.

Stone, D. A. (2011). *Policy paradox: The art of political decision making* (3rd ed.). New York: W. W. Norton.

Sue, D. W. (2010). Microaggressions, marginality, and oppression: An introduction. In D. W. Sue (Ed.), *Microaggressions and marginality: Manifestation, dynamics, and impact* (pp. 3–24). New York: Wiley.

The National Network of State Teachers of the Year (NNSTOY). (2015). *Engaged: Educators and the policy process. National network of teachers of the year.* Arlington: NNSTOY.

United Nations Educational, Scientific and Cultural Organization (UNESCO). 2015. UNESCO guidelines on intercultural education. Paris: UNESCO [Online]. http://unesdoc.unesco.org/images/0014/001478/147878e.pdf. Accessed 10 Jan 2018.

Westerlund, H., Partti, H., & Karlsen, S. (2015). Teaching as improvisational experience: Student music teachers' reflections on learning during an intercultural project. *Research Studies in Music Education, 37*(1), 55–75.

Whitcomb, J., Borko, H., & Liston, D. (2009). Growing talent: Promising professional development models and practices. *Journal of Teacher Education, 60*, 207–212. https://doi.org/10.1177/00224871093372.

Wildavsky, A. (1979). *Speaking truth to power: The art and craft of policy analysis.* New Brunswick: Transaction Publishers.

Winton, S., & Pollock, K. (2012). Preparing politically savvy principals in Ontario, Canada. *Journal of Educational Administration, 51*(1), 40–54.

Zeichner, K. (2012). The turn once again toward practice-based teacher education. *Journal of Teacher Education, 63*, 376–382. https://doi.org/10.1177/0022487112445789.

5

Structure and Fragmentation: The Current Tensions and Possible Transformation of Intercultural Music Teacher Education in South Africa

Albi Odendaal

Abstract The issues of multiculturalism and interculturalism are part of the daily discourse and painful history of South Africa. As such, South African music teacher educators have a unique contribution to make to the international discourse on diversity in music education. This chapter draws on Activity Theory to conceptually position the practices of music teacher education in South Africa, and to place the practices in a wider socio-political environment. Interviews were conducted with four music teacher educators in this interpretative descriptive study, in order to understand their conceptions of multicultural and intercultural music teacher education. Three common practices that are critically framed by the teachers are identified: immersion, interaction and documentation. These practices are then considered in the broader contexts of the structure of the university and the fragmentation of society. The chapter argues on the basis of this analysis that the historically accumulating structural tensions inherent in music teacher education in South Africa should lead to transformation of the activity, but only if music teachers themselves become cognisant of the contradictions inherent in the current practices and collaboratively and creatively expand beyond them.

Keywords Intercultural · Music · Teacher education · South Africa · Activity theory · Transformation · Diversity

1 Introduction

Diversity is a national hallmark that most South Africans are proud of. The appellation "Rainbow Nation" was apparently coined by Archbishop Desmond Tutu, and has until recently been widely used to describe the country (Buqa 2015). South African music teacher educators are typically faced with diverse languages, musical

---

A. Odendaal (✉)
MASARA, North-West University, Potchefstroom, South Africa
e-mail: Albi.Odendaal@nwu.ac.za

practices and social norms in their classrooms. This chapter explores how a group of expert music teacher educators in South Africa think about cultural diversity in their classrooms and in the future classrooms of the music teachers they are preparing. It is a relevant topic to consider, given the various diversities present in South Africa, and the various attempts at dealing with those diversities in the history of the country. The aim of this chapter is to conceptually position the practices that are commonly used in music teacher education in South Africa, both in the ways that the music teacher educators themselves describe them and within the country's broader socio-political environment.

In order to point to the complexity of decision making that music teacher educators face, some central concepts of Cultural Historical Activity Theory are employed (Engeström 2001; Engeström and Sannino 2011). Expansive learning is understood by these scholars as the process where an entire activity, in this case music teacher education, is transformed, developing "culturally new patterns of activity" (Engeström 2001, p. 139). Such expansive learning is theorized to happen as a result of contradictions that exist or are formed between elements of the activity system, resulting in double-bind situations where the activity has to transform in order to keep on existing (Engeström and Sannino 2011). Before discussing the transformation of music teacher education in South Africa, however, the chapter will first give some general background to the idea of cultural diversity in South Africa and how this relates to music, and also briefly discuss how diversity is addressed in the current school curricula. The chapter will then provide conceptualization of current intercultural music teacher education practices and attempt to locate such practices within two main streams of current socio-political activity in the country.

The chapter takes its methodological cue from Interpretative Description (Thorne 2016), an approach which aims to better understand "observable patterns of human subjective experience and behaviour" and to locate that understanding between "theoretical integrity and real-world utility" (p. 37). Interpretative Description is a qualitative research approach which draws on the existing approaches of Ethnography, Phenomenology, and Grounded Theory to address real-world questions through empirical investigation in order to provide theoretically sound ways of addressing the practical issues involved. Although the approach was developed and is used in health disciplines, it is suitable for research in other applied disciplines (e.g. Buissink-Smith and McIntosh 1999), of which education is one. Semi-structured interviews were conducted (Thorne 2016, p. 86) with four music teacher educators, each from a different cultural-linguistic group and each teaching at a different university, in order to discuss and explore their conceptions of multicultural and intercultural music teacher education and the practical ways that they prepare future music educators. As an active music teacher educator, I brought my own understandings to these discussions and the subsequent analysis and also sought to learn from and engage with the views of the colleagues with whom I was interacting; in this way I acted as both a fifth participant and an author. The recorded interviews were analyzed by identifying strategies that teachers employ, and tensions that they experience in attempting to employ the strategies. Because the four music teacher educators are experts in the topic under investigation, they were each provided with early drafts of the chapter and given the opportunity to comment (Thorne 2016, p. 174); in this way the chapter is to some extent a co-construction although filtered by my own understanding of the work of the music teacher educators and the socio-political milieu.

2 The South African Context

As an indication of the range of cultural practices in South Africa it is worth noting that the country boasts 11 official languages. In addition, the Constitution further recognizes four languages that must be promoted and developed and another 11 that must be promoted and respected; in total, 26 languages (*Constitution of the Republic of South Africa Act* 1996) and this total does not count languages of the wide range of people from the rest of Africa and the world who live in South Africa. Each of the people groups who speak these languages have a variety of musical practices that are to a greater or lesser extent unique to the language. Levine (2005), for example, describes the musical practices of the 11 major language groups that were indigenous prior to the arrival of Europeans; albeit with a reified, historical and rural perspective (Harrop-Allin 2005). This plethora of musical practices has coexisted over several centuries and musicians have to a greater or lesser extent appropriated, adapted and exchanged one another's musical ideas, resulting in a variety of modern-day stylistic expressions such as *isicatamiya, ghoema* and *boeremusiek* (Coplan 2008; Martin 2013) alongside musical expressions that are considered traditional by the people who practice them, and those imported from outside of South Africa. Such intercultural exchange is understood in this chapter as an opportunity for enrichment of culture, and not a threat to it (Volf 1996, p. 52; see also Westerlund and Karlsen 2017), and differentiates the intercultural perspective from a multicultural one, which often has a stronger emphasis on the maintenance of cultural identities (Morrow 1998).

Although such intercultural musical interaction is understood in this chapter as mutually beneficial to the parties involved, one should also consider the centuries-long history of violence and oppressive legislation that forms the context for these musical interactions. South Africa is still in many places divided as a result of the long history of colonialism (which started in 1652) and Apartheid (which legally occurred between 1948 and 1994, but is still in many ways ingrained in society). Surprisingly, Morrow (1998, p. 167) points out that the societal divisions and the attendant history is predicated, in the case of Apartheid, upon a multicultural philosophy that argued for the need to "recognise and respect the differences between the different groups that compose the society, and to protect and perpetuate group integrity" by keeping cultural or linguistic groups separate. Although the differences between interculturalism and multiculturalism has been starkly drawn here, and in the history of South Africa, the tension between preservation of my (or our) identity and the embrace of the other is a fluid and perplexing problem, requiring constant negotiation and reevaluation.

The divisions in society that were based on racial, cultural and linguistic classifications have not yet disappeared from the discourses of modern-day South Africa, and are exacerbated by massive class differences resultant from Apartheid and colonial policies – South Africa is currently one of the most unequal societies in the world in terms of income distribution (*Poverty trends in South Africa: An examination of absolute poverty between 2006 and 2011* 2014). The complex issues of race, culture and class intersect in various ways, and are ever present in power negotiations between individuals and groups, resulting in an intricately tangled social environment (Soudien and McKinney 2016) within which music education has to find a suitable approach (see Thorsén 1997 for a dated overview of some of the issues). Due to the ways that culture has been used in the political arena in South Africa, intercultural education has a distinct position in South Africa that should be somewhat differentiated from discourses in the rest of the world.

Prominent topics globally include both the issues of immigration (e.g. Karlsen 2013) and of "infusing the curriculum" with musics from around the globe (e.g. Campbell and Wade 2004, p. 12), neither of which are current topics in South African educational thought. As a result of the multicultural emphasis of the Apartheid policies, curriculum developers since 1994 were wary of multiculturalism, and have instead chosen social cohesion and human rights as bases for curricular development (Soudien and McKinney 2016). Social cohesion is here understood as "a situation where citizens of the state share feelings of solidarity with their compatriots, and act on the basis of these feelings" (Chipkin and Ngqulunga 2008, p. 61). This approach is located in a tension between recognizing the equality and rights of cultural groupings while pursuing the formation of a strong communal identity and cooperation among people in the country (Soudien and McKinney 2016), and is allied to the ways that interculturalism has been described so far in the paper.

The social cohesion agenda of the whole curriculum has not necessarily filtered through to the content of the Music Curricula (Department of Basic Education 2011a, b), and the curricula uncomfortably positions the relationship between indigenous knowledge and Western music educational traditions. By including options to choose a Western Art Music (WAM), Jazz or Indigenous African Music (IAM) stream in subject music in the Further Education and Training phase (grades 10–12), the curriculum acknowledges some of the musical variety of the country, and there is a nod to integration in the mandate that every learner should partake in at least one term of study of the other streams. However, while there is a strong emphasis on indigenous knowledge and practices in the IAM stream, which is coupled with traditional WAM theory, the same is unfortunately not true of the WAM stream, where indigenous knowledge only features in the mandatory term and is not woven throughout like WAM theory is for IAM. There is a danger that this curriculum forces indigenous musical practices into the mould of WAM by allowing the paradigm of WAM to also set the agenda for IAM. Thus, the curriculum may be attempting (intentionally or unintentionally) to "draw indigenous musical practices into western musical referents" (Bradley 2006, p. 11), a practice that is often to the detriment of the indigenous musical practices (see Harrop-Allin and Kros 2014 for a similar critique of the intermediate phase curriculum).

Music teacher education in this context has to address a complex of very difficult topics, and prepare student teachers with skills to grapple with issues such as fostering social cohesion while maintaining the identities of various musics and transcending some of the limitations of the curriculum as printed while keeping in mind the histories and lived experiences of both the country and the students in their classes. As if that is not enough they should also be able to do this with minimal resources and sometimes in dire environmental and socio-economic circumstances that are faced by very many schools (see, for example, the report by *Planning to Fail: Summary of findings from Equal Education's Eastern Cape school visits* 2016).

3 Three Common Practices in Music Teacher Education

The themes discussed in the following section are drawn from the co-created understandings that arose from the interviews with the four music teacher educators and the discussions that took place after the first draft had been distributed. This section identifies three closely related practical approaches that are employed by music teacher educators: immersion, interaction and documentation. These three approaches are perhaps not different from those advocated by European or North American scholars (e.g. Campbell 2002), but differences could include that South Africans are not typically trying to learn about the music of other nations apart from that of the Western Art canon since we have enough musical variety within our borders, and that there is the stated aim of increasing social cohesion on a national level through such interactions (although, see Elliott et al. 2016, p. 4). Further, I briefly discuss the essential element of the critical framing within which these practical approaches are placed, including their contexts and challenges.

3.1 Immersion

Immersion refers to placing future music educators in musical situations that they might not be familiar with for extended periods of time so that they don't only learn the notes or "how it goes", but also gain experience in the practices associated with the music. Music teacher education lecturers who participated in this study have drawn on their own expertise and that of "culture bearers" (Participant 1) to help their students engage in practical music making as a way of immersing them in a different musical and cultural world. Culture bearers are expert musicians who specialize in forms of music making that are typically transmitted orally and who are able to help students experience, not only working with the sonic material, but also with some of the wider practices that surround the songs, dances and accompaniments that they are learning. Future music educators are typically expected to be able to command a variety of musical styles, and also be comfortable in learning and teaching orally and with notational aids. In addition to such learning experiences, students are often involved in community music projects such as UKUSA (Oehrle 2010) or Musikhane[1] where students are expected to teach, not only their own instruments but also a variety of common indigenous instruments such as marimbas and drums together with typical dances and songs.

3.2 Interaction

Interaction refers to fostering musical interactions between students, especially drawing on musics in which students have expertise but that may not be mainstream practices. The diversity of the student population on university campuses and in (higher education) music departments mirrors some of the diversity of the country. This is a major change from the time when people who were classified as non-whites had to gain ministerial approval to be allowed to study music at universities historically intended for people who were classified as white. As an example of such diversity, in one of my Music Education classes last year I had students from five linguistic groups within South Africa. Music teacher educators see this diversity as an opportunity and make use of the varied expertise of the students in their classes, drawing them into teaching each other songs that they learned as children, and fostering greater understanding and cooperation in the process (Joseph 2012). In this way, students have the opportunity to sharpen their teaching skills, learn a range of new musical materials, and have the opportunity to engage with the experiences of their classmates with regards to musical heritage.

3.3 Documentation

Documentation refers to the practices of notating or describing indigenous musical traditions so that non-practitioners can gain some understanding of what may be involved in these traditions. There is a long history of engagement with issues of multicultural and intercultural education among some music teacher educators, officially starting with the founding of the South African Music Educator Society (SAMES) in 1985 (Oehrle 1994). According to Participant 1, teacher educators realized through the discussions that led to the founding of SAMES that there is an urgent need for documenting the educational practices of every kind of musical style in the country, and this led to the founding of the *Talking Drum*, a periodical

---

[1] See http://humanities.nwu.ac.za/music/musikhane

that ran 40 issues over more than 20 years. Although the periodical is out of print, back issues are still available online.[2] This magazine had the explicit aim of publishing practical teaching ideas that can be used in classrooms (Oehrle 2013). Music teacher educators still extensively use this resource with their students, as a means of introducing them to lesson ideas drawing on a wide range of musics. Teacher educators also draw on the massive archive of the International Library of African Music,[3] and all participants noted a growing number of theoretical and practical books that deal with the performance of various styles of South African musics (e.g. McConnachie n.d.; Herbst et al. 2003; Herbst 2005; Mans 2006; Nzewi 2007; Carver 2014; Agawu 2016; Oehrle 2016).

3.4 Critical Framing

The three practices of immersion, interaction and documentation can easily result in the reification and essentialization of culture, where "a single, drastically simplified group identity that is at odds with the complexity of people's lives, their multiple identities and the intersectionalities of those identities" is imposed or inferred (Gouws 2013, p. 39). The music teacher educators I interviewed are careful to engage in critical dialogue with the students around the issues that are raised by engaging in these practices. They point out the need for their students to challenge the narrative that "assumes that there are separate cultures in the first place [...] and assumes that those cultures are distinct" (Participant 3). This works from an understanding that the South African cultural situation is one where we are "many in conversation, not many in isolation" (Participant 2), and where we have deeply "interconnected histories" (Participant 4). The music teacher educators aim, firstly, to help students see the "problematic consequences of thinking that culture is static" (Participant 3), and, secondly, to focus students' attention on little cultures (localized practices and participation in communities) rather than big cultures.

This critical work of undoing assumptions about culture that are widespread in South African society stands in tension with the need to equip students with practical skills that they can employ in schools; repertoires of music and repertoires of teaching that the students can draw from when they stand before a class. Music teacher educators have limited hours in which to engage their students in musics that are unfamiliar to the students, and have to both foster students who have integrated musical skills and repertoires in different styles, and who are able to critically reflect on their own learning and the socio-cultural situation in the country.

---

[2] http://www.disa.ukzn.ac.za/TALKING_DRUM

[3] http://www.ru.ac.za/ilam/

4 The Wider Context

The three practices and the tensions in working with these practices do not stand in isolation, and there are wider social forces that impinge on the work that the music teacher educators do. Here I will discuss two inhibiting forces that the music teacher educators pointed out in our conversations: the structure of the university, and the fragmentation of society. Figure 1 is a schematic representation of the three practices and the context within which they occur.

4.1 The Structure of the University

Music departments situated at universities previously reserved for people classified as white, are copies of European conservatories and typically offer mainly Western Classical music as a course of study. Some universities have thriving Jazz departments, and there are some small departments that specialize in African musics, but inclusion of musical approaches that differ from the Western mainstream is a rare and recent phenomenon. Thus, while the student body has significantly broadened to include a wide representation of the peoples of South Africa in the past 20 years (Spaull 2016), institutional reform – both in terms of the transformation of staff and the reframing the epistemological narratives of universities (Mamdani 2016) – has not kept pace, neither in the university as a whole, nor in the music departments within these universities. Since 2015 until the time of writing South Africa has seen major, and occasionally violent, disruptions at most of the nation's universities. Students are protesting against a wide range of issues, all related to experienced inequities and the perceived lack of action to remedy these (see Hodes 2017 for a history and discussion of the movements). What these protests show is that injustice

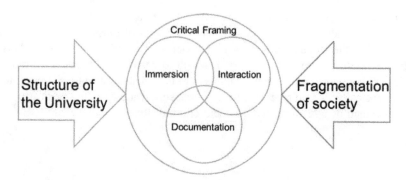

Fig. 1 A schematic representation of three typical practices that teachers employ, together with the forces that impinge on these practices

is still a perceived and experienced part of our society that affects those people who lived through Apartheid as well as the new generations of students who were born after the dawn of democracy in South Africa. It is therefore imperative to consider not only the content of music teacher education as a subject, as many of the music teacher educators have already done, but also the curriculum of the whole degree program within which the subject is taught. If the only intercultural musical contact between students happens in the music education classroom, and there is no further engagement with these issues during the rest of the degree, the kinds of protests that have happened since 2015 are highly likely to continue. There is a tendency among music educators to point out the positive role that music can play in fostering unity (e.g. Joseph 2012), and it is true that music has the potential, if used well, to facilitate this process. One should, however, be careful not to assume that because South Africans are singing each other's songs, the injustices of the past have been resolved.

The structure of the university as a whole and of the offered university music degrees stands in tension with the work that the music teacher educators do, and particularly impinges on the practice of immersion. If immersion only happens once a week in the music education class, it is better than nothing, but true immersion should ideally be a longer and stronger experience than 1 h per week, and should ideally include extended immersive experiences, and reinforcement of similar immersive practices in other subject areas such as theory and aural training.

4.2 The Fragmentation of Society

Running parallel to the increasing calls to decolonize the university, is the increasing fragmentation of society as a result of Apartheid legislation, urbanization and globalization that lead to the not-so-slow decline in communal forms of music making, which older generations in rural areas experienced. This leads Huyssen (2012) to draw on Historically Informed Performance Practice (HIPP) as a perspective when working with traditional musicians. One can extend his argument to state that in the same way that HIPP works to understand the music-making practices of previous generations, South Africans will have to work to understand the traditional musics of our country. Students do not only follow in the musical footsteps of their forefathers, but choose their own paths (Strelitz 2004). Many students who arrive at the university are not versed in the older musics of the country, and many not even in the newer musics. Their musical mother tongues are often globally popular rather than historically local.

This societal fragmentation stands in particular tension with the practice of interaction, which assumes diverse musical backgrounds, and particularly assumes that those diversities are "cultural", and that the students are aware of their musical heritage and able to help others to enjoy it. The fragmentation of society means that the students' cultural heritage is often not of the "traditional" type but rather draws on popular mass media. As a result, universities also play a role as custodians of the variety of musical expressions of the country, and, by introducing students to a wide range of musics, university lecturers have the opportunity to affect the musical life of the country.

5 Conclusion: Visions for the Future

The three practices described in this paper, and the wider societal pressures that impinge on the work of music teacher educators sets up a number of tensions within which music teacher educators must operate. These are not merely superficial dilemmas, but should rather be understood as "historically accumulating structural tensions within and between activity systems" (Engeström 2001, 137), that have developed out of the country's history and the historically developed practices of music education. These structural tensions occur *within* the work of music teacher education – some of these have been highlighted above – and also *between* the system of music teacher education and broader societal forces. The tensions between fostering musical practices and developing critical views of those practices within the classroom, and between the work that music teacher educators do and the forces outside the classroom (the calls for decolonization, and the fragmentation of society) is a source of confusion for music teacher educators in South Africa. However, these tensions may also be the seed for the transformation of South Africa's music teacher education. Such transformation typically only takes place when the problems are no longer understood only as dilemmas (where people express incompatible evaluations) but rather become states of double-bind (when the actors face pressing and equally unacceptable alternatives) (Engeström and Sannino 2011). Engeström (2001, p. 137) argues that such states of double-bind offer the possibility to lead to expansive learning in individuals and, more importantly, in social groupings. Such expansive learning takes place when the activity (especially its object and motive) is reconceptualized to "embrace a radically wider horizon of possibilities". In terms of the argument thus far, this wider horizon of possibilities includes the development of social cohesion through intercultural exchange, both in the music education class and beyond it. This development of social cohesion extends beyond awareness of and respect for the other through engaging with their musical practices, and moves towards embrace of the other as person in radical reconciliation (Volf 1996). Although this is a task beyond what music teacher education could realistically achieve, it is one to which music teacher education may contribute through creating contexts were students may encounter those who are different on an equal footing.

It is possible and likely that such a transformation will occur, but this will only happen to the extent that music teacher educators and their colleagues at the institutions where they work experience the tensions described in this chapter as deeply rooted contradictions, both in their own being and in their own practice. Expansion may happen through individuals taking up the responsibility to initiate change, but is more likely to happen when a collaborative effort is established to enable change. Once such collaborative effort is implemented, and hopefully even before this, a transformation of music teacher education seems inevitable.

Acknowledgements I wish to thank the four music teacher educators who participated in this study for their willingness to discuss their experiences and thoughts about teacher education at their institutions.

References

Agawu, K. (2016). *The African imagination in music.* Oxford: Oxford University Press.

Bradley, D. (2006). Music education, multiculturalism and anti-racism: Can we talk. *Action, Criticism, and Theory for Music Education, 5*, 2–30.

Buissink-Smith, N., & McIntosh, A. (1999). Interpretive description: Advancing qualitative approaches in tourism and hospitality research. *Tourism Analysis, 4*(2), 115–119.

Buqa, W. (2015). Storying Ubuntu as a rainbow nation. *Verbum et Ecclesia, 36*, 1–8. https://doi. org/10.4102/VE.V36I2.1434.

Campbell, P. S. (2002). Music education in a time of cultural transformation. *Music Educators Journal, 89*, 27–32. https://doi.org/10.2307/3399881.

Campbell, P. S., & Wade, B. C. (2004). *Teaching music globally: Experiencing music, expressing culture.* New York: Oxford University Press.

Carver, M. (2014). *Understanding African music.* Grahamstown: International Library of African Music.

Chipkin, I., & Ngqulunga, B. (2008). Friends and family: Social cohesion in South Africa. *Journal of Southern African Studies, 34*, 61–76. https://doi.org/10.1080/03057070701832882.

Constitution of the Republic of South Africa. (Act no. 108 of 1996).

Coplan, D. B. (2008). *In township tonight! South Africa's black city music and theatre.* Chicago: University of Chicago Press.

Department of Basic Education. (2011a). *Curriculum and assessment policy statement grades 10–12: Music.* Pretoria: Department of Basic Education.

Department of Basic Education. (2011b). *Curriculum and assessment policy statement grades 7–9: Creative arts.* Pretoria: Department of Basic Education.

Elliott, D. J., Silverman, M., & Bowman, W. (2016). Artistic citizenship: Introduction, aims and overview. In D. J. Elliot, M. Silverman, & W. Bowman (Eds.), *Artistic citizenship: Artistry, social responsibility, and ethical praxis* (pp. 3–21). New York: Oxford University Press.

Engeström, Y. (2001). Expansive learning at work: Toward an activity theoretical reconceptualization. *Journal of Education and Work, 14*, 133–156. https://doi. org/10.1080/13639080020028747.

Engeström, Y., & Sannino, A. (2011). Discursive manifestations of contradictions in organizational change efforts: A methodological framework. *Journal of Organizational Change Management, 24*, 368–387. https://doi.org/10.1108/09534811111132758.

Gouws, A. (2013). Multiculturalism in South Africa: Dislodging the binary between universal human rights and culture/tradition. *Politikon, 40*, 35–55. https://doi.org/10.1080/02589346.2 013.765674.

Harrop-Allin, S. (2005). Ethnomusicology and music education: Developing the dialogue. *SAMUS, 25*, 109–125.

Harrop-Allin, S., & Kros, C. (2014). The C major scale as index of 'back to basics' in south African education: A critique of the curriculum assessment policy statement. *Southern African Review of Education, 20*, 70–89.

Herbst, A. (2005). *Emerging solutions for musical arts education in Africa*. Cape Town: African Minds.

Herbst, A., Nzewi, M., & Agawu, V. K. (Eds.). (2003). *Musical arts in Africa: Theory, practice, and education*. Pretoria: Unisa Press.

Hodes, R. (2017). Questioning 'fees must fall'. *African Affairs, 116*, 140–150. https://doi.org/10.1093/afraf/adw072.

Huyssen, H. (2012). Music production in the intercultural sphere: Challenges and opportunities. *Acta Academica, 2012*, 43–71.

Joseph, D. (2012). Sharing ownership in multicultural music: A hands-on approach in teacher education in South Africa. *Australian Journal of Music Education*, 10–19.

Karlsen, S. (2013). Immigrant students and the "homeland music": Meanings, negotiations and implications. *Research Studies in Music Education, 35*, 161–177. https://doi.org/10.1177/1321103X13508057.

Levine, L. (2005). *Traditional music of South Africa*. Johannesburg: Jacana Media.

Mamdani, M. (2016). Between the public intellectual and the scholar: Decolonization and some post-independence initiatives in African higher education. *Inter-Asia Cultural Studies, 17*, 68–83. https://doi.org/10.1080/14649373.2016.1140260.

Mans, M. (2006). *Centering on African practice in musical arts education*. Cape Town: African Minds.

Martin, D. (2013). *Sounding the cape: Music, identity and politics in South Africa*. Somerset West: African Minds.

McConnachie, B. (n.d.). In D. Thramm (Ed.), *Listen & learn: Music made easy*. Grahamstown: International Library of African Music.

Morrow, W. (1998). Multicultural education in South Africa. In W. Morrow & K. King (Eds.), *Vision and reality: Changing education and training in South Africa* (pp. 232–244). Cape Town: University of Cape Town Press.

Nzewi, M. (2007). *A contemporary study of musical arts: The root – foundation* (Vol. 1. 5 vols). Cape Town: African Minds.

Oehrle, E. (1994). A history of SAMES. *The Talking Drum*. March. http://disa.ukzn.ac.za/sites/default/files/talkingdrum/TDnewsno3mar1994/tdnewsno3mar1994.pdf

Oehrle, E. (2010). Values infusing UKUSA: A developmental community arts programme in South Africa. *International Journal of Community Music, 3*, 379–386. https://doi.org/10.1386/ijcm.3.3.379_1.

Oehrle, E. (2013). The talking drum: Towards the dissemination of musics in South Africa. *Journal of Musical Arts in Africa, 10*, 135–138. https://doi.org/10.2989/18121004.2013.846991.

Oehrle, E. (2016). *Creative musicking: With African, Indian, and Western musics*. Denver: Outskirts Press.

Planning to Fail: Summary of findings from Equal Education's Eastern Cape school visits. (2016). King William's Town: Equal Education.

Poverty trends in South Africa: An examination of absolute poverty between 2006 and 2011. (2014). Report no. 03-10-06. Pretoria: Statistics South Africa.

Soudien, C., & McKinney, C. (2016). The character of the multicultural education discussion in South Africa. In J. L. Bianco & A. Bal (Eds.), *Learning from difference: Comparative accounts of multicultural education* (pp. 125–145). Dordrecht: Springer.

Spaull, N. (2016, May 13). Black graduate numbers are up. *Mail & Guardian*. [Online]. https://mg.co.za/article/2016-05-2017-black-gradute.numbers-are-up. Accessed 14 Jan 2018.

Strelitz, L. (2004). Against cultural essentialism: Media reception among south African youth. *Media, Culture & Society, 26*, 625–641. https://doi.org/10.1177/0163443704044219.

Thorne, S. (2016). *Interpretive description: Qualitative research for applied practice* (2nd ed.). New York: Routledge.

Thorsén, S.-M. (1997). Music education in South Africa: Striving for unity and diversity. *Svensk tidskrift för musikforskning, 79*(1), 91–109.

Volf, M. (1996). *Exclusion and embrace: A theological exploration of identity, otherness and reconciliation.* Nashville: Abingdon.

Westerlund, H., & Karlsen, S. (2017). Knowledge production beyond local and national blindspots: Remedying professional ocularcentrism of diversity in music teacher education. *Action, Criticism & Theory for Music Education, 16*(3), 78–107. http://act.maydaygroup.org/act-16-3-78-107/.

6

The Discomfort of Intercultural Learning in Music Teacher Education

Alexis A. Kallio and Heidi Westerlund

Abstract Recognizing and ethically engaging with the inherent diversity of music education contexts demands a continuous interrogation of the norms and values underpinning policy and practice in music teacher education. In doing so, teachers and students in higher education are challenged to question why and how students are socialized into particular music education systems, traditions, or perspectives and to consider alternatives. In this chapter, we explore such reflexive processes, employing a theoretical reading analysis through Bourdieu's concepts of *habitus*, and *doxa*. The data consists of group reflections and interviews with student-teachers that the authors conducted as part of an intercultural arts education project between Finnish masters students and two Cambodian NGOs. Based on our analysis, we argue that stepping outside of one's cultural, musical, and pedagogical comfort zone is a necessary component of constructing and (re)negotiating teacher visions in music teacher education. However, this renegotiation may be discomforting for student-teachers, unsettling deep-seated visions of what *good* music education is and ought to be – the taken-for-granted doxa of music teaching and learning. Therefore, for music-teacher education to become transformative and reflexive, there is a need for such educational experiences that engage with processes that are related to the art of living with difference.

Keywords Bourdieu · Discomfort · Intercultural education · Music teacher education · Reflexivity

---

A. A. Kallio (✉) · H. Westerlund
Sibelius Academy, University of the Arts Helsinki, Helsinki, Finland
e-mail: alexis.kallio@uniarts.fi; heidi.westerlund@uniarts.fi

1 Introduction

As school and university populations are increasingly recognized as inherently diverse, visions for higher music education have shifted from the transmission of skills or knowledge to social and ethical commitments to engage with difference. Whereas once, education institutions may have been seen to "provide a haven against social and cultural change" (Gates 2009, xxii), increasing mobility, migration and technological advances now position them at the forefront of learning – what Zygmunt Bauman has called "the art of living with difference" (Bauman 2010, 151). In Finland, national government policy (Opettajankoulutus 2020) has highlighted the need to foster intercultural competencies among future teachers in order to respond to a fast-changing socio-cultural climate and to strengthen democratic practices in schools. Such imperatives require a shift in focus in higher music education from deepening skills and understandings of what is already known, to a "complete reconceptualization of (…) practices and of [the] obligation to partake in global discourses and discussions" (Karlsen et al. 2016, 371). This poses significant challenges to the values and practices that have long been taken for granted – what the sociologist Pierre Bourdieu refers to as *doxa*. With etymological roots in the Greek verb δοκεῖν – to appear, or to accept – doxa functions to naturalize and normalize social practices. As many of our activities in music education are based on historical traditions and are guided by habits and emotions, the musical, pedagogical and onto-epistemological differences encountered through globalization may well appear threatening (Bauman and May 2001), as they disrupt tacit logics and understandings. These disruptions may be felt particularly violently in the context of music teacher education, often within conservatoire settings and structured according to firmly established musical, cultural, and pedagogical values. However, if the social and ethical imperatives of intercultural engagements are to be taken seriously, music teacher education can no longer assume that students can, want to, or should be socialized into a single music education system, tradition, or perspective (Kertz-Welzel 2013). Rather, contemporary societal changes demand an interrogation of why it is that we "teach students *particular* things and socialize them in *particular* ways" (Schubert 2008, 188).

As the norms and values of higher music education are called into question, the underlying doxa may be identified and reflected upon, creating alternatives to the commonsensical scripts of what, why and how we teach and learn. These scripts of music-teacher education can be understood in terms of what Bourdieu referred to as the *logic of the field* (Bourdieu and Passeron 1990). Those who possess cultural capital (in the case of many music-teacher education programs, a strong background in western art music and learning within vocation-based, master-apprentice models) are often comfortable within the field of higher music education. They are able to position themselves strategically, being familiar with the doxa and scripts of how and why things are done. In culturally diverse music education contexts (i.e. all music education contexts), if this logic is available to some and not others, those whose cultural capital does not align with the doxa of the field are excluded. As such, comfort is not an indicator of 'smooth sailing', but of privilege, inequality, and insularity – qualities that music teacher education programs can ill afford in an increasingly globalized world. From this perspective, consensus is impossible and indeed undesirable (Mouffe 2005). Furthermore, the discomforting sense of being outside of one's comfort zone is not a situation to be avoided in music-teacher education, but an essential component of ethical intercultural teaching and learning (see e.g. Westerlund 2017; Westerlund et al. 2015; Saether 2013; Bradley 2007).

In this chapter, we reflect upon the potentials of discomfort in the construction and (re)negotiation of teacher *visions* in higher music education. According to Karen Hammerness (2015), visions of what constitutes *good teaching* establish a sense of purpose with regards to what should be taught, who should be taught, and importantly, how we teach and why. Guiding decision-making and actions, visions are not necessarily utopian goals but represent teachers' strivings, imaginations, commitments, and understandings of classroom actions (Hammerness 2015, 8). However, Hammerness notes that "a program that is too closely focused and organized around a particular vision may deter candidates from expressing or developing alternative perspectives or exploring their own personal visions (...) potentially masking any challenges, differences, or variations" (2015, 6). Furthermore, as Talbot and Mantie explain, this is particularly problematic if visions "operate to advantage certain musical practices over others and, in so doing, advantage some groups of people over others" (2015, 156). If visions are to "promote both a vision of teaching as a professional practice *as well as* teaching as a means of making a difference" (Hammerness 2015, 18), we here consider how visions might challenge the doxa of music teacher education in ethically teaching and learning 'the art of living with difference'; how alternative perspectives are included and welcomed; and what possibilities exist in practice to learn outside of, or in opposition to the institutionalized, unreflective shared understanding of what good music teaching is.

2 Research Context: *Multicultural Arts University*

This chapter draws upon findings from research conducted during the second-cycle of an intercultural project titled *Multicultural Arts University* (see Westerlund et al. 2015 for more on the first-cycle of this project). This cycle of the project involved seven masters-level music education students, one music technology student and one dance student from the University of the Arts Helsinki, travelling to three music and dance programs run by two Cambodian Non-Governmental Organizations (henceforth NGOs) in 2013.[1] The masters student-teachers from the University of the Arts Helsinki were accompanied by four university staff members, including the authors of this chapter, and two music education lecturers. Although facilitated by the university and granting study credits, the project was not a mandatory part of

---

[1] This project was funded by the Ministry for Foreign Affairs of Finland. More information can be found at http://mcau.fi

The Discomfort of Intercultural Learning in Music Teacher Education

their studies but an exceptional situation and opportunity. Participating student-teachers were selected from applicants on the basis of certain criteria, including being in the final stages of their university studies, and having previous travel experiences.

The first NGO that participated in this project, which we here refer to by the pseudonym *New Horizons Children's Community* (henceforth New Horizons), was located on two sites: in Siem Reap in the North of Cambodia, and in the capital city Phnom Penh. New Horizons was primarily a residential home (for approximately 60 children at the Siem Reap community, and over 100 children at the Phnom Penh community), and offered regular lessons in music and dance for the children living there (in traditional Cambodian musics and dance, but also western art and popular music and dance styles). The Finnish student-teachers spent 2 days at New Horizons Siem Reap, and 4 days at New Horizons Phnom Penh. Student teachers conducted small and large group workshops for children, and also engaged in individual instrumental tuition when requested. This work culminated in a one-hour collaborative performance for the New Horizons community, including children and staff. A longer period of time, 10 days, was spent at the second NGO, which we refer to through the pseudonym *Komar Chrieng*. Located in a small town in the rural Southern coastal region, Komar Chrieng was home to a much smaller group of children (approximately 20), but had opened its doors to hundreds of local children to learn traditional Cambodian musics and dances free of charge. The Finnish student-teachers conducted small and large workshops on Finnish folk music and popular music, and in turn, the Cambodian children and staff members taught the student teachers a number of traditional Cambodian musics and dances.[2] At Komar Chrieng the teaching and learning between student-teachers and Cambodian children culminated in a public fundraising-performance for the local community and tourists.

This intercultural teaching and learning project aimed to provide both the Finnish student-teachers and the Cambodian children with opportunities to teach and learn from one another, in many ways following ethnomusicological approaches that are centered on getting to know cultural and musical Others (see e.g., Belz 2006; Campbell 2004; Joseph and Southcott 2009; Schippers 2010; Volk 1998). For the Cambodian children, the project also aimed to create a space of empowerment. This was not only through providing an opportunity for them to teach adult foreigners,

---

[2] These traditions included *Pinpeat* music, *Mahori* music, folk music and dance, classical dance and *Yike* theatre. *Pinpeat* music dates back to the ninth century and is primarily ceremonial or religious music played on wind and percussion instruments; *Mahori* is composed of two music forms, one traditionally designated for the Royal courts, and the other which is primarily performed at wedding celebrations. Folk music and dance often depict scenes of everyday rural Cambodian life and livelihoods. Classical dancers were traditionally sourced from all parts of Cambodian society, from the peasantry to the aristocracy, and were trained from childhood at the Royal Palace. Dancers were seen as the earthly counterparts to the entertainers of the Gods, the Apsara and Devatas, and were revered accordingly. Yike theatre incorporates a singing style reminiscent of Cham and Malay Islamic traditions. Consisting of both singing and dancing, Yike performance depicts local legends, mythology and humour in community settings (see Cravath 2007) and is now a highly endangered tradition in Cambodia.

but also to have a sense of ownership and pride in Cambodia's cultural traditions, some of which are highly endangered due to the genocidal regime of the Khmer Rouge in the 1970s and consequent political conflicts. For the Finnish student-teachers, the project aimed to offer an intercultural "immersive learning experience" (Bartleet 2011, 12). Access to these sites was agreed beforehand by communication between NGO leaders and project leaders (including the two authors of this chapter) which took place via email as well as during a preparatory visit conducted prior to the intercultural exchange. This preparatory visit entailed co-planning the project, aiming for teaching and learning to be context-sensitive and beneficial to all involved. Student-teachers and project leaders all adhered strictly to the ethical guidelines and rules provided by each NGO institution with regards to interacting with children. Data was not collected from children and all interviews with student-teachers were held outside the NGO premises.

3 Methodological Approach

All student-teachers gave their informed consent to participate in this study, and were informed that they could withdraw at any time. The data for this study were collected through: audio recordings of interviews conducted with Finnish student-teachers, both individually and in small groups, by the second author of this chapter and one of the lecturers; a shared pedagogical reflection where both authors of this chapter were present; and eight student-teacher group reflections led by one of the lecturers (see Table 1).

In the interviews, the Finnish student-teachers were asked about the role(s) they assumed during teaching and learning, comparisons between the teaching and learning contexts of Finland and the Cambodian NGOs, their thoughts about working together with the Cambodian staff and children, and how they envisioned that they might apply what they had learnt in the future. The group reflections focused more on their daily activities, teaching, and self-defined learning. The pedagogical reflection centered on a reading of an academic text (relating to intercultural teaching and learning) and the student-teachers' reflections in relation to the intercultural project.

Table 1 Data sources

2 × 3, approx. 45-min-long, semi-structured group interviews (3 student-teachers in each group)[3] at *New Horizons Siem Reap; New Horizons Phnom Penh; and Komar Chrieng*
8 semi-structured, 20- to 50-min-long, individual interviews conducted halfway through the exchange project
45-min-long, shared pedagogical reflection session conducted halfway through the exchange project
8 student-teacher group reflections (2–3 in each reflection group) facilitated by the university lecturer participating in the exchange project; these reflections ranged between 10- and 45-minutes in duration

The interview audio recordings were professionally transcribed and translated into English (the native language of the first author of this chapter).

We (both authors of this chapter) approached the data through what Jackson and Mazzei (2012) term "thinking with theory". As a qualitative "post-framework" (2012, ix), the data was read *with* Bourdieu, approaching the stories and experiences that student-teachers shared not as some "'thing' that has happened 'to' them, but [as] something that has been filtered, processed, and already interpreted" (Jackson and Mazzei 2012, 3). Furthermore, whilst the student-teachers' experiences are the focus of this chapter, as teachers and researchers participating in the same project, we were also contending with our own discomforts, intercultural learnings, and challenges; as such, we could not approach the theory or data as objective outsiders. In acknowledging that student-teachers' shared reflections were already selective and selected, we also note here that "putting philosophical concepts to work" is not merely interpretative. As Bourdieu cautions, researchers should be put "on notice against the fetishism of concepts, and of 'theory,' born of the propensity to consider 'theoretical' instruments-habitus, field, capital, etc. – in themselves and for themselves, rather than to put them in motion and to make them *work*" (Bourdieu and Wacquant 1992, 228). In this sense, our thinking with theory is constitutive (Jackson and Mazzei 2012) – a means to "produce different knowledge and to produce knowledge differently" (St. Pierre 1997, 175). Through pulling the data out of shape through a theoretical frame, and pulling the theory out of shape through the data, the data is lived in new ways, and can be understood as an ethical intervention and invention itself (Lather 2016, 104). The findings presented in this chapter are crafted in the form of composite narrative accounts, a first-person voice that draws upon the stories of many participants (Kallio 2015; Bresler 2005). Illustrating the discomfort and learning that took place, the excerpts here weave together voices of agreement, but also highlight tensions that arose within the group, without sacrificing the anonymity of individual participants (Leavy 2013). In this sense, the excerpts included in this chapter do not represent any single person in particular, but assume a "fiction[al] form... laid over a 'fact-oriented' research process" (Agar 1990, 74).

4 Disrupting the Visions of Good Music Teaching: Student-Teachers' Journeys from Discomfort to Reflexivity

Bourdieu posits that agents mobilize different forms of capital (such as cultural, artistic, religious, pedagogical and so forth) in order to gain currency and position themselves within different fields. "[E]ach field prescribes its particular values and possesses its own regulative principles", delimiting "a socially structured space in which agents struggle, depending on the position they occupy in that space, either to change or to preserve its boundaries and form" (Bourdieu and Wacquant 1992, 17). This suggests that the field is one of continual comparison, conflict and contestation – the site of transformative possibility. In this sense, fields are "a *space of play* which exists as such only to the extent that players enter into it who believe in and actively pursue the prizes it offers" (Bourdieu and Wacquant 1992, 19). Furthermore, agents are able to negotiate or transform the field to various degrees, depending on the capital they may possess, according to the logic of that particular field. In this section of the chapter we present our analysis of the discomfort that student-teachers experienced during the intercultural project. These student-teachers may be seen to be actively pursuing the "prize" of intercultural competence in arts education, and possess considerable cultural and artistic capital within the field of higher arts education in Finland. However, the new fields of the Cambodian NGOs disturbed student teachers' habitus by disrupting the musico-pedagogical scripts of teaching and learning music, and instigating new learnings. Through the narrative excerpts shared in this section, it is possible to follow the student-teachers' journeys from the discomforting of shared and accepted visions of music education, to reflexive and transformative possibility.

4.1 A Crisis of Certainty: Different Agents, Different Fields

As part of the intercultural project, the Finnish participants assumed that all of the children involved in the intercultural immersion project had experienced various hardships, as informed through communications with the Cambodian NGO staff members. These included: the death of parents or other family members; the incarceration of parents or family members; being abandoned or placed in temporary care as the result of economic hardship, disability, or illness; being rescued from child trafficking networks; having been removed from family environments by government agencies in response to various forms of abuse; health conditions such as HIV; and so on. Whilst the Finnish student-teachers were not provided with information regarding particular children or groups, they were aware before they travelled to Cambodia, that the children they were working with represented significantly underprivileged and marginalized social groups and had life experiences very different from their own. However, how these personal histories were manifest in the present often differed greatly from their expectations. The Finnish student-teachers explained that they found it difficult to grapple with their own partial understandings, prejudices, and perspectives as to who the Cambodian children were.

> I was more prepared for very poor conditions, expecting that the children would be huddled together in some sort of sand plot. But, I am surprised that they have very good conditions here. They are more equal to us than I had imagined, I wonder how else we are equal. But then, I also know that this is a whole different world, and I don't understand it. It makes me wonder what I don't understand about Finland, how traumatized Finns are after our own wars. It affects everyone. But how can I approach these children if they are very traumatized? I can't just go teach there in the same way I would with Finnish children.

In (re)considering how the Finnish-students had positioned the Cambodian participants in this project, the student-teachers also experienced discomfort and uneasiness regarding their own roles and positionality as pedagogues.

Do I have to take into consideration that this child is an orphan? Should I approach this in a certain way? Does someone expect me to approach this in a certain way? I feel very confused about the balance between teaching and charity here. I'm not necessarily interested in being a do-gooder, but do I have to be that person, now that I'm here? I probably do. Maybe I am in the wrong place. It would be easier to just teach somewhere else.

The field that the Finnish student-teachers found themselves in, being not only culturally, economically, linguistically, musically, and pedagogically different from that which they were familiar with, but also vastly different to their expectations, disrupted not only their individual habitus, but also the doxa of the music education tradition into which they had all been initiated and grown accustomed. Drawing upon Bourdieu's (1977) writings on habitus as "the strategy-generating principle enabling agents to cope with unforeseen and ever-changing situations" (72), intercultural education scholar Andreas Pöllmann (2016) describes such disruptive experiences amidst "cross cultural mobility" as "habitus dislocation". However, unlike Pöllmann's descriptions of such dislocation, the Finnish student-teachers' "habitus dislocation" was not necessarily experienced as a positive stimulant for "the development of students' intercultural reflexivity and practical intercultural sense" (Pöllmann 2016, 9). Indeed, at times student-teachers described experiencing this dislocation as an act of violence that "brutally disrupted" the "routine adjustment of subjective and objective structures" that constituted their habitus (Bourdieu and Wacquant 1992, 45). Whereas Gesche and Makeham note that intercultural competence is developed as part of a stress–adaptation–growth process that requires the "manoeuvring in and out of challenging situations that push individuals into a developmental upward spiral of increased adaptive capacity" (2010, 245), the intensity and inability for student-teachers to manoeuvre *out* of this uncertainty may have contributed towards experiences of crisis, frustration, and the desire to disengage and take refuge in security.

It would be nice if I could forget about these children's backgrounds. I just want to get on with it and teach.

4.2 Disrupting the Musico-pedagogical Script

Such refuge was often found in familiar scripts of teaching and learning music. Whereas uncertainty arose when the accepted common scripts did not transfer to the intercultural immersion contexts, the discomfort that resulted from such situations also allowed for a growing awareness of the pedagogical doxa underlying their own teaching and learning. For example, student-teachers recognized that much of their education remained unquestioned, as *"in Finland, we are all a part of the same education system. We accept it."* However, in the Cambodian contexts, what student-teachers regarded as commonsensical was at times interpreted in entirely different ways.

Something is happening all the time here, there are never any breaks. I mean, they don't even understand the concept of a break. Yesterday, I told the children that they could have a five-minute break, and they all left and never came back.

In losing a feel for "what is to be done in a given situation" (Bourdieu 1990, 146), student-teachers described a lack of "the practical mastery of the logic or of the imminent necessity of a game – a mastery acquired by experience of the game, and one which works outside conscious control and discourse" (Bourdieu 1990, 61). Furthermore, the "schemes of action" (Bourdieu 1998) that student-teachers had learned and followed in the Finnish university context seemed to be non-transferrable, and were no help in "facilitating the substitutability of one reaction for another (…) enabling the agent to master all problems of a similar form" in new situations (Bourdieu 1990, 94). As such, student-teachers' work was an intensely challenging improvisatory experience, requiring them to "juggle multiple goals as well as handle complexity in [unfamiliar] here-and-now pedagogical situations" (Westerlund et al. 2015, 70).

Here in Cambodia we always have to improvise. There is no ready-made pattern for us to follow. We never know what is expected from us, or what they would like us to do. Our plan-As never work, and our plan-Bs are often impossible – it is like having the rug pulled out from under our feet again, and again, and again.

These complex and unpredictable situations meant that student-teachers experienced new structural forces at work, and consequently a loss of "power to impose the legitimate vision of the social world (…), its present meaning and the direction in which it is going and should go" (Bourdieu 2000, 185). The student-teachers often experienced such forces as a hindrance to progress and development, with some comparing teaching and learning in Finland and in the Cambodian NGOs through deficit narratives of the Cambodian staff and children. These structural forces were experienced not only in teaching but also when learning Cambodian music and dance with the local teachers.

There's no systematic approach to learning to play together. I don't even know if it's controlled chaos or genuine chaos, but it's not very well organized or systematic. If we can't get it right, we are told 'start over', 'start over', 'start over'. It feels very mechanical, like they only have one way to learn a piece. If someone makes a mistake you immediately hear 'NO!' and then it's back to the beginning again. At some point I wanted to scream: 'just let me perform'! In Finland you always have to be encouraging as a teacher, and say something good first before you give negative comments.

Student-teachers' misrecognitions (Bourdieu and Wacquant 1992) of *difference* for *deficit* may be seen as attempts to regain security and certainty by consulting the musico-pedagogical script of Finnish music education. Education scholar David James explains that misrecognition refers to "an everyday and dynamic social process where one thing (…) is not recognised for what it is because it was not previously 'cognised' within the range of dispositions and propensities of the habitus of the person(s) confronting it" (2015, 10). In this way, the Finnish student-teachers attempted to reinstate familiar rules of a familiar game, according to which Cambodian staff or children were labelled as unable to perform, teach, or learn

The Discomfort of Intercultural Learning in Music Teacher Education   95

'properly'. As such, although student-teachers may have recognized that the doxa of Finnish music education was unsustainable in this new context, they still clung to it in search of comfort and security through appealing to what they assumed were universal grounds.

> *The concept of a peaceful work environment is quite weak, and the space is so poorly designed for music with bad acoustics. I mean we can't really achieve good things very efficiently because of the noise. They [the Cambodian staff and children] can tolerate so much noise – whereas I am constantly requiring silence! It is important for them to realize that music starts from silence.*

Susan Conkling (2015) draws upon Ellsworth's (2005) writings in relation to a similar project involving university music education student-teachers traveling from the United States to Bali, noting that those "who invent ways to see and say new things through [pedagogy] do not preexist it but are rather invented in the process.... Teachers [are] in the making themselves" (Conkling 2015, 28). Our analysis here suggests that these processes of "wonderful transformation" (Conkling 2015, 193) amongst pre-service music teachers do not necessarily flow in a single, unwavering direction towards the mastery of visions of intercultural competence. If, as Hilgers states, "[h]abitus is constituted and determined according to a probable future that it helps actualize through anticipation" (2009, 740), it is not surprising that losing a feel for the future – losing the clarity of visions – can result in crisis. Self-making is indeed difficult work.

4.3   *Reflexive Becomings and the Transformation of Habitus*

The aims of the intercultural project were not only to gain an awareness and appreciation of cultural, musical, and pedagogical worlds very different from those with which the Finnish student-teachers were familiar, but also to provide an "experience of themselves while meeting an unknown culture [contributing to an] awareness of their own viewpoints, choices and actions" (Danielsen 2012, 99). In the latter stages of the project, student-teachers noted that the reflection sessions provided essential intercultural learning tools.

> *Coming from a totally different environment and being used to doing things a different way, this has really shaken me up. I can't rely on my assumptions anymore. I have often heard during my studies that the purpose of our education is that we learn to reflect, but it's only now that I realize that reflection is a way of teaching and working all the time. As a teacher you have to be able to analyze what you are doing, and what is happening in your classroom. That's the only way to survive this.*

The pedagogical reflection session held halfway through the project, where student-teachers engaged with an academic text reporting research conducted on a similar intercultural immersion (though in very different cultural and musical contexts), particularly afforded student-teachers some distance to the intensity of their own experiences. Student-teachers found comfort in each other's expressions of uncertainty and discomfort, and also shifted from delineating the boundaries between "us" and "them" to identifying commonalities.

> *I was thinking about how I had learnt to play the folk guitar, and it was actually very similar [to the teaching and learning in Cambodia]. The teacher played first, then I imitated her, and we played it again, and again, and again until it was ingrained in my DNA. So, it's not that different after all. Actually, I really enjoyed learning the guitar.*

Student-teachers were also discovering new ways to teach in the Cambodian context.

> *At some point I just hit a wall – I had to take a fifteen minute break. While I was sitting on the side of the room wondering if I could keep going, I watched the kids. They corrected themselves and guided each other as a group. The noise was infernal, but it was at the same time wonderful. I realised that as soon as I stopped standing right next to them, and stopped giving them advice all the time, they did it much better on their own. I was just messing them up and getting in the way. The second I stopped teaching, one of them took the role, and they worked as a team. I need to trust my students more.*

Through their experiences teaching and learning at the Cambodian NGOs, the student-teachers also came to question some of the most central visions of Finnish music education, such as student-centered pedagogies, and participatory democracy in the classroom. They reflected upon their own discomfort, holding the mirror up to their own assumptions and narrations of what the visions of Finnish or Cambodian music education really are, and the extent to which they are enacted in practice.

> *Are we [Finns] actually a lot more teacher-centered than they are? We are so concerned with holding the reins the whole time – to be in control as a teacher. Initially I thought that teaching here was very authoritarian. But maybe things are not so black and white.*

5 Discomforting Visions of Intercultural Competence

Research has suggested that intercultural music education courses can have "dramatic effects on the attitudes and beliefs of preservice music teachers" (Emmanuel 2003, 39) through the development of *intermusicality* and *intercultural understandings* (Hebert and Saether 2014, 432). Without a shared language, musical or pedagogical repertoire, or cultural history, the intercultural project described in this chapter put the Finnish student-teachers in the situation where they could not always rely upon their pre-existing visions of what music education should be. They were required to negotiate new and unfamiliar interests and agendas, both as individuals and as a group through co-teaching and learning together. Through these negotiations, they identified shared values and principles, and through teaching practice, they learned what did and did not work. As such, the scripted visions and values of good music teaching into which student-teachers themselves had been initiated were also challenged and served as a focus for joint reflection and emerging reflexivity towards what is considered good music teaching in Finland. It was through such enhanced reflexivity, and growing self-awareness, that student-teachers began

The Discomfort of Intercultural Learning in Music Teacher Education   97

to "identify and [gain] (...) (relative) control over their own disposition[s]" (Hilgers 2009, 738). In other words, student-teachers were able to identify and gain control over the doxa of Finnish music education – the taken-for-granted good of teaching and learning of music, and reconstruct their own habitus as sites of transformation. As discussed in this chapter, this was not comfortable work. Challenging doxa and one's own habitus is perhaps *necessarily* discomforting work – not in the sense that transformation and learning requires student-teachers to feel uncomfortable and threatened all the time, but in the sense that leaving their comfort zones is productive (in the generative sense). As Bourdieu (1999) states, some degree of discomfort may be necessary in opening "the possibility of an emancipation founded on awareness and knowledge of the conditionings undergone and on the imposition of new conditionings designed durably to counter their effects" (Bourdieu 1999, 340).

As seen through the composite narrative excerpts, student-teachers' achievements were not necessarily framed as the acquisition of skills or knowledge regarding the musics or pedagogies of cultural Others. And as Deardorff (2009) suggests, knowledge and skills do not equate with intercultural competence. According to her framework, intercultural competence is comprised of five interrelated elements: *attitudes* (respect, openness, curiosity, discovery), *knowledge* (cultural self-awareness, culture-specific knowledge, sociolinguistic awareness), *skills* (observation, listening, evaluating, analyzing, interpreting, relating), *internal outcomes* (flexibility, adaptability, an ethnorelative perspective and empathy), and *external outcomes* (behavior, communication). In light of the research reported in this chapter, this framework raises an important question: when can we deem a teacher to be interculturally competent? We would argue that in gaining control over one's dispositions in order to negotiate and navigate new spaces of intercultural teaching and learning, one can never acquire the 'correct' attitude, knowledge, skills or outcomes to transcend all fields of play (cf. Pöllman 2016). If such attainment were possible, one could simply replace the old doxa of music education with new, unreflected values and practices. In other words, whilst institutional reflexivity "has its roots in how expert knowledge promotes radical doubt, this reflexivity is itself the basis of *re-envisioning* order and security" (Heaphy 2007, 83, italics added). As the world shifts towards a globalized, unitary framework of experience (Giddens 1994, 97) in which there are no 'Others', all are expected to be able to transcend the taken-for-granted games. Such an intercultural world can be described through what Chantal Mouffe has called "agonistic pluralism" (Mouffe 2005, 105). We cannot avoid the hegemonic nature of social relations and identities, but only come to terms with it, and be receptive to the multiplicity of voices and to the complexity of their power structures, to leave room for heterogeneity (Mouffe 2013, 49).

Hence, "heightened reflexivity" (Giddens 1994, 17) is then only the starting point for intercultural competence, rather than the end goal. Intercultural visions of music education allow for students (and their teachers) to have "a small chance of knowing what game we play and of minimizing the ways in which we are manipulated by the forces of the field in which we evolve" (Bourdieu and Wacquant 1992, 198–199). Thus, "reflexive vigilance" may well be an essential component of intercultural competence, as the ability and willingness to constantly analyze how power operates, "no matter how painful it may be" (Bourdieu and Wacquant 1992, 88–89). This is an unsettled and unsettling, lifelong process of 'becoming' (Deardorff and Jones 2012), rather than one of acquiring knowledge or cultivating attitudes and skills.

Acknowledgements We would like to acknowledge that this project and research would have not have been possible without the generosity of the three Cambodian NGO sites who participated in this intercultural project. We would also like to thank the Ministry for Foreign Affairs of Finland for partially funding the project. This publication has been undertaken as part of the Global Visions through Mobilizing Networks project funded by the Academy of Finland (project no. 286162).

References

Agar, M. (1990). Text and fieldwork: Exploring the excluded middle. *Journal of Contemporary Ethnography, 19*(1), 73–88.

Bartleet, B.-L. (2011). Stories of reconciliation: Building cross-cultural collaborations between indigenous musicians and undergraduate music students in Tennant Creek. *Australian Journal of Music Education, 2*, 11–21.

Bauman, Z. (2010). *44 letters from the liquid modern world*. Malden: Polity Press.

Bauman, Z., May, T. (2001). *Thinking sociologically* (2nd edn). (orig. 1990). Malden: Blackwell Publishers.

Belz, M. J. (2006). Opening the doors to diverse traditions of music making: Multicultural music education at the university level. *Music Educators Journal, 92*(5), 42–45.

Bourdieu, P. (1977). *Outline of a theory of practice* (R. Nice, Trans.). New York: Cambridge University Press.

Bourdieu, P. (1990). *In other words: Essays towards a reflexive sociology*. Stanford: Stanford University Press.

Bourdieu, P. (1998). The scholastic point of view. In *Practical reason: On the theory of action* (R. Johnson et al., Trans.). Stanford: Stanford University Press.

Bourdieu, P. (1999). Scattered remarks. *European Journal of Social Theory, 2*, 334–340. https://doi.org/10.1177/13684319922224563.

Bourdieu, P. (2000). *Pascalian meditations*. Stanford: Stanford University Press.

Bourdieu, P., & Passeron, J-C. (1990). *Reproduction in education, society and culture* (R. Nice, Trans.). London: Sage.

Bourdieu, P., & Wacquant, L. J. D. (1992). *An invitation to reflexive sociology*. Chicago: University of Chicago Press.

Bradley, D. (2007). The sounds of silence: Talking race in music education. *Action, Criticism and Theory for music education, 6*(4), 132–162.

Bresler, L. (2005). What musicianship can teach educational research. *Music Education Research, 7*(2), 169–183.

Campbell, P. S. (2004). *Teaching music globally*. Belmont: Wadsworth.

Conkling, S. W. (2015). Utopian thinking, compliance, and visions of wonderful transformation. In S. W. Conkling (Ed.), *Envisioning music teacher education* (pp. 181–194). Lanham/Boulder/New York/London: Rowman & Littlefield.

Danielsen, B. A. B. (2012). Praksisbegrepet i musikklærerutdanningen [The notion of practicum in music teacher education]. In B. Å. B. Danielsen & G. Johansen (Eds.), *Educating music teachers in the new millennium. Multiculturalism, professionalism and music teacher education in the contemporary society. A report from a Research and Development project* (pp. 89–108). Oslo: NMH.

Deardorff, D. (Ed.). (2009). *The SAGE handbook of intercultural competence*. Thousand Oaks: Sage.

Deardorff, D. K., & Jones, E. (2012). Intercultural competence: An emerging focus in post-secondary education. In D. K. Deardorff, H. de Wit, J. Heyl, & T. Adam (Eds.), *The Sage handbook of international higher education* (pp. 283–303). Thousand Oaks: Sage.

Ellsworth, E. (2005). *Places of learning: Media, architecture, pedagogy*. New York: Routledge.

Emmanuel, D. T. (2003). An immersion field experience an undergraduate music education course in intercultural competence. *Journal of Music Teacher Education, 13*(1), 33–41.

Gates, T. (2009). Introduction: Grounding music education in changing times. In T. A. Regelski & J. T. Gates (Eds.), *Music education for changing times: Guiding visions for practice* (pp. xiv–xxx). London: Springer. https://doi.org/10.1007/978-90-481-2700-9.

Gesche, A. H., & Makeham, P. (2010). Creating conditions for intercultural and international learning and teaching. In M. Hellstén & A. Reid (Eds.), *Researching international pedagogies. Sustainable practice for teaching and learning in higher education* (pp. 241–258). London: Springer.

Giddens, A. (1994). *Beyond left and right: The future of radical politics*. Cambridge, MA: Polity Press.

Hammerness, K. (2015). Visions of good teaching in teacher education. In S. W. Conkling (Ed.), *Envisioning music teacher education* (pp. 1–20). Lanham/Boulder/New York/London: Rowman & Littlefield.

Heaphy, B. (2007). *Late modernity and social change. Reconstructing social and personal life*. London/New York: Routledge.

Hebert, D., & Saether, E. (2014). 'Please, give me space': Findings and implications from an evaluation of the GLOMUS intercultural music camp, Ghana 2011. *Music Education Research, 16*(4), 418–435.

Hilgers, M. (2009). Habitus, freedom, and reflexivity. *Theory and Psychology, 19*(6), 728–755.

Jackson, A. Y., & Mazzei, L. A. (2012). *Thinking with theory: Viewing data across multiple perspectives*. London: Routledge.

James, D. (2015). How Bourdieu bites back: Recognising misrecognition in education and educational research. *Cambridge Journal of Education, 45*(1), 97–112. https://doi.org/10.1080/030 5764X.2014.987644.

Joseph, D., & Southcott, J. (2009). Opening the doors to multiculturalism: Australian pre-service music teacher education students' understandings of cultural diversity. *Music Education Research, 11*(4), 457–472.

Kallio, A. A. (2015). Factional stories: Creating a methodological space for collaborative inquiry in music education research. *Research Studies in Music Education, 37*(1), 3–20.

Karlsen, S., Westerlund, H., & Miettinen, L. (2016). Intercultural practice as research in music education: The imperative of an ethics-based rationale. In P. Burnard, E. Mackinlay, & K. Powell (Eds.), *The Routledge international handbook of intercultural arts research* (pp. 369–379). New York: Routledge.

Kertz-Welzel, A. (2013). "Two souls, alas, reside within my breast": Reflections on German and American education regarding the internationalization of music education. *Philosophy of Music Education Review, 21*(1), 52–65.

Lather, P. (2016). The work of thought and the politics of research: (Post)qualitative research. In N. K. Denzin & M. D. Giardina (Eds.), *Qualitative inquiry and the politics of research* (pp. 97–118). Oxon: Routledge.

Leavy, P. (2013). *Fiction as research practice: Short-stories, novellas and novels*. Walnut Creek: Left Coast Press.

Mouffe, C. (2005). *The democratic pradox*. New York/London: Verso.

Mouffe, C. (2013). *Agonistics. Thinking the world politically*. London/New York: Verso.

Pöllmann, A. (2016). Habitus, reflexivity, and the realization of intercultural capital: The (unfulfilled) potential of intercultural education. *Cogent Social Sciences, 2*(1), 1149915. https://doi.org/10.1080/23311886.2016.1149915.

Saether, E. (2013). The art of stepping outside comfort zones: Intercultural collaborative learning in higher music education. In H. Westerlund & H. Gaunt (Eds.), *Collaborative learning in higher music education: Why, what and how?* (pp. 37–48). London: Ashgate.

Schippers, H. (2010). *Facing the music: Shaping music education from a global perspective.* Oxford: Oxford University Press.

Schubert, J. D. (2008). Suffering. In M. Grenfell (Ed.), *Pierre Bourdieu: Key concepts* (pp. 183–198). Stocksfield: Acumen.

St. Pierre, E. A. (1997). Methodology in the fold and the irruption of transgressive data. *International Journal of Qualitative Studies in Education, 10*(2), 175–189.

Talbot, B. C., & Mantie, R. (2015). Vision and the legitimate order. Theorizing today to imagine tomorrow. In S. W. Conkling (Ed.), *Envisioning music teacher education* (pp. 155–180). Lanham/Boulder/New York/London: Rowman & Littlefield.

Volk, T. (1998). *Music, education, and multiculturalism.* Oxford: Oxford University Press.

Westerlund, H. (2017). Visions for intercultural teacher identity in C21st super diverse societies. In P. Burnard, V. Ross, H. J. Minors, K. Powell, T. Dragovic, & E. Mackinlay (Eds.), *Building intercultural and interdisciplinary bridges: Where theory meets research and practice* (pp. 12–19). Cambridge: BIBACC Publishing.

Westerlund, H., Partti, H., & Karlsen, S. (2015). Teaching as improvisational experience: Student music teachers' reflections on learning during an intercultural project. *Research Studies in Music Education, 37*(1), 55–75.

7

Assessing Intercultural Competence in Teacher Education: A Missing Link

Sapna Thapa

Abstract This chapter discusses the importance of developing intercultural competence as a foundational strategy in teacher education. The primary argument asserts that specific, mandated-content assessments do not help newly trained teachers to develop skills and knowledge related to thoughtfulness, criticality, cultural responsiveness, and caring for the young individuals with whom they work. The author attributes this to the lack of intercultural sensitivity and intercultural communication in teacher education discourses. Researchers suggest that caring in schools and other such institutions have diminished as there are distinct gaps in the relationships between teachers and culturally diverse students causing these students to fall out of the school systems. The chapter informs about the need to equip teachers with intercultural sensitivities and intercultural communication skills to help them navigate the changing demographics in classrooms. Finally, it provides some insight into discovering missing links in teaching and pedagogical approaches and offers some strategies for bridging the ever-widening intercultural gaps.

Keywords Intercultural competence · Diversity · Teacher education

1 Introduction

Teaching in a mid-western University in Wisconsin (University of Wisconsin-Stout), as a foreign instructor (non-American, Asian–Nepali), I discovered that my group of pre-service teachers view the rest of the world through, what many researchers call, a "monolingual-mono-cultural" lens (Fonseca-Greber 2010, 102; Kayes 2006; Dean 1989). Most of my pre-service teachers belong to a homogenous group of 'white Americans' who claim that teaching young children is what they want to do in the future. Almost all believe that their classrooms will consist of mostly 'white' children from middle-class families, who will speak English and

---

S. Thapa (✉)
Early Childhood Teacher Education, University of Wisconsin-Stout, Menomonie, WI, USA
e-mail: thapas@uwstout.edu

will have experiences similar to their own and their ancestors. Some acknowledge that their classrooms might have a few children from 'other' cultures and to accommodate these children, they would learn a few words and songs from the 'other' culture, display pictures of diverse people and talk about 'their' food. This narrow and deficit outlook towards children/people from different cultural backgrounds was very alarming to me. It was not surprising to note that many of them were unaware of the changing demographics in classrooms across the United States and those who were aware assumed that they would not be affected (Maxwell 2014; Florian 2017). I was worried about this outlook and their attitude towards diversity and the lack of knowledge regarding intercultural communication as it would limit their practice and become a barrier in their future profession, especially if they aimed to become inter-culturally competent, global leaders in education. Class discussions about culture, inclusiveness, and, intercultural competence/communication (ICC) also disclosed some disturbing comments. Similar to Weaver (1999) and Rottenburg's (2008) studies, many of my students indicated that culture was outside their 'American-ness' and that they were 'just white, middle-class Americans' who valued 'hard work and success'. So, in an attempt to develop strategies to help my pre-service teachers and students expand their knowledge about world cultures and acquire some semblance of intercultural competence, I participated in a research project called "Infusing diversity across the curriculum." In this chapter, I will give an overview of the project and explain why ICC discourses in teacher education are essential pedagogical approaches. I will argue the importance of understanding one's own culture and cultural background, beliefs and values as essential tools in understanding other world cultures, diversity and inclusion, and address the importance of applying a "caring pedagogy" and its inter-connectedness with ICC when working with very young children (Soto 2005). In conclusion, I will highlight the implications of ICC and its importance in teacher education and provide some strategies that could help pre-service teachers develop intercultural competence and connectedness in a highly evolving, globalized world (Soto 2005).

2 Impacts of Mandated Assessments on Teacher Education and the Development of ICC

As mentioned earlier, I have been teaching Early Childhood Teacher Education at UW-Stout for the past 5 years. The research assumptions below disclose how my pre-service teacher's attitudes and dispositions are related to the artifacts derived from socio-cultural interactions, cultural background and upbringing. I argue that encouraging pre-service teachers to critically reflect on their attitudes and dispositions will help them to develop a level of intercultural sensitivity and enhance their intercultural competence. Critical reflections will also help them to become empathetic and caring individuals rather than simply the savior of "poor minority children" as discovered by some scholars (Garmon 2005, 207; see also Madrid, Baldwin and Belbase 2016). Campbell, Thompson and Barrett suggest that "critical examination and analysis" of the self are the "means through which personal beliefs and images of teaching are explored" (2012, 80). Campbell et al. (2012), citing Britzman (1991), further add that teachers are influenced by the practices in social environments and by the values, beliefs and histories of self. Therefore, if we are to prepare successful and effective teachers who will care for *all* children and strive to "improve [the] human condition, and meet the challenges of a changing world" we have to begin by "sensitizing" them "to the values of others and seeing/experiencing the world through the language and culture of another" (Fonseca-Greber 2010, 102).

However, these suggestions could be pipedreams as recent shifts towards systemic and standardized assessments for pre-service teachers has changed the landscape of teacher education in the United States. Several teacher preparation programs across the country are scrambling to succeed in the competitive licensure examination called the "edTPA" (Educator/tion Teacher Performance Assessment). Many university courses are being revised to fulfill the assessment's objectives. According to Legwell and Oyler, the edTPA is a "high-stakes summative assessment for teaching candidates while generating formative feedback for candidates and programs" (2016, 131). Recent literature has accused the edTPA assessment system of excluding contextualized cultural issues and ignoring the development of important skill sets such as cultural and intercultural competence despite the relevance of inclusivity and diversity in many school systems today (Cochran-Smith et al. 2016). Many scholars agree that standardization is an outcome of the intense emphasis on globalization. Globalization authorizes success through competitive means and the enhancement of productivity through skilled citizens, which then translates into economic efficiency of nations. Sahlberg suggests that globalization benefits education by integrating "world cultures" but also segregates and marginalizes individuals and communities (2004, 66).

Barton suggests "marriages between capitalism and education" accentuates commercialism "at the expense of social justice and human dignity" (2001, 847). Due to this massive corporate movement, newly trained teachers are going out into the field with little or no skills or knowledge related to thoughtfulness, criticality, cultural responsiveness, and caring for young individuals with whom they work (Trainer 2012). These mandates and standardization are very relevant in UW-Stout's teacher education. As instructors, we are more focused on supporting our preservice teachers to pass the edTPA rather than developing intercultural sensitivity and competence in cultural diversity, inclusion etc. Although we include and teach topics, such as differentiation and adaptations to help pre-service teachers plan appropriate lessons for young children, we forget to include the important pedagogy of care in our lectures. In the absence of care, celebrations of differences and support for diverse children cannot be possible as minority children will always need differentiation and adaptations. Weiner states, targeting "specific students, those presumed to need extra help" is an assumption that "poor, minority children do not succeed in schools because they and their families are defective" (2007, 276). This is true in our teacher education, since we direct our pre-service teachers to focus on meeting specific and targeted needs of academically challenged children in technical and robotic ways rather than guiding them to look for reasons behind that need – in other words, we intentionally tell them to forego care and avoid relationships; we are teaching teachers to identify weaknesses of students rather than guiding them to work with the strengths of students.

With the mandated assessments, we are moving further and further away from developing meaningful relationships with students. We are negating the value of critical self-reflection, intentionality, flexibility and care. This could very well be one of the reasons that many of my students declared that all they had to do was learn a few words of another language, hang pictures and have some cultural items to accommodate diverse groups of children. According to high volumes of research, many parents want more for their children than just a score on a standardized test (Zeichner 2006). Zeichner adds that focusing on higher test scores eliminates teachers from supporting their students in achieving success in other important areas such as "social learning, aesthetic learning and civic learning" (2006, 333). We cannot only focus on preparing "good enough" teachers who are "low-level technicians" adjusting to the needs of specific minority children but must also support our pre-student teachers in understanding the complexity of the teaching profession and its intimate relation to care and empathy (Zeichner 2006, 333; see also Hartlep et al. 2015). Hence, I argue that, if our teachers are to become successful leaders, it is critical for them to care about the children and families with whom they work by becoming knowledgeable about their culture, their backgrounds and their values. We must encourage teachers to move away from the deficit model of working with the weaknesses of children from poor and marginalized groups. Pre-service teachers must be guided to investigate their biases through critical reflections and discussions about their own cultures, backgrounds and their life experiences. They must be encouraged to be sensitive towards others and their cultures and to be competent in navigating the changing demographics and contribute towards bridging the widening gaps between cultures, ethnicities and socio-economies.These would then enhance efficiency, professionalism, flexibility and intentionality.

3 Culture: Definitions and Care Theory as a Basis for Intercultural Sensitivity

Wursten and Jacobs (2013) suggest that the dominant cultural trait of the USA is 'masculinity,' and often Americans view culture objectively through "institutional aspects" such as art, music, cuisine and peoples (Bennett and Bennett 2004, 150). Fonseca-Greber perceives this simplistic view as a the "monolingual-mono-cultural national identity" and informs that "sensitizing Americans to the value of seeing the world through the language-culture of another" can be challenging (2010, 102). The word 'culture,' many scholars agree, is ambiguous. There is a myriad of definitions, which are co-constructed and contextualized based on values, polices, practices and on the nature of social interactions. Many scholars also agree that the dominant cultural, social, political and economic value of any particular context play a vital role in the development of intercultural competence and intercultural communication. For example, Dai and Ming-Chen (2014) state that ICC is influenced by the predominant culture and becomes obvious only through a rigorous process of socialization. Similarly, Rissanen, Kuusisto and Kuusisto suggest that ICC is a "contextual, never-ending and unpredictable process" whereby "intercultural sensitivity" forms the basis of accepting others despite their differences (2016, 447). Based on the development model provided by Bennett and Bennett, intercultural sensitivity is achieved when one is able to change oneself affectively, cognitively, and behaviorally and "move from ethnocentrism to ethno-relativism" (2004, 1). They designate six distinct stages of experiences during the transformation from ethnocentrism to ethno-relativism with "denial of cultural differences" being the most extreme experience. This stage is followed by "defense and minimization" of cultural differences. The final stage, Bennett and Bennett state, is to accept cultural differences so that one is able to adapt and integrate those differences into personal "identity" (2004, 1). Other definitions of ICC suggest that it is the ability to "adeptly navigate complex environments marked by a growing diversity of peoples, cultures and lifestyles" (United Nations Educational Scientific and Cultural Organization 2013, 5). A large volume of literature suggests that ICC is more apparent in professions related to care, such as medicine and nursing. However, recent discourses propose that the foundational principle of teaching is also based on *caring*. Care in education relates to intentionality, flexibility, developing meaningful relationships, and openness towards cultural and other differences; these are the attributes of intercultural sensitivity (Garmon 2004; Soto 2005; Zeichner 2006). Dai and Ming-Chen suggests that ICC requires one to develop a "global mind-set," which is "closely related to individuals' affective, cognitive, and behavioral abilities" (2014, 6). In other words, individuals with a global mind-set are culturally sensitive (affective), open, knowledgeable and flexible (cognitive) and think critically and holistically (behavioral) to benefit the larger community (Dai and Ming-Chen 2014). (On this matter see recommended reading at the end of this chapter.)

However, masculine cultures support individualistic values of "achievement and success," hence there is little emphasis and motivation to cultivate caring for others or to acquire cultural knowledge of people from another culture (Wursten and Jacobs 2013, 10). For example, Darling-Hammond informs that many American schools "offer fewer opportunities for teachers to come to know students well during long periods of time" (2006, 6), even when most "students perceive the school community as a caring institution" (Soto 2005, 859). Care theory, according to Soto, accentuates fostering positive relationships between teachers and students to validate "students' cultural values and beliefs" and to promote engagement and commitment between the two parties (2005, 864). Soto adds that most often teachers fail to "recognize and understand the emotional impact" faced by culturally or ethnically diverse students, resulting in non-retention of such students in educational institutions (Soto 2005, 860). The flip side of this discourse (sometimes requiring critical judgements and discussions) is the emotional impact on teachers who work in a global environment or specifically with diverse children in the

USA. Care in this instance could be displayed as an evangelical action to emancipate, save, or help the 'marginalized other' rather than celebrating the differences by applying intercultural sensitivity. For example, Madrid, Baldwin and Belbase inform that many teachers especially from affluent Western countries undergo an emotional trauma when their "deeply held cultural ideologies" are disrupted (2016, 3). Their research with six American pre-service teachers in a cross-cultural context reveals some disturbing themes, such as the perpetuation of "the privileged Westerner and the Marginalized Other," and attitudes of agency based on the "cultural practices of the host country" (2016, 8). Their conclusive findings disclose the "frustration" of these American teachers with the "educational practices" in the host country and a "national love for their own Western ideologies" (2016, 8). They warn that ignoring such responses may lead newly trained teachers to problematically "reproduce dominant assumptions about the education of young children" in diverse contexts (2016, 3). Therefore, it is essential to deconstruct the pedagogy of 'care' for our pre-service teachers so that they recognize that caring in education is not about saving or emancipation, but rather about accepting differences and making an effort to cultivate intercultural communication through intercultural sensitivity.

4   Infusing Diversity Across the Curriculum: Approaches in Developing ICC and a 'Caring Pedagogy'

"Infusing diversity across the curriculum" is a yearlong project supported and funded by the Nakatani Teaching and Learning center at UW-Stout. During the year 2014–2015, I participated in this project to understand personally perceived and co-constructed conceptions of culture and diversity through a semester-long assignment with my Early Childhood Education (ECE) students. The primary aim of this project was to develop definitions of culture and diversity through a subjective inquiry into the personal lives of my students via reflective journal writings. I conducted this inquiry to understand how my group of predominantly white, female students from a mid-western, semi-rural university represented and perceived their culture and what understandings they had about world cultures and diversity. The ethical application was approved on the fifth of April 2015 under the Code of Federal Regulations Title 45 Part 46 by the UW-Stout Institutional Review Board (IRB). The IRB is a federally mandated review board that protects the "rights and welfare of human research subjects" (See http://www.uwstout.edu/rs/irb.cfm). Informal consent was obtained from all students as the project was designed as a class assignment. Students were randomly assigned numbers and instructed to write this number on their narrative submissions to maintain anonymity. If students wished to withdraw from the project, they were asked to submit the narratives with their names on them instead of the random number. There were no consequences for withdrawing from the project.

The design for this research project was based on a qualitative model. Data was collected through descriptive and reflective narratives written by 38 students (mainly sophomores) of two different sections of an ECE class. The project was introduced at the beginning of the semester as a writing assignment using letters of the English alphabet. Each week students from both sections were instructed to choose words from an alphabetical list and write a short reflective paragraph relating the word to their personal experiences. Section 001 students were allowed to choose random words from a prescribed list while Section 002 were instructed to choose specific words related to values, beliefs and/or culture. The initial data analysis revealed that 90% of section 001 had chosen simpler words from the given list, i.e., words such as 'adventure' and 'athletics' for letter A and 'basketball' and 'burger' for letter B were predominant. The narratives from the section 002 students were related to their experiences in the American context and expressed their thoughts on topics, such as 'anti-bias,' 'competition,' 'divorce,' 'family,' 'heritage,' etc. The descriptive data (written narratives) from both the sections were compared, contrasted and eventually analyzed, utilizing a thematic coding model provided by Braun and Clarke (2006). Similar ideas were grouped to reflect perceptions regarding culture, values, and cultural and ethnic differences through the experiences they expressed in the writings. Class discussions were conducted to collect views regarding the assignment and to assess student learning with both the sections each week. More in-depth discussions were conducted with student of section 002 regarding their narratives. The initial ideas that emerged from the data were relative to positive/negative life experiences, such as: family heritage, religion and church, individuality, competition, contentment, entitlement, divorce, separation, race, color, gender, socioeconomy, etc. These emerging themes were further analyzed and grouped into distinct categories of: individuality, pride, power, privilege, faith and whiteness. The limitations of the data are apparent due to the constrained size of the respondents (38 in total) and the fact that most, if not all, came from middle-class, white families from mid-western, semi-rural settlements and were predominantly female (32 female). Bennett's developmental model of intercultural sensitivity suggests that most people who grow up in culturally homogeneous environments and have limited contact with people outside their own culture group are often in the "denial stage" (1993, 110). They are either "indifferent" or ignorant about other cultures and peoples (Paige et al. 2003, 469). Limitations in the interpretations are also obviously based on the biases that my positionality (that of a non-American–Nepali–Asian instructor) imposed on the data. Although I needed to maintain a degree of "ongoing self-awareness during the research process" so as not to skew the data, there were times when I had to acknowledge my predisposition to natural and human characteristics (Pillow 2003, 178). A small group of scholars suggest that assessments of ICC are based on human characteristics and that there are few who know how to measure these (Bennett 1993; Paige et al. 2003). In line with this observation, the interpretations below do not measure levels of ICC, rather they are my thoughts on and perceptions of the student-written narratives influenced by my positionality and my personal values and beliefs.

4.1 Individuality and Competitiveness

Several students articulated the influence of their social upbringing on their individuality and competitive nature. Most students were involved in competitive activities such as sports and believed that winning mattered as it was an expected norm. Rottenberg describes these characteristics as "performativity" and suggests that they are linked to race, gender, and class. She further adds that "class norms" in the USA for example, "urged subjects to live up to regulatory ideals linked to the middle class" (2008, 12).

> *He would challenge us and try to beat us in everything. But it was never an ego complex or anything.*
> *Winning was also introduced during this period.*
> *I gravitated to individual sports but still competing in team sports.*
> *(...) the ability to be competitive played an incredible role.*

According to Rottenberg (2008), the class discourse disallows subjects to be initiated into society from the lower class and encourages climbing from one class to another. Therefore, performativity as the dominant norm influences the creation of one's identity through "repetitive effects on a subject through the discursive reiteration of its regulatory ideals" as the following excerpts illustrate.(Rottenberg 2008, 13).

> *Throughout high school, I had never believed in the word quit.*
> *I think being so competitive and having victory [being] a huge part of me has to do with how I was raised.*
> *There's always quotes hung up that say "Never give up" or "quitters never win."*

Triandis describes individualism as an aspect of personality and states that individualist cultures perceive "the self as stable" while the context around the individual is fluid; therefore, individuals shape the environment to suit their personalities (2001, 920). Several respondents in this research were first-generation college attendees. Some of them came from rural areas and were from families who had lived in the same regions for many generations. These students stated that they were *"taught from a young age to put [on]their town's glorious jersey and play hard."* Wolfson suggests that American individualism has mutated over the last three decades and individualism has become more about competition and winning (1997, 77). Contrary to the trend of competitive individualism, most of the respondents belonged to families that romanticized the "conforming American of the 1950s," who, in search of "natural rights to life, liberty and the pursuit of happiness," joined and became part of a civil society to escape obscurity and poverty (Wolfson 1997, 79). For example, many students who participated in this research expressed that they *"live in a great community"* and some were very aware of what was expected of them, such as *"successfully completing their studies and getting a good job"* or *"getting married and settling down."* However, *"winning"* and *"being ahead"* were primary responses.

4.2 Heritage and Family: Pride and Power

There was a strong sense of pride among the participants regarding their familial and ancestral heritage. For example, many of them mentioned being blessed to have acquired a particular first or last name as it was considered a valuable family legacy. This could be an expression of historically situated social policies that underpin the predominance of families as the "basic unit of society" although many scholars note the rapid changes occurring in American family units today (Kagan 2009, 4). For example, Angier writes that recent research reveals that families are "becoming more socially egalitarian" and are more "ethnically, racially, religiously and stylistically diverse" than before (2013). Despite the changes in family structures across the United States, this research noted that most of the respondents' families were homogeneous, with white parents of opposite sexes, and religiously affiliated to a Church, which was their prime source of community support. The male respondents were proud to uphold the family name, indicating the dominant masculine culture and elitist attitudes. The white female respondents outnumbered the handful of male participants, and, in a similar mindset, indicated that working with children is a woman's job and an expectation of the society. The data was devoid of discussions regarding ethnicity and/or race, signifying an intergenerational trend of white, middle-class conformity shaped by the experiences of their ancestors.

> To this day, I thank my father for naming me after him because I know it's a piece of family heritage that he passed down to me.
> At an early age, my Aunt instilled pride into my life. She used to repeat regularly remember you're a "_____" act like it!
> I think pride is incredibly important because it's something local communities all the way up to our federal government need to instill in its citizens. If individuals weren't prideful we couldn't have advanced and progressed as much as we have.

4.3 Privilege of Whiteness and Socio-economy: Opportunity and Entitlement

Jean and Feagin suggest that "a family's memory is crucial to its identity and to its members' identity" (1998, 297). Cross and Madson describe this identity as the "self." They argue that the self is a "dynamic cultural creation" formed by "self-views, and emotions" and impacted by the "cultural values, ideals, structures and practices" of a particular context (1997, 6). The participants of this research revealed several instances where their self-identity was based on values and ideals such as family, status, whiteness and socio-economy. These, they claimed, were responsible for their success as they were *"blessed to have so many opportunities to develop"* and were aware that *"opportunity and advantages really are key predictors for success."* Socio-economy played a crucial role in the formation of their self and some participants stated that *"money means a lot more than that; it means a way of living, experiencing new things and also a way to go out and get away or go out and have fun*." Being and belonging to white families and communities was an indicator of socio-economical emancipation and entitlement as some students noted that "*socio-economic status can have a lot to do with many types of things, usually being in your favor*." This emancipatory assertion subtly specifying their white-privilege showed through in their affluence, as some of them owned "*a cabin they would go to for weekend getaways*" while others owned a "*sailboat*." While participants claimed to be aware of classism and their designated place in the societal class structure, the data and research outcome did not divulge much dialogue regarding race and ethnicity. For example, few participants mentioned the Black or African-American experience and suggested that "*all children are the same*," indicating a "color-blindedness" (Apfelbaum et al. 2012). Apfelbaum et al. note that this kind of behavior is "routinely exhibited by teachers seeking to model equality in their class-rooms" (2012, 206).

4.4 Faith and Religion

Volumes of research studies have confirmed that children in families and communities who regularly practice some form of religious practice have healthier and positive outcomes (Smith 2003). This was evident in this research as several respondents mentioned how "*God and faith*" were "*very important*" in their lives. Some stated that "*God loved them*" and "*has a plan for their lives*." These imply that the participants' behavior and actions are highly influenced by their beliefs, faith and religion. Several research studies also mention that individuals who are religiously affiliated are better able to cope with stressful events as their "religious and spiritual systems may be a valuable source to make meaning from their experiences" (Krok 2015, 202).

4.5 Afterthoughts

Through these excerpts, most students revealed that their culture consisted of things that they valued, loved or respected. However, it was evident that these individual intricacies were difficult for them to acknowledge as their individual "culture" or cultural identity. Most assumed that their cultural identity was based on a whole (white and American and at times white-American Wisconsinites) rather than in smaller parts (immigrant heritage, family belief systems, religion, upbringing, socio-economy, race, gender etc.). These narratives confirm that most students were never guided to investigate their cultural identities through a reflective or a subjective lens. Dedeoglu and Lamme emphasize that "views of reality" are social constructions given "personal meaning by their life experiences" (2011, 470). As mentioned above and suggested by Bennett and Bennett (2004), objective views of culture are institutional and can pertain to "political and economic systems" while subjective views relate to the "experiences of the social reality formed by the society's institution." They inform that both views subsist as a dichotomy. According to them, "objective culture is internalized through socialization" while "subjective culture is externalized through role behavior" (2004, 150). Through the narratives above, it can be assumed that internalized values (from their families and upbringing, education, and/or, religious communities) were being externalized through their actions (individualistic, competitive and prideful) and that this was probably the reason why all students insisted, that their predominant culture was that of *"middle class, white and American,"* and that *"hard work"* to be *"successful"* was their primary value or belief. Several scholars confirm that teachers' beliefs and values impact their instructional approaches and how they view children from other cultures (Hachfeld et al. 2015; Gay 2010; Milner 2010). Therefore, it can be assumed that beliefs about one's own culture and upbringing influence how teachers view teaching and working with children from diverse backgrounds. Commonly held beliefs about the importance of individualism, competition, pride and entitlement among my pre-service teachers perpetuate hegemony and reject the notion of intercultural sensitivity. This in turn, eliminates the very essence of a caring pedagogy because one can only care or empathize with other people and other cultures if one becomes aware of their own culture and socio-cultural backgrounds. A pedagogy of care can only be indulged if one rejects the "white knight going to teach in inner-city schools to save the poor minority children" attitude and entitlement and see "others" eye to eye and treat them like human beings just like themselves (Garmon 2005, 207).

5 Conclusion: Visions and the Step Forward

Developing ICC, as the literature claims, is not an easy overnight task. It requires participants to be introspectively mindful of not only their own culture but to be able to "deconstruct the discourse of mono-culturalism" (Rhedding-Jones 2007, 39). Teachers need to delve deeply into understanding their ethnocentric views regarding development, teaching and learning and replace them with ethno-relativity through a reflective process (Bennett and Bennett 2004). The development model of intercultural sensitivity (DMIS) by Bennett and Bennett (2004) relies on the theoretical premises of "personal construct" and "radical constructivism," both of which are intimately related to human emotions. Madrid et al. state that it is imperative for teachers to recognize these emotions and the "discomfort" that becomes apparent when their "deeply held cultural ideologies" are threatened while trying to develop intercultural sensitivity (2016, 3).

Therefore, the development of ICC is reliant on how teachers interpret these underlying tenets of the self; and, it is contingent on how teachers explore and interpret their own values, beliefs and prejudices (Campbell et al. 2012). ICC requires a critical examination of thoughts through reflective actions, problem-solving skills, an ability to recognize and deconstruct assumptions, and a resolution to constantly question personal dogmas. Instructors in teacher education must continuously challenge the "deficit thinking" model by "engaging in a critique of society's socio-political structures" with pre-service teachers, and by encouraging them to discover the missing link that will bridge the widening gap that social constructs such as "race, gender roles, and culture" accentuates. However, these gaps can only be re-conceptualized if we learn to care for and about others (Hartlep et al. 2015, 142) because without care and empathy – these visions will not be realized.

If you find it in your heart to care for somebody else, you will have succeeded.
Maya Angelou

References

Angier, N. (2013). The changing American family. *The New York Times.*

Apfelbaum, E. P., Norton, M. I., & Sommers, S. R. (2012). Racial color blindness: Emergence, practice, and implications. *Current Directions in Psychological Science, 21*(3), 205–209.

Barton, A. C. (2001). Capitalism, critical pedagogy, and urban science education: An interview with Peter McLaren. *Journal of Research in Science Teaching, 38*(8), 847–859.

Bennett, J. M. (1993). Cultural marginality: Identity issues in intercultural training. In R. M. Paige (Ed.), *Education for the intercultural experience* (pp. 109–135). Yarmouth: Intercultural Press.

Bennett, J. M., & Bennett, M. J. (2004). An integrative approach to global and domestic diversity. In D. Landis, J. M. Bennett, & M. J. Bennett (Eds.), *Handbook of intercultural training* (pp. 147–165). Thousand Oaks: Sage.

Braun, V., & Clarke, V. (2006). Using thematic analysis in psychology. *Qualitative Research in Psychology, 3*(2), 77–101.

Britzman, D. P. (1991). Decentering discourses in teacher education: Or, the unleashing of unpopular things. *The Journal of Education, 173*(3), 60–80.

Campbell, M. R., Thompson, L. K., & Barrett, J. R. (2012). Supporting and sustaining a personal orientation to music teaching: Implications for music teacher education. *Journal of Music Teacher Education, 22*(1), 75–90.

Cochran-Smith, M., Stern, R., Gabriel, J., Sánchez, A. M., Keefe, E. S., Fernández, M. B., Chang, W. C., Cummings, M., Carney, S. B. Baker, M., 2016. Holding teacher preparation accountable: A review of claims and evidence. Boulder: National Education Policy Center. [Online] http://nepc.colorado.edu/publication/teacher-prep. Accessed 10 Jan 2018.

Cross, S. E., & Madson, L. (1997). Models of the self: Self-construals and gender. *Psychological Bulletin, 122*(1), 5.

Dai, X., & Chen, G. M. (2014). On interculturality and intercultural communication competence. *China Media Research, 11*(3), 100–114.

Darling-Hammond, L. (2006). Constructing 21st-century teacher education. *Journal of Teacher Education, 57*(3), 300–314.

Dean, T. (1989). Multicultural classrooms, monocultural teachers. *College Composition and Communication, 40*(1), 23–37.

Dedeoglu, H., & Lamme, L. L. (2011). Selected demographics, attitudes, and beliefs about diversity of preservice teachers. *Education and Urban Society, 43*(4), 468–485.

Florian, L. (2017). Teacher education for the changing demographics of schooling: Inclusive education for each and every learner. *Teacher Education for the Changing Demographics of Schooling: Issues for Research and Practice, 2,* 9.

Fonseca-Greber, B. (2010). *Social obstacles to intercultural competence in America's language classrooms.* Center for Educational Resources in Culture, Language and Literacy (CERCLL) (NJ3).

Garmon, M. A. (2004). Changing preservice teachers' attitudes/beliefs about diversity: What are the critical factors? *Journal of Teacher Education, 55*(3), 201–213.

Garmon, M. A. (2005). Six key factors for changing preservice teachers' attitudes/beliefs about diversity. *Educational Studies, 38*(3), 275–286.

Gay, G. (2010). *Culturally responsive teaching: Theory, research, and practice.* New York: Teachers College Press.

Hachfeld, A., Hahn, A., Schroeder, S., Anders, Y., & Kunter, M. (2015). Should teachers be colorblind? How multicultural and egalitarian beliefs differentially relate to aspects of teachers' professional competence for teaching in diverse classrooms. *Teaching and Teacher Education, 48*, 44–55.

Hartlep, N. D., Porfilio, B. J., Otto, S., & O'Brien, K. (2015). What we stand for, not against: Presenting our teacher education colleagues with the case for social foundations in PK-12 teacher preparation programs. *The Journal of Educational Foundations, 28*(1–4), 135.

Kagan, S. L. (2009). American early childhood education: Preventing or perpetuating inequity. In *Equity matters: Research review* (Vol. 3). New York: The Campaign for Educational Equity, Teachers College, Columbia University. [Online]. http://citeseerx.ist.psu.edu/viewdoc/downlo ad?doi=10.1.1.526.5604&rep=rep1&type=pdf. Accessed 10 Jan 2018.

Kayes, P. E. (2006). New paradigms for diversifying faculty and staff in higher education: Uncovering cultural biases in the search and hiring process. *Multicultural Education, 14*(2), 65.

Krok, D. (2015). The role of meaning in life within the relations of religious coping and psychological well-being. *Journal of Religion and Health, 54*(6), 2292–2308.

Ledwell, K., & Oyler, C. (2016). Unstandardized responses to a "standardized" test: The edTPA as gatekeeper and curriculum change agent. *Journal of Teacher Education, 67*(2), 120–134.

Madrid, S., Baldwin, N., & Belbase, S. (2016). Feeling culture: The emotional experience of six early childhood educators while teaching in a cross-cultural context. *Global Studies of Childhood, 6*(3), 336–351.

Maxwell, L. A. (2014). US school enrollment hits majority-minority milestone. *The Education Digest, 80*(4), 27.

Milner, H. R., IV. (2010). What does teacher education have to do with teaching? Implications for diversity studies. *Journal of Teacher Education, 61*(1–2), 118–131.

Paige, R. M., Jacobs-Cassuto, M., Yershova, Y. A., & DeJaeghere, J. (2003). Assessing intercultural sensitivity: An empirical analysis of the hammer and Bennett intercultural development inventory. *International Journal of Intercultural Relations, 27*(4), 467–486.

Pillow, W. (2003). Confession, catharsis, or cure? Rethinking the uses of reflexivity as methodological power in qualitative research. *International Journal of Qualitative Studies in Education, 16*(2), 175–196.

Rhedding-Jones, J. (2007). Monocultural constructs: A transnational reflects on early childhood institutions. *TCI (Transnational Curriculum Inquiry), 4*(2), 38–54.

Rissanen, I., Kuusisto, E., & Kuusisto, A. (2016). Developing teachers' intercultural sensitivity: Case study on a pilot course in Finnish teacher education. *Teaching and Teacher Education, 59*, 446–456.

Rottenberg, C. (2008). *Performing Americanness: Race, class, and gender in modern African-American and Jewish-American literature.* New England: UPNE.

Sahlberg, P. (2004). Teaching and globalization. *Managing Global Transitions, 2*(1), 65.

Smith, C. (2003). Religious participation and network closure among American adolescents. *Journal for the Scientific Study of Religion, 42*(2), 259–267.

Soto, N. E. (2005). Caring and relationships: Developing a pedagogy of caring. *Vill L Rev, 50*, 859.

St. Jean, Y., & Feagin, J. R. (1998). The family costs of white racism: The case of African American families. *Journal of Comparative Family Studies*, 297–312.

Trainer, T. (2012) *'Education' under consumer-capitalism, and the simpler way alternative* (Simplicity Institute Report 12m, 2015). [Online]. http://simplicityinstitute.org/wp-content/ uploads/2011/04/TrainerEducationSimplicityInstitute.pdf. Accessed 10 Jan 2018.

Triandis, H. C. (2001). Individualism-collectivism and personality. *Journal of Personality, 69*(6), 907–924.

United Nations Educational, Scientific and Cultural Organization (UNESCO). (2013). *Intercultural competences: Conceptual and operational framework.* Paris: UNESCO.

Weaver, G. (1999). American cultural values. *Kokusai Bunka Kenshu (Intercultural Training)* (Special Edition, pp. 9–15). [Online]. http://trends.gmfus.org/doc/mmf/American%20 Cultural%20Values.pdf. Accessed 10 Jan 2018.

Weiner, L. (2007). A lethal threat to US teacher education. *Journal of Teacher Education, 58*(4), 274–286.

Wolfson, A. (1997). Individualism: New and old. *The Public Interest, 126*(Winter), 75–88.

Wursten, H., & Jacobs, C. (2013). The impact of culture on education. Can we introduce best practices in education across countries. *ITIM International, 1,* 1–28.

Zeichner, K. (2006). Reflections of a university-based teacher educator on the future of college- and university-based teacher education. *Journal of Teacher Education, 57*(3), 326–340.

8

Expanding Learning Frames in Music Teacher Education: Student Placement in a Palestinian Refugee Camp in Lebanon

Brit Ågot Brøske

Abstract The purpose of this chapter is to discuss how intercultural music projects can contribute to expansive learning in music teacher education. Based on cultural-historical activity theory (CHAT), I explore expansive learning on the student-music-teacher and institutional levels. The inspirational starting point for the chapter is the professional placement of student music teachers in the Palestinian refugee camp Rashedieh in South Lebanon. Both students and staff from the Norwegian Academy of Music are involved in this project, and both the context and the content of the setting are experienced by student-music-teachers and staff as highly unfamiliar, unpredictable, and challenging—although highly valuable. A particular focus of the discussion relates to the concepts of complexity and contradictions, and how they can function as potential sources for change, development, and expansive learning. I argue that student-music-teachers' involvement in intercultural projects can create rich opportunities for expansive, intercultural learning. However, in order to achieve this, we have to design educational programs that enhance reflection and dialogue, provide a solid intercultural competence, and create possibilities for existential meetings and placement settings in which student-teachers experience being "the other". Consequently, students, teachers, and institutions can learn something that is "not yet there", and be prepared for the crucial challenges of the future.

Keywords Music teacher education · Intercultural projects · Professional placement · Expansive learning · Palestinian refugees

---

B. Å. Brøske (✉)
Music Education and Music Therapy Department, Norwegian Academy of Music, Oslo, Norway
e-mail: brit.a.broske@nmh.no

1 Introduction

This chapter explores learning by taking student music teachers to an intercultural project held in a Palestinian refugee camp in South Lebanon. The Norwegian Academy of Music (NMH) has been involved in a project in Lebanon (known as the "Lebanon Project")[1] since 2005 (for more information, see Storsve and Danielsen 2013). This project can in different ways be seen as an important learning arena for both the student music teachers participating in the professional placement training and for NMH as an institution.

In this chapter, cultural-historical activity theory (CHAT) is used as a way of understanding learning opportunities within the music project in the refugee camp. Activity theory is particularly useful when exploring and understanding learning that involves the interaction of at least two activity systems (Engeström 1987; Engeström and Sannino 2010; Vennebo 2016). This is one way of considering the interaction between NMH and the professional placement arena in Lebanon. In particular, the present study will focus on complexity and contradictions as potential sources for change, development, and expansive learning. When encountering an unfamiliar context characterized by a high degree of complexity and unforeseen challenges, questioning and reflecting on one's own competence seem to be central catalysts for learning in projects where different cultures meet; I label this 'intercultural projects' in this chapter. I posit that intercultural projects can create opportunities to expand on the aim of the activity, which in this context is both to teach children music as well as to better understand music teaching within higher music teacher education. The following research question is posed: *What kind of expansive learning takes place in an intercultural professional placement in music education at the individual and institutional levels? How can such learning inform music teacher education?*

This chapter is divided into three sections. In the first part of the chapter, I present the context: the Lebanon Project, theoretical perspectives, and previous relevant research. Then, I turn to discussions and reflections on expansive learning at the student-music-teacher level. This is based on my own previous research on students' learning experiences after partaking in a professional placement in Rashedieh (Brøske-Danielsen 2013). Activity theory is especially valuable for focusing not only on learning at the individual level, but also at the institutional, or system, level. In the third part of the chapter, I discuss how such a project can contribute to expansive learning at the institutional level, and in what ways such learning can inform music teacher education.

---

[1] https://nmh.no/forskning/prosjekter/libanonprosjektet

2 The Lebanon Project: Context and Content

In 2002, Norwegian music teachers introduced community music activities for children in the Palestinian refugee camp Rashedieh in South Lebanon. This has grown into a large project called the Lebanon Project, and the Norwegian Academy of Music (NMH) has been a central partner in it since 2005. The refugees in Rashedieh lack basic human rights and access to education; moreover, the unemployment rate is high, the economy is poor, and the camp lacks clean water and adequate health care. Further, there are few or no opportunities for children and adolescents to continue their music education outside of the camp, due to their refugee status. The music activities in Rashedieh take place in a cultural center run by a non-governmental organization: Beit Atfal Assumoud. Local instructors run the music activities and teach music as a permanent, weekly activity. A large orchestra with a mixture of instruments forms the core of the project, in which children and adolescents from 7 to 20 years old play together, all with different skills and musical backgrounds. In addition to the music activities offered in the refugee camp, the Lebanon Project establishes music as part of the curriculum in Lebanese schools, and trains Lebanese and Palestinian music teachers in Lebanon—all led by music teachers from NMH.

The student music teachers' professional placement occurs mainly within a Muslim cultural context in which music is neither common as a leisure activity nor as a school subject. Music is considered by some Muslims as *haram* (forbidden), while others deem it a valuable and desirable activity (Harris 2006; Izsak 2013). Through community music activities, the project in Rashedieh aims to promote equal rights and contribute to cultural democracy (Brøske-Danielsen 2016; Brøske 2017). Such ideologies can occasionally be seen as being in opposition to the social and religious hierarchical structures in the camp (Brøske-Danielsen 2016), and the project is itself replete with internal ideological contradictions (Brøske 2017). Relevant issues arise about gender (views on what girls could or could not do), on what kinds of music are acknowledged, and to what extent and how children with special needs could be included in the musical practices. These are issues that undergraduate student music teachers at NMH encounter during their professional placement in Rashedieh. The professional placement aims to broaden the students' understanding of their role as music teachers and to prepare them for a varied professional career. When placed in the refugee camp, student teachers administer and teach music activities for children and give concerts in the camp and in Lebanese schools. By doing so, the students are given the opportunity to encounter unfamiliar people, music, traditions, and cultures, as well as to gain knowledge that extends the context- and discipline-specific aspects of music teaching and learning.

Although currently limited to a group of Norwegian researchers and teachers, the Lebanon Project offers much greater potential for participation. Future areas for research and developmental work encompass the fields of music education, music therapy, and community music. Thus far, project-related publications have focused on the value of music activities for participating Palestinian children in terms of offering them new roles and possibilities to experience mastery, meaning, and improved quality of life (Ruud 2011; Storsve et al. 2012). Research studies have found that interaction between Palestinian and Lebanese children and Norwegian teachers facilitates new ways of understanding the self, experiencing recognition, and gaining respect and equality for the Palestinian refugee children (Boeskov 2013).

Other studies have focused on the need for competence development among music teachers working in Rashedieh refugee camp (Ruud 2012), and student music teachers learning in refugee camps or similar settings (Brøske-Danielsen 2013). When leading and carrying out music activities in a different and unfamiliar culture, several dilemmas and contradictory values and goals seem to arise. Recently, I have critically discussed these phenomena, theorizing how aiming to create a culture of equality and cultural democracy can conflict with the ideology and social structures of the local culture (Brøske 2017). My finding demonstrates the importance of focusing on learning and building formalized organizational structures within this specific community music project.

3 Sociocultural Activity Theory

Activity theory (CHAT) is based on the notion that learning and development takes place in and through social participation (Engeström 1987). It has its roots in the works of Vygotsky and the notion of mediating artifacts (Vygotsky 1978). CHAT has developed over several generations. Leont'ev (1981) developed the understanding that individual and group actions are embedded in a collective activity system. Activity systems can be defined as a group of people sharing a joint objective or motive (de Lange 2014); they are multi-voiced, object-oriented, and negotiated and constructed by participants (Engeström 2001). Six components—subject, object (referring to what the activity is directed towards), mediating artifacts, community, rules and division of labor—together constitute an activity system in which the components are interconnected and interdependent (Engeström 1987, 1999, 2001; de Lange 2014).

The third generation of CHAT includes at least two interacting activity systems (de Lange 2014). These activity systems consist of different perspectives, understandings, traditions, and interests at the same time. Such multiplicity is included in the term *multivoicedness* and is related to the notion of *contradictions* as driving forces and the basis for development and change (Engeström 2001). *Multivoicedness* and *contradictions* constitute two of total five central principles in activity theory. Taking an activity system as *the prime unit of analysis* is another central principle, and the fourth principle is that activity systems transform over periods of time and have to be understood against their *historical* development (Engeström 2001). Negotiating institutional boundary areas contributes to creating contradictions, which enable expansive learning cycles. Expansive learning cycles entail that the learner constructs new objects and concepts for the collective activity (Engeström

1999; Engeström and Sannino 2010); learning "new forms of activity which are not yet there" (Engeström 2001, p. 138). Expansive learning cycles start with questioning existing practice (Engeström 1999), and are followed by analyzing and modeling new solutions and consolidating the new practice (Engeström 1999; Vennebo 2016). The possibility of *expansive transformations* is the fifth principle of activity theory (Engeström 2001). Expansive transformations are discontinuous by nature, as the learning process is often full of leaps, disruptions, misunderstandings, and conflicts, yet: "discontinuities between communities, although potentially troublesome, also represent opportunities for learning" (Hubbard et al. 2006, p. 17). Such discontinuous and expansive learning processes can take place throughout the activity system, in the objective of the activity, or in the people involved. There are some similarities between this complex idea of learning processes and Bollnow's (1976) understanding of the term *existential meeting*, entailing a decisive, existential, and paramount experience which forces the individual to reorient as their very existence is affected. In particular, there are similarities in focusing on learning as discontinuous and dependent on questioning one's own understanding and actions, on the one hand, and, in Bollnow's understanding, learning that demands personal involvement (Bollnow 1976), on the other.

This chapter considers the interaction of two activity systems: (1) NMH; and (2) Rashedieh camp and its music activities. In several obvious ways, these two systems are very different; however, that is not the primary focus here. Instead, the focus is on how multivoicedness and contradictions are driving forces for expansive learning both at a student and an institutional level when operating in a boundary practice (Star and Griesemer 1989). A boundary practice is a practice in which two communities engage; it becomes "established and provides an ongoing forum for mutual engagement" (Wenger 1998, p. 114). In addition to briefly touching upon the six components of the activity systems: subject matter, objective, mediating artifacts, rules and division of labor, I deal with expansion of the object, understood as the outcome of the activity in great detail. Perspectives from and research on CHAT (Engeström 1987) and boundary practices (Akkerman and Bakker 2011; Star and Griesemer 1989) provide a theoretical framework for examining and understanding common challenges faced by partnerships (Waitoller and Kozleski 2013).

4 Expansive Learning: The Student Perspective

I will now turn to perspectives on the involvement of student music teachers in the Lebanon program. I base my examination on previous research about what student music teachers have learned from participating in the Lebanon program. In this previous research, the students' data was collected through reflective journals where the student teachers reflected on their experiences of participating in the professional training at Rashedieh camp (Brøske-Danielsen 2013). The study showed that the student teachers' experience in the Palestinian refugee camp could be characterized by encountering the unfamiliar and unexpected, which forced the students to confront new dilemmas and issues to which they had to adjust and handle, and on which they were required to reflect. The setting presents both cultural and pedagogical unfamiliarities and differences that contribute to increased reflection and questioning (Brøske-Danielsen 2013). In the following, I will focus on these two areas of interest – cultural differences and pedagogical complexity – incorporating perspectives from activity theory as a central part of the discussion. In the concept of CHAT, cultural differences and pedagogical complexity can be seen as multivoicedness and as central issues leading to contradictions (Engeström 2001). What students learn from the Lebanon program, how the learning takes place, and what conditions lead to this learning will be addressed in the following. But first, I will describe a typical day for the Norwegian students in Rashedieh camp.

4.1 A Typical Working Day in Rashedieh Camp

In Rashedieh camp, around 50 children welcome the Norwegian students through a small concert featuring both Arabic and western music. Then the students teach and lead for the rest of the day, starting with some musical games and warm-up activities, before moving on to prepared musical material: a multi-use arrangement[2] based on a song or tune. A multi-use arrangement entails having ideas and sketches of different voices and possibilities for different instruments, and several issues still to be decided, depending on the students' ability to make professional decisions on the spot. There are several challenges encountered throughout the day, such as working with translators as several of the children do not speak English very well. There is a lack of rooms suitable for practicing in smaller instrumental groups, and student-teachers and children face communication challenges, creating the need for regular breaks to translate instructions. There are several breaks and interruptions made throughout the session as the electricity comes and goes, leading to no sound on the keyboards, electric guitars, or the bass, and when the boys attend Friday prayers. After the workshop in Rashedieh, the teachers from NMH lead afternoon reflective sessions for the student-teachers that focus on sharing and making sense of their experiences; adjusting to various classroom material and teaching strategies; organizing for the next day; and exchanging feedback among students and between students and teachers.

4.2 Cultural Differences

As exemplified in the description of an average working day, the professional placement in Rashedieh camp is rife with unfamiliar and unpredictable experiences for the students. The context is characterized by the lack of a common language between

---

[2] For more information on this, see Brøske-Danielsen and Storsve (2016).

student-teachers and children, the lack of a mutual understanding regarding gender and religious issues, and the reality that the children are refugees with little hope and few prospects for the future. The student-teachers are moving from one activity system, represented by NMH and music education in Norway, to another activity system represented by Rashedieh camp and the music activities there. They experience the context in Rashedieh camp featuring both intrinsic multivoicedness and contradictions, as well as contradictions between the unfamiliar Rashedieh system and their familiar situation in Norway. Contradictions are found on several levels, which is a central feature in activity theory and a driving force for expansive learning (de Lange 2014). Based on this understanding, the context can be considered well suited to enabling expansive learning. Within expansive learning cycles, contradictions lead to questioning, and "the object and motive of the activity are reconceptualized to embrace a radically wider horizon of possibilities than in the previous mode of the activity" (Engeström 2001, p. 137). The contradictions and unfamiliarities can then be seen as key conditions for the reconceptualization of the objective of the activity and for the learning that takes place.

A previous study (Brøske-Danielsen 2013; Danielsen 2012) shows that teaching in collaboration with fellow student-teachers in this challenging context contributes to increased awareness of competence, as students experience and acknowledge both themselves and the other students as competent music teachers (Brøske-Danielsen 2013). When the student-teachers have to implement all their previous achieved competence, they realize how their competences are useful and valuable in other contexts than where the competence was first gained. For student-teachers, participating in the program positively impacts their self-confidence as developing professionals and in their personal lives (Brøske-Danielsen 2013). Furthermore, the study shows that when the student-teachers encounter refugee children who are part of a vulnerable group, it contributes to the student-teachers' reflections on the value of music, giving them a renewed understanding of their own role. As a result, student-teachers shift their focus from their own personal, artistic achievements to consider the refugee children's needs in the teaching situation (Danielsen 2012). This shift leads to a reconceptualization of the students' prior understanding, biases, choices, and actions (Danielsen 2012). Building on perspectives of expansive learning, this reconceptualization can be understood as *the students expanding their understanding of the object of music education.*

4.3 Pedagogical Complexity

The context in Rashedieh camp is characterized by a high degree of pedagogical complexity, underlining the multivoicedness (Engeström 2001) of this activity system. There are extremely large variations in age and skill among the participating children. We do not know in advance how many children will attend or how many interruptions there will be, for example, owing to electricity outages or absences when all the boys leave to attend Friday prayers. Throughout the workshops, it is unfamiliar and challenging for the student-teachers to collaborate and teach together in a large group, and to work with a translator. These challenges place special demands on the teachers' choice of musical material, teaching strategies, and organization of activities (Brøske-Danielsen and Storsve 2016). This demanding situation for the teacher is similar to experiences in a collaboration between Finland and Cambodia (Westerlund et al. 2015). In both situations, student-teachers were required to step out of their comfort zones and engage in deep reflections on the nature of teaching and the purpose of music education. Both these studies show that language barriers contributed to a more nuanced understanding of the use and value of verbal instructions, while favoring the use of body language and instrument-demonstrations as the primary means of communication and teaching (Brøske-Danielsen 2013; Westerlund et al. 2015).

The context in Rashedieh constitutes an unpredictable, complex, and challenging teaching situation (Brøske-Danielsen 2013). This finding contradicts the proposal that professional placements should be of *reduced complexity*, where student-teachers can practice on specific components of their vocational tasks within a manageable context (Grossman et al. 2009). In Rashedieh camp, the student-teachers encounter a context that demonstrates a higher degree of complexity than normal, and—as something else appears to be more important, such as playing music with refugee children—the student-teachers seem to handle the complex situation together. The student-teachers are forced to gain experience in facing the unknown, while seeing themselves and their fellow students as competent music teachers. At the same time, the student-teachers collaborate with each other, which seems to make it possible for them to handle challenging situations. It seems that being able to handle and act on the unknown and unfamiliar constitutes an important part of their intercultural competence by being able to adjust to different cultures and settings and make sense of different ways of approaching music and music education.

4.4 The Need for Reflection

A central element of professional placement is the emphasis on reflection, carried out through reflective dialogues to which both teachers from the Academy and peer students contribute. As mentioned above, encountering this complex and rather different culture and context forces the student-teachers to step out of their comfort zones, which, in part, forces them to question their teaching strategies and conceptions of the value of music (Brøske-Danielsen 2013). In CHAT, *questioning* is considered the first step in the expansive learning cycle (Engeström and Sannino 2010; Rantavuori et al. 2016). Reflection is then crucial for making sense of the students' daily experiences. Reflection was also found to be crucial for Master's students studying performance who participated in a complex and challenging professional placement, according to the research study of Brøske and Sætre (2017). Their study shows that as students experience and encounter things that they find challenging, reflective everyday conversations become a necessity. When encountering a variety of unfamiliar elements, reflective conversations become a valuable and familiar part of the students' day (Brøske and Sætre 2017). Although this has not been studied within the Lebanon program, it is reasonable to hypothesize that similarities could be confirmed, as the student-teachers in the Lebanon program also experienced the setting as challenging and unfamiliar. It seems that this comparison confirms the importance of reflective conversations between students within placements that are complex, challenging, and unfamiliar.

4.5 Questioning as a Starting Point

An important aspect of the reflective dialogues is their *questioning* of the accepted practice and existing wisdom; and this questioning constitutes the first step in an expansive learning cycle (Engeström 1999). Joint reflections can be seen as conditions for the learning that takes place in the Lebanon program. Encountering, or meeting, the unfamiliar teaching context forces the student-teachers to draw on all their previously gained competence (Brøske-Danielsen 2013). Subsequently, as the unknown becomes familiar, they can consider what they know and reflect on this knowledge in new ways and through new lenses. By identifying, reflecting on, and assessing unspoken conditions, student-teachers gain new understanding. Personal involvement is then crucial for this development. The feeling of doing something that matters to others is important for the student teachers, and makes it impossible for them to continue unaffected (Brøske-Danielsen 2013).

This feeling is in line with Bollnow's (1976) understanding of an existential meeting, as well as Engeström's (2001) understanding of the role of contradictions as a driving force for questioning within the theory of expansive learning. When meeting something unusual and paramount, in which the individual is fully engaged and involved, the learner must reorient her view and start questioning her own preconceptions and prior understanding. The students' questions and reflections not only concern the actual teaching in the refugee camp, but may even extend to their overall ideas on the value of music and teaching, teaching strategies, understandings of culture, and their role as music teachers (Brøske-Danielsen 2013). Such questioning can contribute to new approaches and understandings when teachers meet other target groups, both in familiar and unfamiliar teaching contexts. This questioning can be further expanded to a way of operating and thinking, or, in other words, to new habits of mind and action, and to expanding learning cycles (Engeström 2001). This is one of the most valuable outcomes and one of the most important reasons for carrying out this program. The student teachers encounter people from another culture through and in music, thereby experiencing being "the other", and hence being forced to question things hitherto taken for granted. Creating the conditions for this to happen would be a good starting point for intercultural music education. Based on the established value of the process and outcome, the professional placement can be considered highly relevant for the student teachers' future work, although it is not authentic or similar to contexts that the student-teachers will probably encounter later in life. The students gain experience in learning "what is yet not there" (Engeström 2001, p. 138), as they cannot anticipate the competences and skills they will need to employ in such an unimagined teaching context.

4.6 The Value of Encountering the Unforeseen

As shown thus far, there are several reasons for bringing student music teachers to professional placement settings like the Lebanon program, including to increase student-teachers' intercultural competence. I would, however, underline that the significance of such programs is not primarily about learning specific cultural content, such as learning Arabic music; rather, it is about encountering a demanding and contradictory situation in which meeting a marginalized group of people offers new understandings, and leads to a questioning and enrichment of the object of the activity. Student-teachers gain new understandings of themselves as people and as professionals, and have the opportunity to unconditionally welcome everyone in a musical community.

5 Expansive Learning: The Institutional Perspective

The theory of expansive learning focuses on learning processes in which subjects of learning are transformed from isolated individuals into collectives and networks, and the focus is on "communities as learners" (Engeström and Sannino 2010). Nevertheless, the complex interrelations between the individual subject and her community is at the core of CHAT and the theory of expansive learning (Engeström 2001). In expansive transformations and in interactions between two or more activity systems, the object of the activity can be reconceptualized to embrace a radically wider horizon of possibilities than in the previous mode of the activity (Engeström 2001). The collaboration or interaction between NMH and Rashedieh can be understood as the overlap of two activity systems. This overlap occurs in a boundary practice as these two communities are mutually engaged (Waitoller and Kozleski 2013). In themselves, as well as between one another, the two systems are both filled with multiple voices and contradictions (Brøske 2017) that can be a driving force for change and expansive learning, and can lead to a reconceptualization of the object of the activity (Engeström 2001). In the following, I will focus on expansive learning at an institutional level, and specifically on possibilities for and barriers to expansive learning in a higher music education institution like NMH when interacting with a community music project, such as the one in the Rashedieh refugee camp.

5.1 Expansive Learning Among Higher Education Staff

The fact that higher education staff from NMH participate differently in the professional placement and in the Lebanon Project as a whole can, on a system level, contribute to developing a common and joint understanding of perspectives and needs in an intercultural field, and expansion in music teacher education. This new understanding and expansion relates not only to how to operate within an international project, but also to how we can bring perspectives and experiences from the project into the ongoing work at NMH, wherever they are relevant. In the same way that student-teachers are forced to reconstruct and adjust their understandings, values, and objects for the activity, higher education staff and researchers must adapt when participating in intercultural projects. Such participation can contribute to gaining valuable experience in communicating and operating within an unfamiliar context, facilitating music education in a Muslim culture, and understanding cultural and religious issues and contradictory dilemmas. Understanding cultural issues and contradictory dilemmas can lead to an enrichment of the repertoire of being a music teacher, or expansion of the object of the activity in terms of activity theory (Engeström and Sannino 2010).

As society changes, so too must music teachers and musicians in order to consider how to include refugees and immigrants in music activities in society, and how to engage all members of society in music education. Music teacher education needs to cover a broad range of issues relating to democracy and equity, and be able to engage with current matters in society. To initiate such changes, enhancing expansive learning could be the starting point for music teacher education, starting with questioning accepted practice and moving on to modeling new practices (Engeström 2008). This process could lead to expansion of the object, not only as it relates to cultural and religious issues, but as it challenges the understanding of basic issues in music teaching that are often taken for granted. These could be issues such as the concepts of talent, progression, and practice as cornerstones when learning music.

5.2 Educating Music Teachers to Meet Societal Needs

Municipal Music and Art Schools in Norway constitute an important professional field for educating music teachers. If the music teacher education at NMH and similar institutions are to be relevant to the field of teacher education, meeting the needs of these schools is important in terms of what kinds of competence music teachers need. There is now a call from national authorities to the Norwegian Municipal Music and Arts Schools to take greater part in cultural activities in reception centers for asylum seekers and in activities to promote the inclusion of immigrants granted residence (Brøske and Rønningen 2017).[3] There is also a shift in focus for the Municipal Music and Arts Schools through a new curriculum plan, emphasizing a broad ranging program, including scope for artistic activities organized in large groups that do not require pupils to have certain skills or put in extra effort (Kulturskolerådet 2017).[4] Incorporating intercultural projects into music teacher education, such as the Lebanon program, can contribute to building competence among music teachers in how to adjust musical material to a varied and complex ensemble, and how to develop teaching strategies suitable for both working with refugees or immigrants as well as more generally working with varied and large groups of children.

Furthermore, encountering Muslim culture can contribute to creating new understandings of refugees from Muslim countries, and challenge biases on this issue. Finally, experiences gained from participating in such intercultural projects could lead to a more nuanced and renewed understanding of the joy of music and the value of the community of practice within music activities. When meeting refugees in Rashedieh, contradictions between the expectations of high quality, development, and progress in Norwegian children's musical learning and among refugees in Lebanon is brought to the fore (Brøske and Rønningen 2017). It seems that participating in intercultural projects can contribute to challenging the notion of quality and musical progress as conditions for quality and learning in music teaching. Debates on progress, development, and quality are ongoing in the whole field of music teaching in Norway, where a common understanding seems to be that the goal of instrumental instruction is always to become the best possible performer. First-hand experiences from music activities in Rashedieh can enrich and nuance music teacher educators' understanding of progression and development as basic notions of quality and purpose in music teaching, and be a catalyst for expansive learning.

5.3 Obstacles and Challenges

Enabling expansive learning among NMH staff, and at NMH as an institution, requires that staff participate in international projects in several areas and ways, engage in intercultural music education practices and discussions in Norway, and are motivated to start to question their own understandings. This is not at the moment a realistic scenario, mostly due to few staff members participating in the project for

---

[3] A small-scale study was carried out among four music teachers working in Municipal Music and Art Schools in Norway, participating in the music activities in Rashedieh in August 2016 (Brøske and Rønningen 2017).

[4] http://kulturskoleradet.no/_extension/media/4683/orig/Strategidokument%20Fokusomrade%20 flyktninger%20og%20kulturskole%205.1%20per%2020170512.pdf

several different reasons. One research study has underlined the importance of being willing to question prior understandings and assumptions. This study focused particularly on identifying barriers to collaboration within a partnership between primary schools and higher education (Waitoller and Kozleski 2013). Results from this study suggest that boundary practices where artifacts are questioned and expanded in a collective and democratic manner offer rich opportunities for development (Waitoller and Kozleski 2013).

Operating in a new and unfamiliar activity system as the "unknown" can contribute to creating disturbances and interruptions to the norm, thereby constituting the starting point for expansive learning. Boundary crossing entails contradictions and facing multivoicedness, and collaboration and dialogue are important for doing terms and understandings explicit and available for everyone involved (Waitoller and Kozleski 2013; Brøske 2017). Subjects may act as boundary-crossing change agents, carrying, translating, and helping to implement new ideas between the activity systems involved (Engeström and Sannino 2010). When participants shift their roles and tools and reconstruct the object of the activity, it can lead to changes in the activity systems (Waitoller and Kozleski 2013). Such changes demand that the subjects involved are willing and flexible enough to start questioning the established practice, and really interested in learning from the collaboration. Reticence to become personally involved and an unwillingness to challenge one's own understandings and practices is often easier, meaning that allowing intercultural projects to simply become exotic and interesting novelties is a real risk. Such simplification could lead to cultural fascination, or "cultural peeking", rather than expansive learning. Enabling expansive learning in intercultural projects on an institutional level is therefore dependent on the subjects' willingness to step out of their comfort zones and make a brave jump into the unknown (Sæther 2013).

6 Towards Expansive Music Teacher Education

If being able to encounter new and unfamiliar situations and people from a variety of cultures and traditions is a central part of intercultural competence in music teacher education, it is essential to move beyond a fascination with the exotic and the different. Focusing on embracing difference and contradictions, questioning one's own preconceptions, and reconstructing the competences and skills needed when meeting people from across different cultures, ethnicities, and religions could be a starting point. Such a starting point creates possibilities to move beyond "cultural peeking" (Knudsen 2010) when approaching the intercultural field. Doing so involves shifting the focus away from what is different, and embracing contradictions as a starting point for learning and development in terms of people, contexts, and cultures in all situations. Then, multiculturalism extends beyond ethnic labeling. Experiencing being "the other" through encountering a new and unfamiliar culture via the Lebanon program can be a push in this direction. The resulting hope is that an intercultural attitude can pervade everything we do, becoming a part of our everyday life, our behavior, and our work. When facing new or unfamiliar expressions and culture, it is then central to explore what is similar rather than what is (at first glance) different (Knudsen 2010). To have intercultural competence could then be about having a basic attitude that emphasizes respect and curiosity for all people rather than focusing on the exotic and different representations of cultural expression.

Several of the aspects discussed in this chapter concern the known and the unknown, the familiar and unfamiliar, and similarity and difference. Seeing the Lebanon program from the perspective of expansive learning provides additional ways of understanding how such intercultural projects have the potential to enhance and enable expansive learning. Both on-campus and regular placement settings are familiar to the students and hence characterized by routines and taken-for-granted elements. When placing student music teachers in professional placement settings, like primary and secondary schools or in Municipal Music and Art Schools, they enter an arena in which they have several years of experience and possess a lot of knowledge. Although this is a necessary placement for educating music teachers, I think that in order to meet future demands, especially related to intercultural challenges, it is necessary to bring student teachers to placement settings that are fundamentally intercultural. Such settings could, to a greater extent, stimulate new questions about teaching and learning practices, about elements taken for granted throughout their own upbringing and education, and contribute to creating a habit of questioning one's own practices, biases, and understandings. Then, I hope, that when returning to their own activity systems, or at least to known activity systems, they will have changed and will see music education, people, and challenges differently. This is expansive learning. Since contradictions are the driving forces of expansive learning, especially when dealt with through analyzing, testing out new models, and reflecting (Engeström 1999), intercultural projects can indeed function as particularly useful tools to enhance expansive learning.

The endeavor to educate music teachers for the future requires what I am tempted to call *expansive music teacher education*. The discussion and ideas presented in this chapter outline a vision for such music teacher education, and some of it can be summarized as follows:

- Creating conditions for expansive, intercultural learning by bringing student music teachers to intercultural projects where they experience being the "other" and meeting the unfamiliar;

- Meeting marginalized groups, such as refugees, during the educational program to contribute to new and nuanced understandings of concepts as quality, talent, and progress;

- Creating learning environments in which stepping out of comfort zones (high risk) is considered a low-risk endeavor;

- Establishing rich arenas for reflection in order to make sense of the unfamiliar, and for analyzing and creating new models and understandings;

- Creating collaborative intercultural networks among higher education staff; and

- Creating a learning environment among higher education staff to enable questioning, analysis, and reconceptualization.

We have to design educational programs that potentially foster expansive learning, enhance reflection and dialogue, provide a solid intercultural competence, create possibilities for existential meetings, and create placement settings in which student-teachers experience being "the other". Hopefully, an expansive music teacher education may give students, teachers, and institutions access to experiences and possibilities to learn something that is *not yet there* and to be prepared for the crucial challenges of the future.

References

Akkerman, S. F., & Bakker, A. (2011). Boundary crossing and boundary objects. *Review of Educational Research, 81*(2), 132–169. https://doi.org/10.3102/0034654311404435.

Boeskov, K. (2013). Meningsfyldte møder – om norsk-palæstinensisk kulturudveksling. In V. R. Storsve & B. Å. B. Danielsen (Eds.), *Løft blikket – gjør en forskjell: erfaringer og ringvirkninger fra et musikkprosjekt i Libanon* (pp. 127–148). Oslo: Norges musikkhøgskole.

Bollnow, O. F. (1976). *Eksistensfilosofi og pedagogikk.* Copenhagen: Christian Ejlers.

Brøske, B. Å. (2017). The Norwegian Academy of Music and the Lebanon Project: The challenges of establishing a community music project when working with Palestinian refugees in South-Lebanon. *International Journal of Community Music, 10*(1), 71–84.

Brøske, B. Å., & Rønningen, A. (2017, March). Encountering the unfamiliar – Building intercultural competence. Experiences from a pilot project bringing music teachers to a Palestinian refugee camp in South-Lebanon. Paper presented at the *Cultural Diversity in Music Education International Conference (CDIME XIII),* Nepal.

Brøske, B. Å., & Sætre, J. H. (2017). Becoming a musician in practice: A case study of professional work placement as part of specialist higher music education programmes. *Music + Practice, 3*(1) [Online]. http://www.musicandpractice.org/volume-3/becoming-musician-practice-case-study/. Accessed 16 Feb 2018.

Brøske-Danielsen, B. Å. (2013). Community music activity in a refugee camp – Student music teachers' practicum experiences. *Music Education Research, 15*(3), 304–316.

Brøske-Danielsen, B. Å. (2016). Norges musikkhøgskole og Libanonprosjektet. Refleksjoner omkring et community music-prosjekt med palestinske flyktningbarn i Sør-Libanon. Paper presented at *The 20th Conference of Nordic Network for Research in Music Education.* Hamar, Norway, March, 2016.

Brøske-Danielsen, B. Å., & Storsve, V. R. (2016). Musikkarbeid med palestinske flyktningbarn i Libanon. Et community music perspektiv. In K. Stensæth, V. Krüger, & V. Fuglestad (Eds.), *I transitt – mellom til og fra. Om musikk og deltagelse i barnevern* (pp. 173–190). Oslo: Norges musikkhøgskole.

Danielsen, B. Å. B. (2012). Praksisbegrepet i musikklærerutdanning. In B. Å. B. Danielsen & G. Johansen (Eds.), *Educating music teachers in the new millennium* (pp. 89–108). Oslo: Norges musikkhøgskole.

de Lange, T. (2014). Aktivitetsteori og læring. In L. Wittek & J. H. Stray (Eds.), *Pedagogikk – en grunnbok* (pp. 162–177). Oslo: Cappelen Damm Akademisk.

Engeström, Y. (1987). *Learning by expanding: An activity-theoretical approach to developmental research*. Helsinki: Orienta-Konsultit.

Engeström, Y. (1999). Innovative learning in work teams: Analyzing cycles of knowledge creation in practice. In Y. Engeström, R. Miettinen, & R.-L. Punamäki-Gitai (Eds.), *Perspectives on activity theory* (pp. 377–404). Cambridge, UK: Cambridge University Press.

Engeström, Y. (2001). Expansive learning at work: Toward an activity theoretical reconceptualization. *Journal of Education and Work, 14*(1), 133–156.

Engeström, Y. (2008). *From teams to knots: Activity theoretical studies of collaboration and learning at work*. Cambridge: Cambridge University Press.

Engeström, Y., & Sannino, A. (2010). Studies of expansive learning: Foundations, findings and future challenges. *Educational Research Review, 5*(1), 1–24.

Grossman, P., Hammerness, K., & McDonald, M. (2009). Redefining teaching, re-imagining teacher education. *Teachers and Teaching, 15*(2), 273–289.

Harris, D. (2006). *Music, education and Muslims*. Stoke on Trent: Trentham Books.

Hubbard, L., Mehan, H., & Stein, M. K. (2006). *Reform as learning: School reform, organizational culture, and community politics in San Diego*. New York: Routledge.

Izsak, K. (2013). Music education and Islam: Perspectives on Muslim participation in music education in Ontario. *The Canadian Music Educator, 54*(3), 38.

Knudsen, J. S. (2010). Musikkulturelt mangfold – forskjeller og fellesskap. In J. H. Sætre & G. Salvesen (Eds.), *Allmenn musikkundervisning* (pp. 156–178). Oslo: Gyldendal Akademisk.

Kulturskolerådet. (2017). *Strategidokument for oppfølging av Landstingsvedtak 5.1. Flyktninger og kulturskolen*. http://kulturskoleradet.no/_extension/media/4683/orig/Strategidokument%20Fokusomrade%20flyktninger%20og%20kulturskole%205.1%20per%20170512.pdf

Leont'ev, A. N. (1981). *Problems of the development of the mind*. Moscow: Progress.

Rantavuori, J., Engeström, Y., & Lipponen, L. (2016). Learning actions, objects and types of interaction: A methodological analysis of expansive learning among pre-service teachers. *Frontline Learning Research, 4*(3), 1–27. https://doi.org/10.14786/flr.v4i3.174.

Ruud, E. (2011). Musikk med helsekonsekvenser. Et musikkpedagogisk prosjekt for ungdommer i en palestinsk flyktningleir. In S. E. Holgersen & S. G. Nielsen (Eds.), *Årbok for Nordisk pedagogisk forskning* (pp. 59–80). Oslo: Norwegian Academy of Music.

Ruud, E. (2012). The new health musicians. In R. Macdonald, G. Kreutz, & L. Mitchell (Eds.), *Music, health and wellbeing* (pp. 87–96). Oxford: Oxford University Press.

Sæther, E. (2013). The art of stepping outside comfort zones: Intercultural collaborative learning in the international GLOMUS camp. In H. Gaunt & H. Westerlund (Eds.), *Collaborative learning in higher music education*. Farnham: Ashgate Publishing Limited.

Star, S. L., & Griesemer, J. R. (1989). Institutional ecology, 'translations' and boundary objects: Amateurs and professionals in Berkeley's Museum of Vertebrate Zoology, 1907–39. *Social Studies of Science, 19*(3), 387–420.

Storsve, V. R., & Danielsen, B. Å. B. (2013). KAMP i Libanon. Prosjektprkasis i Kandidatstudiet for musikkpedagogikk (KAMP) ved NMH. In V. R. Storsve & B. Å. B. Danielsen (Eds.), *Løft blikket – gjør en forskjell: erfaringer og ringvirkninger fra et musikkprosjekt i Libanon* (pp. 67–90). Oslo: Norges musikkhøgskole.

Storsve, V. R., Westby, I. A., & Ruud, E. (2012). Hope and recognition. A music project among youth in a Palestinian refugee camp. In B. Å. B. Danielsen & G. Johansen (Eds.), *Educating music teachers in the new millennium* (pp. 69–88). Oslo: Norwegian Academy of Music.

Vennebo, K. F. (2016). Innovative work in school development: Exploring leadership enactment. *Educational Management Administration & Leadership, 45*(2), 298–315.

Vygotsky, L. S. (1978). *Mind in society: The development of higher psychological processes*. Cambridge: Harvard University Press.

Waitoller, F. R., & Kozleski, E. B. (2013). Understanding and dismantling barriers for partnerships for inclusive education: A cultural historical activity theory perspective. *International Journal of Whole Schooling, 9*(1), 23–42.

Wenger, E. (1998). *Communities of practice: Learning, meaning, and identity.* Cambridge, MA: Cambridge University Press.

Westerlund, H., Partti, H., & Karlsen, S. (2015). Teaching as improvisational experience: Student music teachers' reflections on learning during an intercultural project. *Research Studies in Music Education, 37*(1), 55–75.

9

Narrating Change, Voicing Values and Co-Constructing Visions for Intercultural Music Teacher Education

Laura Miettinen, Heidi Westerlund and Claudia Gluschankof

Abstract Researchers have suggested that higher education institutions need to be re-thought as 'imagining universities' that continually engage in re-imagining themselves, in order to be able to justify their own existence in a fast-changing world. It can be expected that music teacher education programs, as part of higher education, would benefit from envisioning their shared future from the same starting point. This chapter presents the second-stage inquiry of "Co-creating visions for intercultural music teacher education in Finland and Israel," an ongoing collaborative research project between the Sibelius Academy of the University of the Arts Helsinki and the Levinsky College of Education in Israel. The study is based on the constructionist pre-understanding that music teacher education programs ought to be developed by conversations and collective reflections, and that it is through these reflections that we narrate change. As an overall methodological framework, the study draws from Appreciative Inquiry (AI), emphasizing the positive as the basis from which to envision together what the future of intercultural music teacher education would look like. The data was collected through four workshop discussions, two at each site, totaling 24 participating teacher educators. The forward-looking themes of these second-stage discussions were developed from the groundwork of the first-stage focus group interview inquiry that mapped the present situation. This study suggests that there is an increasing need to create spaces where music teacher candidates and music teacher educators creatively face uncertainty rather than security, and where risk-taking can be encouraged and practiced safely. There is also a need to increase flexibility and openness, and to continue working more collaboratively within the institutions.

Keywords Music education · Teacher education · Intercultural · Diversity · Co-construction · Organizational change

---

L. Miettinen (✉) · H. Westerlund
Sibelius Academy, University of the Arts Helsinki, Helsinki, Finland
e-mail: laura.miettinen@uniarts.fi; heidi.westerlund@uniarts.fi

C. Gluschankof
Faculty of Music Education, Levinsky College of Education, Tel Aviv, Israel

1 Introduction

Due to the effects of increasing global mobility and migration, teacher education and schooling worldwide are on the verge of change regarding their approach to diversity. Although multiculturalism as a larger phenomenon has been influencing education for decades, the recent wave of global movement has challenged educational institutions and teacher educators to re-evaluate their curricula and pedagogical approaches. To counteract professional education that relies on tacit knowledge, socialization, and the 'apprentice model,' researchers have suggested that universities and teacher education units should be considered as learning institutions, particularly in such complex matters as engaging with diversity in education (e.g. Ball and Tyson 2011; Jacobowitz and Michelli 2008).

The discussion around cultural diversity has taken different perspectives in previous music education research, such as embracing the value of diverse musical practices (Campbell 2004; Campbell et al. 2005; Schippers 2010; Volk 1998), emphasizing the music teacher's role as a social change agent in culturally responsive teaching in music education (Abril 2013; Lind and McKoy 2016; Robinson, 2006), and understanding social justice in music education (Benedict et al. 2015). In their recent publication, Roberts and Campbell (2015) examine the connections between multiculturalism and social justice in music education by exploring how the five levels of multicultural curriculum reform formulated by J. Banks (2013) can be applied in music education to establish multicultural social action and social justice. However, Westerlund and Karlsen argue that multiculturalism as a dominant ideology of diversity in music education is insufficient, and although it is in many ways beneficial, it also works to "obscure forms of inequality and injustice that fall outside of its conceptual frames" (2017, 80). Instead, they offer a more heterogeneous and intercultural approach, which allows for the "development of a wider ethical reflexivity and critical awareness of the paradoxes involved" (2017, 100). Similarly, Ballantyne and Mills (2008, 2010, 2015, 2016) have engaged with this area of research through their studies and meta-analyses of research literature on diversity and social justice, in both general teacher education and music teacher education. In addition, Howard et al. (2014) have explored in more detail the process by which the multiculturalism movement has had an influence on the diversification of music teacher education in the United States.

As a response to the need for further scholarly discussion and empirical inquiry into diversity in music teacher education programs, this chapter examines the second-stage inquiry of "Co-creating visions for intercultural music teacher education in Finland and Israel," an ongoing collaborative research project between the Sibelius Academy, University of the Arts Helsinki and the Faculty of Music Education, Levinsky College of Education in Tel Aviv. In 2015, the study became a part of the larger cross-national research project "Global visions through mobilizing networks: Co-developing intercultural music teacher education in Finland, Israel, and Nepal." Using the concepts 'mobilizing networks' (Davidson and Goldberg 2010, 13) and 'networked expertise' (Hakkarainen 2013) as theoretical starting points, the Global Visions project explores what future learning institutions would look like if their practices were developed through collaboration, networking, and sharing that increases local and global reflexivity on issues of diversity. Socio-politically, Finland and Israel are in different phases when it comes to facing the challenges and opportunities created by cultural diversity. In Finland the population structure has only fairly recently started to change toward becoming more culturally diverse due to migration and global mobility whereas in Israel the challenges of promoting peaceful co-existence and social justice between culturally and ethni-cally diverse populations have been, and are still, a constant feature, even before the state was founded. The collaborative study between the Levinsky College of Education and the Sibelius Academy was initiated based on mutual institutional interest in the co-creation of knowledge and visions for more collaborative and interculturally competent music teacher education, in other words "trans-organizational development" (Bouwen and Taillieu 2004; also Gergen 2015, 211).

The first stage of this study mapped the music teacher educators' own intercul-tural competences, as needed in their work and described by themselves, and the competences their institutions aim to provide. We also asked the music teacher edu-cators to discuss the future needs and challenges on an institutional level, regarding these competences. There have been many attempts in the past to define the concept of intercultural competence (see e.g. Bennett 1993; Byram 1997; Lustig and Koester 2003; Hammer 2015), and here we refer to a definition in Deardorff's (2006) study agreed upon by a group of leading intercultural scholars and administrators: inter-cultural competence is "the ability to communicate effectively and appropriately in intercultural situations based on one's intercultural knowledge, skills, and attitudes" (2006, 247–248).

An intercultural approach in education thus emphasizes the inter-action and communication between people from different cultural backgrounds and, aspiring to be interculturally competent, music teacher educators call out the desire to enhance and promote intercultural dialogue and understanding in the music class-room. The first-stage inquiry showed that there is a pressing need for creating opportunities for music teacher educators to discuss and share their experiences on an institutional level, in this case around the topics of diversity and interculturality. The objective of this chapter is to elaborate upon the themes that emerged from the focus-group interviews in the first stage of the study in order to further explore how change is narrated for intercultural music teacher education at the Levinsky College of Education and the Sibelius Academy.

2 Theoretical Lenses: Visions for Organizational Change

The second-stage inquiry presented here is based on the constructionist pre-understanding that music teacher education programs ought to be developed by conversations and collective reflections, and that it is through these reflections that we narrate change. Instead of seeing a teacher education unit simply as a collection of individuals, or as a hierarchical system or place, it is seen as a fluid social collective that constructs shared meanings and understandings (Gergen 2015; Hosking and McNamee 2006). Like in any organization, music teacher educators ought to "create the meaning of work" and "negotiate their visions and goals" together with colleagues (Gergen 2015, 194). When attention is paid to the relational social processes of co-creation, the program can "move creatively with the times" (Gergen 2015, 194) and "*with* the conversations in the surrounding culture" (2015, 200).

Language, discussion, and stories therefore are seen both as constituents of the organization itself (Gabriel 2015, 275) and as "building blocks" encouraging members to 'think outside the box' (Gergen 2015, 196). In other words, collegial conversation provides a cultural record of not just 'who we are' as a music teacher education unit, but also "what we hope to achieve" (Faber 2002, 21). In the process of discussing and telling stories of our experiences, we add different expressions, we leave out unimportant details and issues we would rather not remember, and we suppress competing voices and conflicting dogma (Faber 2002, 21). Discussions "help us negotiate between those factors that restrict and limit our possibilities and our free ability to pursue our own choices" (Faber 2002, 25). According to the organizational researcher Brenton Faber, this *is* how we "narrate change" (2002, 21).

Moreover, we assume that music teacher education ought to be developed not just through local discussion, but also global discussion. This study has therefore provided a space for the institutional co-construction of visions, and collectively *recognized new possibilities* through networking between music teacher educators in two vastly different contexts. By sharing ideas that have been articulated in focus-group interviews amongst teachers of the music education programs, and by continuing collective discussions, the researchers of this study co-created institutional spaces for conversations to take place; conversations that would not otherwise have been held in the everyday life of the teacher educators. Gergen uses the metaphor of organization as "the co-active flow of conversation" (2015, 199), or "conversational co-creation," for a constructionist approach to opening a new way of thinking about organizational change, one in which all workers bring their experiences, knowledge, and values to the table. Here, we would like to add two more spatial metaphors, namely: (1) music teacher education as a "space" for negotiation that reshapes the program, including the pedagogical and curricular space (Barnett 2005, 2011, 77), and (2) music teacher education as a "mobilizing network" of knowledge building

(Davidson and Goldberg 2010), in this way highlighting the role of teacher education in knowledge-production. The spaces within the study's two programs can be seen as knowledge-building communities (Westerlund and Karlsen 2017) that, through this project, feed discussion both in their local spaces and also across their institutional borders, creating networked knowledge around visions for change in music teacher education.

3 Research Contexts

The participants in this study all teach at the music teacher education programs at either the Faculty of Music Education at the Levinsky College of Education in Israel, or the Sibelius Academy in Finland. The two teacher education programs are vastly different, and the study therefore provides maximized opportunities for mutual institutional learning (Stake 1995).

The Sibelius Academy offers a five-and-a-half-year "extended and integrated program" (Zeichner and Conklin 2005, 647) leading to a bachelor's and master's degree in music education, a degree that is required for music teachers in Finnish secondary schools (13–18-year-old students). By holding a master's degree in music education, one is also qualified to teach in other learning institutions such as conservatories and adult learning centers. The program has separate study lines for Finnish and Swedish-speaking students. The program's curriculum includes a wide range of musical genres and styles, including popular music, and emphasizes peer-teaching and -learning practices. Students are selected through an extensive entrance examination process where only approximately 15% of the over 200 applicants annually are accepted. This means that the level of musicianship among the accepted students is high from the beginning.

In Israel, the educational system supports parallel but separate education systems: state-secular Jewish Hebrew speaking, state-religious Jewish Hebrew speaking, state-Arabic, and state-funded independent schools. Levinsky College belongs to the state-secular Jewish stream; therefore the official teaching language of the institution is Hebrew. At the time of this study's data generation, the Faculty of Music Education at Levinsky College offered four undergraduate programs leading to the certificate required for K-12 teaching: a 4-year B.Ed. program in music education that certifies the students to teach at Hebrew-speaking, state educational institutes, and a 3-year B.Ed. program in music education with three separate study lines in collaboration with other institutions: the Rimon School of Jazz and Contemporary Music, the Ron-Shulamith music school for ultra-orthodox Jewish female students, and the Safed Academic College, where most of the students are Israeli Palestinians who intend to teach in the Arab-speaking schools. About 90% of applicants are accepted to these programs, and for some of the students these studies offer them their first opportunity to systematically develop their musicianship. The Levinsky music curriculum is mainly based on Western art music and Hebrew singing traditions except in the joint study program with the Safed Academic College, where teachers from Levinsky teach only pedagogical courses and music courses include music from the Arabic tradition.

4 Facilitating Institutional Space for Conversational Co-creation: The Research Design of the Study

As mentioned above, the first-stage inquiry mapped the understandings of and practices for enhancing intercultural competences in the two institutions through focus-group interviews (see, Miettinen et al. 2018). In the interviews, the music teacher educators discussed cultural responsiveness related to (1) their own and their students' musical style background; (2) the heterogeneity of their students and these students' future students (language, background, religion, abilities, and disabilities); and (3) awareness of formal and non-formal repertoires, and other limitations related to the religiosity of the students. Issues related to curriculum and instruction included the explicit curriculum, especially related to the degree of openness to a variety of musical cultures. Their wishes included more collaboration between colleagues, new courses, the use and place of technology, and their own learning about other musical cultures to be able to include them in the curriculum. Following these discussions, and as part of the first-stage inquiry, four semi-structured interviews were conducted individually with two teacher educators, one from each institution, who had longer experiences of having to step outside their comfort zones when teaching diverse student populations at home and abroad (see Miettinen In print). The two teacher educators were chosen as interviewees because of their input in the first stage group interviews, where they shared their experiences in the discussions. The purpose of these individual interviews was to gain in-depth information on some of the topics that were brought up in the group interviews.

4.1 The Research Approach: Appreciative Inquiry

Based on our experiences from the first-stage focus group discussions, we decided that the second stage of discussions would be inspired by Cooperrider and Srivastva's (1987; Cooperrider et al. 2008) appreciative inquiry approach, with its premise that "appreciative narratives unleash the powers of creative change" (Gergen 2015, 205). Appreciative Inquiry (AI) emphasizes the positive past and present as the grounds upon which a group or organization can envision what the future could look like. AI has been described as a "generative learning process that uncovers narratives of success and builds upon them" (Ridley-Duff and Duncan 2015, 1580). According to Cooperrider et al. (2008), AI's "aim is to generate new knowledge of a collectively desired future" (2008, xi). The research process of AI includes four stages of inquiry: "discovery, dream, design, and destiny." The first stage of this study was "discovery," where the participants engaged in dialogues and shared their views on the positive aspects of the program, particularly what works and what is valuable regarding their work. These discoveries were then cultivated in the "dream" stage, where the participants started to envision "a desired future" for their program, asking what possibilities there might be to further develop the present situation (2008,

5–7). Since the first two stages of "discovery" and "dream" are more researcher-led, and thus easier to facilitate and control by the researchers than the latter two, we decided at this point to carry out only these first two stages in order to test the approach in practice.

Altogether four workshops were held, two at each site, with a total of 24 participants. We designed the AI workshops in three parts: (1) introduction; (2) small-group discussions; (3) reports and whole group discussion. The aim of the half-hour introduction (given by the first author of this study) was to present the preliminary findings of the first-stage focus-group interviews from both countries. For the second part, the participants were asked to divide into two to three small groups to discuss among themselves, in their own language, the four questions (sent via email prior to the workshop) based on AI-models: (1) What do you see as the core values of your institution, and how are these values articulated and communicated to you as a staff member? (2) If you were to imagine the future of your own institution with respect to the changes occurring in the surrounding diverse society, what would the main challenges be? (3) What qualities would the next generation of music teachers/music-teacher educators need? And (4) If you had three wishes for your institution regarding how to address cultural diversity in the music education program, what would they be? The nature of the small-group discussions was not primarily researcher-participant interviews, as in the first-stage study, but rather shared discussions between the colleagues, facilitated by the researchers. This part lasted between 45 and 60 min. The third part gathered all the participants together, where each of the small groups reported their discussions to the other groups and researchers. These small-group reports were followed by a joint reflection period. The researchers recorded the small-group reports and the subsequent joint reflections; these recordings comprise the data set of this second-stage study.

4.2 Limitations of the Second-Stage Inquiry

The data has limitations in terms of whose voices are represented. The groups of participating teacher educators were relatively small, and a wider range of ideas could have been generated if more opportunities for discussion would have been organized. Moreover, a group discussion that is reduced into a summarizing report, presented by one person, is naturally limited in terms of how individual ideas are finally given space. The negotiation that took place during the small-group discussions, and the potential disagreements between the teachers, did not necessarily end up in the data as such. Furthermore, there were clear limitations due to language preferences. In both contexts, there were teacher educators who were not confident in expressing their ideas in English. However, as the questions were sent to the participants beforehand, the data brings out ideas that the teacher educators had already reflected upon before the workshop; it was thus of their own volition that they wanted to discuss these ideas together with their colleagues, and during the small-group discussions they were also able to converse in the language in which they usually communicate at their institution. Despite these limitations, the data provides us with valuable insights on how the music teacher educators perceived their institutions, their own roles within the institutions, and the organizational future in terms of diversity.

5   Research Question and Data Analysis

The question that we posed for the second-stage inquiry and the data was: *How is change narrated in music teacher educators' conversational co-creation for intercultural music teacher education at the Levinsky College of Education and the Sibelius Academy?* In our analysis, we applied a process of "narrative creation" (Bold 2012, 148) in which the different accounts in the data were first organized based on how they fit together with each other, and then in the next stage based on how they "made the narrative flow" (2012, 148). We wanted the "representative constructions" (2012, 153) to include the variety of views and experiences from both institutions, without comparisons being made between them. The shared voice of "we" is not to be understood as a unison, nor to be representative of all people who participated the interviews, but rather to "act more as examples of experiences from different perspectives" (2012, 153), yet interpreted as "the professional voice." The constructions include data from both contexts and all group interviews, and is predominantly composed through direct data quotations with no preliminary categories or themes. By following the ethos of AI, the analysis aimed at uncovering "narratives of success" (Ridley-Duff and Duncan 2015, 1580) by constructing the *full spectrum of ideas,* along with the potential tensions, on how music teacher education programs could be developed to better respond to issues of diversity. The co-constructed representations that condense the data are thus not aiming to represent reality as such in the two contexts, but rather the reality of ideas and ideologies, as co-created through the discussions and collectively conducted analysis.

The 'conversational co-construction' of this study has taken place at various levels: the workshop discussions were fueled by our main findings from the first-stage focus group discussions held at both institutions, as well as by other studies in the larger project. In the second-round workshops, teacher educators had a chance to discuss their individual views in a smaller group, and to formulate shared ideas together with their colleagues. The group reports can be seen as compromises, with any disagreements faded into the background; however, they also created further discussion that likewise informed our data. In this way, the discussions had several layers of co-construction. Importantly, our analysis adds one more layer of co-construction, as we selected and combined ideas from the data by blending the collective and individual voices in the reports of the two institutional contexts.

The co-constructed narratives that were created through the bottom-up principle can be seen to cover two larger thematic areas, namely, how to deal with uncertainty related to diversity, and how to better support the development of a collaborative institutional mindset. For the purpose of presenting the findings of the analysis, we have divided the two thematic areas into four emerging themes: problematizing endless diversity; addressing flexibility and openness as desired qualities for both music teacher education and future music teachers; envisioning music teacher education as a space for the pedagogical co-construction of knowledge; and change through collegial dialogue and sharing.

6 Living in 'Epistemological Pandemonium'

6.1 Problematizing Endless Diversity

In an expert culture, 'super-diversity' (Vertovec 2007) and 'supercomplexity' (Barnett 2000) appear as problems when too many knowledges fight over the educational space. The music teacher educators discussed questions such as: how is specialization related to the core value of versatility, and how could such values guide the pedagogical and musical underpinnings in a music education program? The term of the "Renaissance man" was used to describe the envisioned contesting qualities and demands of the next-generation music teacher and music teacher educator. As a solution, an important distinction was made between expertise and versatility at the program level, on the one hand, and versatility as an aspired competence at the individual student teacher's level, on the other hand.

> *Multiculturalism keeps coming up as an issue. There is always a desire to do something about it. How do we deal with that as teachers? How diverse can we be and still maintain a good, high level? We can't all be an expert in African and Cuban and Indian music. The issue is, what does it mean to be an expert? Multiculturalism might be mediocrity. So that's not what we want. We think that we need to have courage and take the best students and the best teachers. It raises the level. The curriculum of the program has to be multicultural, but not every teacher [in teacher education] has to be multicultural. That's why we have several teachers – numerous teachers, because no-one could teach everything. Our job as teachers is maybe helping the student to construct some kind of meta-knowledge about the ways in which they make music.*

Inclusion of diverse values touches upon the question of value relativism, and the limits of music teachers' cultural identity.

> *It's an interesting discussion, whether there is a music teacher mentality in terms of cultural diversity. Are we kind of expecting that everybody has to tolerate as much as possible? And is it realistic or not?*

This discussed notion of tolerance can be interpreted through the 'dilemma of multiculturalism' that divides the world into cultural wholes, and takes all possible diversities *as positive*. This phenomenon has been discussed, for instance, by Zygmunt Bauman, who argues that when mutual tolerance is combined with mutual indifference, "cultural communities may live in close proximity but they will rarely

Narrating Change, Voicing Values and Co-Constructing Visions... 141

speak to one another" (2011, 59). According to Bauman, "A 'multicultural' world allows cultures to coexist, but the politics of 'multiculturalism' does not make it easier, indeed possibly makes it more difficult, for these cultures to gain benefits and enjoyment from their coexistence" (ibid).

Teachers identified the importance of entrance examinations in hindering diversity in the student population. The academic frame was considered as setting the criteria for who is accepted in music teacher education, and how those selections are made.

And does that actually reflect the entrance examinations?
You're leaving so many people out who are wonderful musicians.... But then it's an academic institution. We cannot base our teaching on intuition and experience.

This also raises the question of teacher educators' need for security. Instead of accepting students from different musical traditions and cultural backgrounds into their programs, and in that way challenging themselves to think differently and strive for versatility in their teaching, an institution's "quality requirements" can be used as an excuse to avoid the hard work of stepping out of one's comfort zone as a teacher.

6.2 Addressing Flexibility and Openness as Desired Qualities for Music Teachers

Dealing with uncertainty requires risk-taking, flexibility, and openness. Whilst examining the challenges of higher education in 'supercomplex societies', Barnett (2000) argues that there is an urgent need for universities to *generate* uncertainties and self-reflexivity. Students graduate and are then forced to grasp unpredictable intersections of knowledges, and they must not be afraid of either uncertainty or making daring interventions (2000, 167). Paradoxically, this occurs at the same time universities and higher education need to help "to assuage that uncertainty" and "to multiply accounts of the world" (Barnett 2011, 123). How higher music education can provide spaces for students to face uncertainty, whilst at the same time multiplying accounts that assuage that uncertainty, seems an essential question to reflect upon in music teacher education. Here, the teachers' reflections pointed out that being prepared for facing uncertainty can mean that one's vision is open and free from fixed answers.

It's really important that we could share some of the weird situations that we face, that they don't stay in the classroom. Then it helps everyone to <u>build up the vision that anything can happen,</u> but you just have to resolve the situation without considering all the possible options beforehand. That's usually what students ask: they want to have those manuals. But there aren't those kinds of practical manuals; they don't exist. And you don't need them, you just need to learn how to be interested, listen, and meet every student.

Envisioning flexibility and openness again took place on two levels: the need to make the curriculum of music teacher education more flexible and open, and the vision of future music teachers being able to meet the needs of an ever-changing society. The program level flexibility was related to the basic assumptions that frame the program.

> Are we an institution that is about transmitting a musical culture? Keeping it alive for the next generation. Is that maybe a core value? The challenge may not be breaking a hegemony, 'cause maybe there isn't one, but maybe rethinking them. Maybe we need to reframe core courses. Every kind of action that rocks the boat is good and is needed. We need to be courageous enough to take true risks and to see what happens, and that is needed with the changes that cultural diversity is bringing to us. Is it true that you need to begin with Western classical? Is that the very beginning, so to speak? But who said Gamelan doesn't have pedagogies, or is not systematic.

Even when a music teacher education program involves plenty of options and musical diversity, these options may not encourage the student teachers to develop their self-reflexivity toward cultural diversity by forcing them to step out of their comfort zones. The idea of obligatory engagement with issues of diversity arose as an identified need for program-level change.

> We talked about openness and listening – opening up to the new and reaffirming the old. Being able to absorb new ideas. Also, in terms of interhuman relationships. And the flexibility to absorb other musical contexts and contents. We talked about adaptability, and about the ability to identify the musical elements within different genres. And situations where anything can happen. You need to just go out there, and then you just survive, facing these new situations. It's a capability to communicate outside your own competence, outside your own comfort zone and your own field. In teacher training, that could be fortified, for example by encouraging students to follow the news, to be active, to be activists.

When discussion moves to the realm of the 'strange,' 'different,' or 'unknown,' teaching-learning processes can then be constructed as spaces for risk-taking – both for teachers and students. MacPherson (2010) emphasizes that such "safe" spaces in diverse educational contexts are not simply places to represent one's culture or identity, as in the multicultural education approach, but spaces in which constant discussions should be encouraged, and where students should be allowed to make mistakes and practice how to interact or respond (2010, 279). Opening up these shared spaces or 'third spaces' (Bhabha 1994) can become places "where all the existing practices and conceptions ... can be left behind in order to come up with new understandings and ways of interacting" (Miettinen In print). In these spaces, supporting the student's autonomy becomes equally important as embracing diversity. Consequently, music teacher educators need to learn to live in an 'epistemological pandemonium' where risk-taking and openness, on the one hand, and stability and safety, on the other hand, can co-exist enabling a shared space for creative interaction.

7 Co-construction of Knowledge as an Institutional Mindset

7.1 Envisioning Music Teacher Education as a Space for Pedagogical Co-construction of Knowledge

Teacher educators pondered the ways that they could support students taking part in pedagogical knowledge creation. Encouraging risk-taking and cultivating openness and sensitivity toward diversity were seen as necessary means in this endeavor, although it was hard for them to pinpoint particular ways to do this in class.

> We thought that the task of the teachers is to support the student while she finds her own pedagogical path, and in that all the values of being open, of being sensitive. We need to support teachers and students to be courageous and to take risks, both artistically and pedagogically. But it's really difficult to give any practical advice about how to do this. However, we can all individually affect the general atmosphere, of not only tolerating but embracing cultural diversity. It can happen in really, really small things, in small, small steps, and they can all build this atmosphere. Also, we construct reality at the same time as we talk, depending on what kind of words we use.

Teachers identified one common way to respond to diversity, namely, learning from each other.

> One core value is flipped learning.[1] That the teacher supports the autonomy of the pupil. And the whole idea is that you learn in a group. And the basic question in this kind of group activity is what good can you do for the others via your own learning.

> Yesterday, for the first time, I took them [the students] down to the practice room. They've never been. And they walked into the practice room like children into a candy store.... Here I am sitting, I'm the teacher. But I'm totally in the corner. And I'm letting them make their music. Now in doing this I'm observing the ways in which they make music, and their concept of music teaching and learning, because they're teaching each other and they're learning.... In this way, I'm letting them make music as they know how to make music.... And my job as a teacher here, is maybe helping them construct some kind of meta knowledge ... about the ways in which they are making music. As a teacher I will learn, and I will maybe be able to implement some ideas from this later in my career.

As the findings of our first-stage inquiry showed (Miettinen et al. 2018), the teacher educators expressed a willingness to learn from and with the students, for instance in situations where the teacher educator did not speak or understand the mother tongue of the students or did not have enough knowledge about the students' musical tradition. The teacher educators' accounts in both data sets reinforce the view that 'learning from each other' (Darling-Hammond and Lieberman 2012) can be an effective way to respond to the everyday challenges created by cultural diversity in

---

[1] In the pedagogical approach of flipped learning, the traditional teacher-centered model shifts to a learner-centered approach as the students are actively involved in knowledge construction when the opportunity to access the learning material before the class allows the in-class time to be "dedicated to exploring topics in greater depth and creating rich learning opportunities" (Flipped Learning Network, 2014).

a classroom context. This mutual learning can happen both within and across institutions, given favorable circumstances.

7.2 Initiating Change Through Collegial Dialogue and Sharing

Considering that engaging in conversation, talking aloud, and reflecting together with your peers is a common practice in teacher education, this study highlights that this very same practice of facilitating conversation is equally important amongst the teacher educators themselves, when aiming at professional development. Similarly, as teacher education programs should provide their students spaces for thinking out loud and sharing their experiences, and in this way develop future teachers' reflexivity (e.g. Juntunen and Westerlund 2013; O'Connell Rust 2002), the staff members also need these spaces in order to develop themselves and enhance "institutional learning" (Senge 2006). This paradoxical difference between classroom practices and organizational practices came out in discussions, as the teacher educators called for more opportunities to meet, discuss, and share their experiences. The teachers had several suggestions for how to enhance collaboration, and how to prepare not just their students, but also themselves, for culturally diverse teaching situations.

> We envisioned an institution where the dialogue is part of it. Dialogue among all the teachers, and also with other institutions. We want to create a dialogue. People do not seem to meet enough. We talked about the personal experiences; how the teachers in different music genres don't necessarily meet or hear each other, and also that there are not enough opportunities to even have these meetings. This is the opposite of segregation. We've been talking about doing mutual concerts. Meeting each other in its creative power. Teachers playing together. We talked about how to teach collaborative courses and interdisciplinary courses, to work together to produce books. Teachers developing teaching programs together. We were talking about using a website as a platform.

Part of the conversation involved realizing that a reflective community in music teacher education does not need to be a harmonious whole, and that discussion, indeed, is related to change.

> So, basically, the community changes, constantly. We constantly change. So, it's a never-ending story. But it needs to be done in respectful ways, and by giving space to other opinions, and we don't have to agree. Why can't we create such a dialogue within our program? Why do we need people to be so far away to talk freely? If we are talking together, everyone has an agenda.

As Faber writes, "change can be a stabilizing and recursive force as an organization's stories pull discordant images and narratives back into a sense of temporary alignment" (2002, 39). In this way, change is "rarely associated with unity, continuity, or agreement" (ibid.). The key, then, is to be aware of how disagreeing views and opposing arguments can be included in the same space, conversation, and process. More importantly, however, during the discussions the teachers realized, as Gergen argues, that "major shifts in the organization can be achieved just through talking!"

and that such dialogic practices can become a "major game changer" (Gergen 2015, 206). At the Sibelius Academy, the discussion did indeed continue, and later resulted in a decision to include sensitivity to cultural diversity as one of the goals that is expected to permeate all subjects in the new music teacher education curriculum.

8   Concluding Thoughts

Researchers have suggested that higher education institutions need to be re-thought as 'imagining universities' (Barnett 2011) that continually engage in re-imagining themselves, in order to be able to justify their own existence in a fast-changing world. In the same way, it has been suggested that teacher education programs need to be re-imagined from the perspective of moving away from a curriculum focused on teachers' *knowing*, and towards a curriculum organized around what teachers *need to be able to do*. It can be expected that music teacher education programs, as part of higher education, would benefit from envisioning their shared future from the same starting point.

To conclude, this study suggests that there is an increasing need to create spaces where music teacher candidates and music teacher educators creatively face uncertainty rather than security, and where risk-taking could be encouraged and practiced safely. More discussion and the sharing of thoughts, emotions, and fears regarding issues of diversity in teaching could make it easier to handle the ambivalence between resistance and openness to change. There is also a need to increase flexibility and openness, and to continue working more collaboratively within the institutions. Moreover, if institutional collaboration is taken seriously in developing future music teacher education, this also has consequences for how leadership in music teacher programs ought to be understood. Conversational co-creation requires "relational leading" of the flow of conversation to generate, sustain, and create the meanings that can move the organization forward, as the relational processes become a focus of concern (Gergen 2015, 199). The effort put into the co-creation of visions pays itself back, as people tend to support what they create (2015, 203). Also, coming back to Faber's idea of the potential of collegial conversations, co-constructed understandings of 'who we are' as music teacher educators, staff members, and as a music teacher education unit paves the way for envisioning together 'what we hope to achieve' (Faber 2002, 21). Judging by the many comments from the participants on how the discussions initiated by this study should be continued, the need for sharing and co-creating within their programs is great. Unveiling that need and developing the collaboration further are the central goals of the whole "Global visions through mobilizing networks" project. The study presented in this article has aimed to facilitate the envisioning process within and across the two participating institutions, with a vision that the re-imagining and collaboration would continue to re-shape the ways that music teacher education responds to the challenges of cultural diversity as part of our rapidly changing world.

Acknowledgements This publication has been undertaken as part of the Global Visions through Mobilizing Networks project funded by the Academy of Finland (project no. 286162).

References

Abril, C. R. (2013). Toward a more culturally responsive general music classroom. *General Music Today, 27*(1), 6–11.

Ball, A. F., & Tyson, C. A. (2011). Preparing teachers for diversity in the twenty-first century. In A. F. Ball & C. A. Tyson (Eds.), *Studying diversity in teacher education* (pp. 399–416). Lanham: Rowman & Littlefield.

Ballantyne, J., & Mills, C. (2008). Promoting socially just and inclusive music teacher education: Exploring perceptions of early-career teachers. *Research Studies in Music Education, 30*(1), 77–91.

Ballantyne, J., & Mills, C. (2015). The intersection of music teacher education and social justice: Where are we now? In C. Benedict, P. Schmidt, G. Spruce, & P. Woodford (Eds.), *The Oxford handbook of social justice in music education* (pp. 644–657). New York: Oxford University Press.

Banks, J. A. (2013). Approaches to multicultural curriculum reform. In J. A. Banks & C. A. M. G. Banks (Eds.), *Multicultural education: Issues and perspectives, 8th ed.* (pp. 181–199). Hoboken: Wiley.

Barnett, R. (2000). University knowledge in an age of supercomplexity. *Higher Education, 40*(4), 409–422.

Barnett, R. (2005). Concluding note. In R. Barnett (Ed.), *Reshaping the university. New relationships between research, scholarship and teaching* (pp. 192–193). Berkshire: Open University Press.

Barnett, R. (2011). *Being a university*. London: Routledge.

Bauman, Z. (2011). *Culture in a liquid modern world*. Malden: Polity Press.

Benedict, C., Schmidt, P., Spruce, G., & Woodford, P. (2015). *The Oxford handbook of social justice in music education*. New York: Oxford University Press.

Bennett, M. J. (1993). Towards ethnorelativism: A developmental model of intercultural sensitivity. In R. Michael Paige (Ed.), *Education for the intercultural experience* (2nd ed. pp. 21–71). Yarmouth: Intercultural Press.

Bhabha, H. K. (1994). *The location of culture*. London: Routledge.

Bold, C. (2012). *Using narrative in research*. London: Sage Publications.

Bouwen, R., & Taillieu, T. (2004). Multi-party collaboration as social learning for interdependence: Developing relational knowing for sustainable resource management. *Journal of Community and Applied Social Psychology, 14*, 137–153.

Byram, M. (1997). *Teaching and assessing intercultural communicative competence*. Clevedon: Multilingual Matters.

Campbell, P. S. (2004). *Teaching music globally: Experiencing music, expressing culture*. New York: Oxford University Press.

Campbell, P. S., Drummond, J., Dunbar-Hall, P., Howard, K., Schippers, H., & Wiggins, T. (Eds.). (2005). *Cultural diversity in music education: Directions and challenges for the 21st century*. Bowen Hills: Australian Academic Press.

Cooperrider, D. L., & Srivastva, S. (1987). Appreciative inquiry in organizational life. In R. W. Woodman & W. A. Pasmore (Eds.), *Research in organizational change and development* (Vol. 1, pp. 129–169). Stamford: JAI Press.

Cooperrider, D. L., Whitney, D., & Stavros, J. M. (2008). *The appreciative inquiry handbook: For leaders of change* (2nd ed.). Brunswick: Crown Custom Publishing.

Darling-Hammond, L., & Lieberman, A. (2012). Teacher education around the world: What can we learn from international practice? In L. Darling-Hammond & A. Lieberman (Eds.),

Teacher education around the world. Changing policies and practices (pp. 151–169). London: Routledge.

Davidson, C. N., & Goldberg, D. T. (2010). *The future of thinking. Learning institutions in a digital age.* London: MIT Press.

Deardorff, D. K. (2006). Identification and assessment of intercultural competence as a student outcome of internationalization. *Journal of Studies in International Education, 10*, 241–266.

Faber, B. D. (2002). *Community action and organizational change: Image, narrative, identity.* Carbondale: Southern Illinois University Press.

Flipped Learning Network (FLN). (2014). *What is flipped learning?* [PDF file]. Retrieved from: https://flippedlearning.org/wp-content/uploads/2016/07/FLIP_handout_FNL_Web.pdf

Gabriel, Y. (2015). Narratives and stories in organizational life. In A. De Fiona & A. Georgakopoulou (Eds.), *The handbook of narrative analysis* (pp. 275–292). Oxford: Wiley Blackwell.

Gergen, K. J. (2015). *An invitation to social construction* (3rd ed.). London: Sage.

Hakkarainen, K. (2013). Expertise, collective creativity, and shared knowledge practices. In H. Gaunt & H. Westerlund (Eds.), *Collaborative learning in higher music education* (pp. 13–26). London: Ashgate.

Hammer, M. R. (2015). Intercultural competence. In J. M. Bennett (Ed.), *The SAGE encyclopedia of intercultural competence* (pp. 483–485). London: Sage Publications.

Hosking, D. M., & McNamee, S. (Eds.). (2006). *The social construction of organization.* Copenhagen: Copenhagen Business School Press.

Howard, K., Swanson, M., & Campbell, P. S. (2014). The diversification of music teacher education: Six cases from a movement in progress. *Journal of Music Teacher Education, 24*(1), 26–37.

Jacobowitz, T., & Michelli, N. M. (2008). Diversity and teacher education: What can the future be? In M. Cochran-Smith, S. Feiman-Nemser, D. John McIntyre, & K. E. Demers (Eds.), *Handbook of research on teacher education. Enduring questions in changing contexts* (3rd ed., pp. 679–685). New York: Routledge.

Juntunen, M-L., & Westerlund, H. (2013). Laadukas arviointi osana oppimista ja opetusta [High-quality assessment as part of learning and teaching] In *Musiikkikasvattaja: kohti reflektiivistä käytäntöä* [Music educator: Toward reflexive practice.] (Eds.), M-L. Juntunen, H. M. Nikkanen, & H. Westerlund (pp. 71–92). Jyväskylä: PS-Kustannus.

Lind, V. R., & McKoy, C. L. (2016). *Culturally responsive teaching in music education. From understanding to application.* New York: Routledge.

Lustig, M. W., & Koester, J. (2003). *Intercultural competence: Interpersonal communication across cultures* (4th ed.). Boston: Allyn & Bacon.

MacPherson, S. (2010). Teachers' collaborative conversations about culture: Negotiating decision making in intercultural teaching. *Journal of Teacher Education, 61*(3), 271–286.

Miettinen, L. (In print). Religious identities intersecting higher music education: An Israeli music teacher educator as boundary worker. In A. A. Kallio, P. Alperson, & H. Westerlund (Eds.), *Music, education, and religion: Intersections and entanglements.* Bloomington: Indiana University Press.

Miettinen, L., Gluschankof, C., Karlsen, S., & Westerlund, H. (2018). Initiating mobilizing networks: Mapping intercultural competences in two music teacher programmes in Israel and Finland. *Research Studies in Music Education, 40*(1), 67–88. https://doi.org/10.1177/13211 03X18757713.

Mills, C., & Ballantyne, J. (2010). Pre-service teachers' dispositions towards diversity: Arguing for a developmental hierarchy of change. *Teaching and Teacher Education, 26*(3), 447–454.

Mills, C., & Ballantyne, J. (2016). Social justice and teacher education: A systematic review of empirical work in the field. *Journal of Teacher Education, 67*(4), 263–276.

O'Conell Rust, F. (2002). Professional conversations: New teachers explore teaching through conversation, story, and narrative. In N. Lyons & V. K. LaBoskey (Eds.), *Narrative inquiry in practice. Advancing the knowledge of teaching* (pp. 173–188). New York: Teachers College, Columbia University.

Ridley-Duff, R. J., & Duncan, G. (2015). What is critical appreciation? Insights from studying the critical turn in an appreciative inquiry. *Human Relations, 68*(10), 1579–1599.

Roberts, J. C., & Campbell, P. S. (2015). Multiculturalism and social justice. Complementary movements for education in and through music. In C. Benedict, P. Schmidt, G. Spruce, & P. Woodford (Eds.), *Oxford handbook of social justice in music education* (pp. 272–286). New York: Oxford University Press.

Robinson, K. M. (2006). White teacher, students of color: Culturally responsive pedagogy for elementary general music in communities of color. In C. Frierson-Campbell (Ed.), *Teaching music in the urban classroom. A guide to survival, success, and reform* (pp. 35–56). Lanham: Rowan & Littlefield Education.

Schippers, H. (2010). *Facing the music: Shaping music education from a global perspective.* New York: Oxford University Press.

Senge, P. M. (2006). *The fifth discipline: The art and practice of the learning organization* (2nd ed.). London: Random House.

Stake, R. E. (1995). *The art of case study research.* Thousand Oaks: Sage.

Vertovec, S. (2007). Super-diversity and its implications. *Ethnic and Racial Studies, 30*(6), 1024–1054.

Volk, T. M. (1998). *Music education and multiculturalism: Foundations and principles.* New York: Oxford University Press.

Westerlund, H., & Karlsen, S. (2017). Knowledge production beyond local and national blindspots: Remedying professional ocularcentrism of diversity in music teacher education. *Action, Criticism and Theory for Music Education, 16*(3), 78–107.

Zeichner, K. M., & Conklin, H. G. (2005). Teacher education programs. In M. Cochran-Smith & K. M. Zeichner (Eds.), *Studying teacher education: The report of the AERA panel on research and teacher education* (pp. 645–735). Mahwah: Lawrence Erlbaum Associates for AERA, Washington, DC.

10

To Honor and Inform: Addressing Cultural Humility in Intercultural Music Teacher Education in Canada

Lori-Anne Dolloff

Abstract In this chapter I address the need for reshaping the way we think about Indigenous inclusion in the intercultural curriculum. While Canada has prided itself on its multicultural heritage, the nation's relationship with the First Peoples – First Nations, Inuit and Métis – has been immoral, genocidal and assimilationist. The 2015 publication of the findings of the Truth and Reconciliation Commission's Calls to Action details a way forward from the colonial patriarchy of the past. Education in general, and music education in particular are charged with finding ways to incorporate Indigenous knowledge, perspectives and history into the curriculum. After an introduction to the issues of the marginalization of Indigenous voices I discuss several arts-based curricular and extra-curricular initiatives that reframe intercultural music education. I propose that developing cultural humility in music teacher education will be a step forward in the decolonization of our teaching and learning spaces. This includes a move from generic cultural competencies toward an attitude of 'Cultural Humility'. Cultural Humility is discussed as an attitude toward engagement with peoples of cultures other than one's own. The stance is based on life-long, self-reflective inquiry, and seeks to disrupt the power imbalance that defines 'othering', seeking to establish partnerships and collaboration.

Keywords Cultural humility · Intercultural education · Music education · Truth and reconciliation · Indigenous issues

I am a second-generation settler on the land we know as Canada. I would like to acknowledge the ancestral keepers of the land on which I live and work:

> The sacred land on which the University of Toronto, Faculty of Music operates has been a site of human activity for 15,000 years. This land is the territory of the Huron-Wendat, the Seneca, and most recently, the Mississaugas of the Credit River. The territory was the subject of the *Dish With One Spoon Wampum Belt Covenant*, an agreement between the

---

L.-A. Dolloff (✉)
Faculty of Music, University of Toronto, Toronto, ON, Canada
e-mail: lori.dolloff@utoronto.ca

Iroquois Confederacy and the Ojibwe and allied nations to peaceably share and care for the resources around the Great Lakes. Today, the meeting place of Toronto is still the home to many indigenous people from across Turtle Island and I am grateful to have the opportunity to work on this land.

I wish to further acknowledge that I am writing this chapter during the year that Canada is celebrating 150 years of nationhood, a celebration not without contention for it erases the thousands of years of nations that existed in the land we call Canada prior to colonization by Western European countries. This historical erasure and the means by which it was achieved are evident in everything from history textbooks to national celebrations, from the puerile, caricatured manner that Indigenous people are portrayed as sports mascots, to the ways that indigenous music has been censured, appropriated in performance, and indiscriminately consumed.

In this chapter I address current issues for music teacher education that are grounded in a need to reconcile intercultural curriculum policies in music education, as currently practiced, with the reclaimed musical and cultural identities of Indigenous peoples in Canada. This is framed within the movement in Canada toward reconciliation of relationships with Indigenous peoples. Issues in the provision of music education in schools and communities include claims of cultural appropriation as music teachers include acontextual or improperly pan-Indigenous music into their programs, without the voices or lives of Indigenous peoples as part of a discussion around inclusion, or as a contextualizing resource for the music. Many of Canada's First Peoples have traditions of familial or local 'ownership' of individual songs and dances. It is considered inappropriate for other groups of First Peoples, let alone non-Indigenous peoples to perform those songs. The goal of ongoing efforts must be to honor the Indigenous peoples and their cultural protocols as well as to inform ongoing practice as educators seek to include the music and voices of Indigenous experience in non-indigenous music classes.

In seeking a path forward to this goal, I aim to disrupt the rhetoric of cultural reconciliation to move toward an attitude of cultural humility. Following a brief discussion of the role of education in the erasure of Indigenous culture in Canada, I will propose "Cultural Humility" as the framework of our music education response to historical abuse. As inheritors of educational systems that both suppressed Indigenous reality, and exploited certain cultural art forms, participants in current teacher education programs, both instructors and students, need examples of current national and local efforts to re-organize education and teacher education. Examples will be included throughout this chapter as resources for curriculum development in university music teacher education, and as possible models for musical engagement in the university classroom.

1 A Brief History of Residential Schooling

First, a bit of context. Although colonization has resulted in many forms of cultural – and sometimes literal – genocide, there has been an ongoing willful ignorance of the Indigenous experience of colonization in many parts of the world. Canadian national focus has at last been firmly drawn to the trauma caused by the educational colonial practice of residential schooling. The history of residential schooling is not in the distant past; residential schools operated from 1840 to 1996. During this time 15,000 First Nations, Inuit, and Métis children were taken from their homes, many forcibly by social workers accompanied by the police force. These schools were often in isolated communities sometimes hundreds of miles from the children's homes. They were forbidden to speak their native language, their traditional clothes were burned, and their hair, worn long in cultural traditions, was cut. The punishments for speaking languages other than English were strapping, starvation, and isolated confinement. In addition to these various kinds of physical and emotional abuse, many survivors of residential schooling speak of sexual abuse. The children were taught that they were less human than those in power, and that their traditional ways were evil, demonic and to be exterminated. In fact, the Canadian policy was to 'kill the Indian in the child' in order to save the child.

The lingering emotional trauma is evident in the following quote from a witness to testimony of a survivor of the 'education' of residential schooling.

> I know someone who was in residential school [...] and I know how ashamed she is of being Native, and the deep hatred she has for herself because of her schooling. It seems like every single child who did not die was left without a soul, and who pays the price for that? Everyone. The pain filters through the generations and touches us all. ("Anonymous" respondent on the blog of "Jill" a non-indigenous witness to a truth-telling session cited in Robinson and Martin 2016, p. 45)

2 The Truth and Reconciliation Commission (TRC)

After many failed attempts to bring this miscarriage of educational goals and cultural genocide to light, including a Royal Commission in 1994, the Canadian government mandated the Truth and Reconciliation Commission of Canada to document the allegations surrounding residential school experiences, and the legacy of this schooling. A brief summary of the work of the commission follows:

- The commission operated from 2009 to 2015
- Court-mandated hearings recorded the stories of survivors and intergenerational survivors of Canada's governmental instituted Residential Schools
- Judge Murray Sinclair, First Indigenous High Court Justice (1988), headed the commission hearings

- Thousands of hours of statements were recorded from over 7000 survivors, including documentation of artifacts and music

The documentation will be housed with participants' permission at the National Centre for Truth and Reconciliation in Winnipeg. Further, the commission's process resulted in 94 Calls to Action. Addressed to the government and national institutions, these calls are presented as a blueprint for a way forward, and several are recommendations for educational settings. But these proposals and actions are not without controversy. They are premised on the notion of reconciliation – a return to *right relationships*; the responsibility for reconciliation is fraught with emotional and legal pitfalls.

3 Reconciliation and Education

Amagaolik (2012) argues that a focus on reconciliation presupposes a right relationship to which to return. Certainly, colonial history of the last 150 years, particularly in the history of education, boasts no such right relationship. Indigenous artistic practices were treated with mistrust and superstition, and were thus banned. The Indigenous knowledge of the land was ignored, except in cases of extreme need for survival, and traditional wisdom and teaching ways were not included in the education of Indigenous children. Thus, we need to assume a posture of *conciliation*. Amagaolik describes conciliation as the effort to overcome mistrust and ill will, and to become compatible (2012, p. 91). Is there a role for music making in bridging mistrust and ill will?

Although I am basing my work on the Canadian context, this is not only a North American issue. Indigenous peoples the world over have been subjugated and their histories erased (Maracle 2015). The work of Alexis Kallio with Sami peoples in Finland (2013), and Bartleet et al. (2016a, b) in Australia, among others, speak of the same intergenerational trauma, loss of identity and social issues. Sami musician, Sofia Jannok sees music as an integral part of moving past colonialism. In an interview entitled "Life Beyond Colonialism", Jannok states:

> The national media in Sweden are only now opening their eyes to what is happening in *Sápmi*, because music is bringing these things to the fore. But music has always been an essential part of the decolonization work that *Sápmi* has undertaken for as long as I have lived and long before my time. (Blomqvist 2016, online article)

The effects of nationalist canons of music also have the effect of homogenizing repertoire and shutting out voices of minority and marginalized voices. Hebert and Kertz-Welzel (2012) explore the results of a move toward creating state-affirming national repertoires, which often silence other realities towards hegemonic reinforcement of patriotism and assimilation into a unified nation-state. Their study echoes the discourse surrounding colonialization in many parts of the world.

Yet, there is a need to beware of forced dualisms, or essentializing either the Indigenous or the Colonizer. Citing Orner (1992), Madden and McGregor remind us that thinking in dualisms is a Western-European construct, often positioning Colonizers in a stance of power over Indigenous peoples. In this discussion of curriculum, however, there is an additional issue. Who are included in the dualism? Whose perspectives are excluded? Which Indigenous perspectives are we representing? There is a reason why we list First Nations, Inuit and Métis (FNMI) peoples when we discuss Indigenous Canada. Each of these designations is a collective of local traditions, including sometimes widely varying perspectives. And, even as there is a diversity of indigenous cultures, so too there is a diversity of colonizing cultures and newcomer participants to the colonial project known as Canada. As Madden and McGregor caution,

> A brief reading of scholarly literature that focuses on non-Indigenous peoples […], however, reveals a situation in which the term non-Indigenous is often synonymous with white and of European heritage. The binary opposition then becomes Indigenous/white European, as opposed to Indigenous/non-Indigenous, and regardless of the order the terms are presented, Indigenous can be investigated as the abject [sic.]. From this vantage point, the term non-Indigenous excludes a discussion of the complex experiences of peoples of color who simultaneously participate in and are subject to the colonial project while facing marginalization themselves, as well as unique decolonizing sites, strategies, and goals that may be available from this standpoint. (2013, p. 380)

So, it is not a matter of Indigenous/Non-Indigenous/Classical/Non-Classical or Formal/Informal materials and pedagogies. Addressing the need for conciliation, for creating a relationship, disrupting power relationships and overcoming mistrust, requires a deconstruction and reconstruction of music education.

Many of our current flailing attempts to address Indigenous issues do not overcome this deep mistrust. Many continue to inflame it as we add and stir pan-indigenous musics to the curriculum, grabbing songs and music from the 'global songbook'. Moreover, the addition of indigenous material in the music curriculum cannot just be a unit of listening to decontextualized pan-aboriginal music as suggested in many curriculum guidelines. That does little to: address the centuries of prohibiting drumming, dancing and singing in traditional styles; draw attention to contemporary Indigenous artists creating ongoing artistic expressions; or the ongoing social issues facing Indigenous communities.

4 Becoming Engaged as a Learner

In June 2009, I was invited to 'go North' and teach in the schools of Iqaluit, the capital city of the territory of Nunavut. Nunavut is the newest political territory established in Canada, the first to be locally governed by Indigenous people – the Inuit. Not being well acquainted with the particulars of modern Inuit life, I was uncertain about what I could add to the musical lives of the children in this community. After my first visit, it was evident that I needed to work at contextualizing my teaching and materials in the local context, and I have returned 17 times since June 2009, teaching in schools, music camps and teacher development sessions. I have enjoyed the challenges of creating musical materials that reinforce the local language –Inuktitut, and collaborating to create yearly festival performances that included music in English, French and Inuktitut, dealing with themes that speak to the community. The collaboration resulted in bringing a local drum dancer to teach at the university of Toronto, in local high schools and to teach and perform as part of a cultural massed choir event with the Toronto District School Board. In March 2013, I was accompanied by two graduate students who taught alongside me, and immersed themselves in the schools for a week. All of these 'events' are secondary to the ongoing effect of decolonializing my attitudes and waking me up to the appalling continuing effects of colonialism on the Indigenous peoples of Canada. I have recounted the specifics of several of these visits in previous research (Dolloff 2016), and theorized my reflections as a movement toward 're-(in)forming' and decolonializing my teaching practice.

I became determined to bring issues relevant to the effects of colonialism on the Indigenous peoples of Canada to my practice as a music teacher educator. Since I started my travels north I am often asked to come and share music that I have learned during the visits I made to the Arctic. I have done so in collaboration with a Toronto-based Inuk colleague, Raigelee Alorut, on many occasions. I did not understand this collaboration as cultural appropriation because I was framing my work to introduce groups to the cultures of the Inuit and encouraging students to seek out and listen to the artists that I showcased through video, or in the children's songs that I taught them to sing. Increasingly, however, I am feeling uneasy with Southern groups performing indigenous music outside of Indigenous gatherings and contexts. For years prohibitions of indigenous cultural expression in many countries have resulted in incarceration, physical trauma, and even death of Indigenous peoples – most famously, perhaps, when the spiritual ritual known as the Ghost Dance was seen as a threat to the US government and precipitated the showdown that ended in the 1890 massacre at Wounded Knee, as Wente (2017) reminds us. When non-indigenous groups publicly perform music that was formerly prohibited, they are moving beyond cultural appropriation, they are gaining cultural capital from something that was denied to its originators. Wente, an indigenous film producer and radio commentator spoke recently about a film produced circa 1894, documenting the Ghost Dance. The indigenous performers were in regalia and danced with passion. However, what the public failed to understand as they consumed this culture was that this same group of dancers could have been imprisoned for performing this dance if it had not taken place as part of a documentary filming (Wente 2017).

My colleague Raigelee Alorut was a guest artist at the Faculty of Music, and led a throat singing, drum dancing ensemble for a term. She felt validated by being able to share her music. Other Inuit did not agree; Tanya Tagaq, renowned throat singer and vocal artist, reportedly told Raigelee, that she would never teach throat singing to Qallunaat [non-Inuit]. This gave Raigelee pause, but, as she worked through the issue, she realized that in teaching the music she is celebrating being able to perform it (Alorut and Dolloff 2016). Raigelee's addition to the university curriculum framed as a 'world music' ensemble was problematic. In team teaching this course with Raigelee, she and I ensured that much of the two hour session each week included stories of the experience of colonization of the North, the history of the song-making, and current issues in the North. This was a different mandate from the rehearsal format of a performance ensemble, but important to both of us in our effort to bring Indigenous knowledge of the North to the university students, to challenge the often romanticized popular notions of the 'Great White North'.

5   The Colonial Curriculum: A Canonic Fantasy

In a discussion of addressing the canon of university music education, Madrid (2017) problematizes the inclusion of Ibero-American music in the music history curriculum. He rejects the inclusion of 'marginalized music' in the colonial framework that seeks to homogenize the way music is viewed. To those who would claim that inclusion of world music constitutes expanding the canon, Madrid responds that this view presupposes that:

> [the] canon is actually a list of works or a given repertory. However, [...] the canon is an epistemology; it is a way of understanding the world that privileges certain aesthetic criteria and that organizes a narrative about the history and development of music around such criteria and based on that understanding of the world. In other worlds, the canon is an ideology more than a specific repertory. (2017, p. 125)

So, following Madrid, merely incorporating indigenous music into music classrooms, without reorienting the teaching–learning context to incorporate indigenous epistemology is an exercise in re-inscribing colonialism, 'new wine in old skins' if you will. This is the effect of current efforts to 'indigenize' the music academy: replacing white bodies with indigenous bodies, and graciously making space for indigenous titles to the lists of performance repertoire, all with the conductor firmly on the podium, sometimes joined by a 'guest' artist. Although this would seek to respond to the Calls to Action, it does not adequately address the issue of the power differential. Indigenous voices are still guests allowed into the academy, rather than part of the foundation of the enterprise.

6   Indigenizing or Decolonializing Music Education?

I choose to look at curriculum reform in music teacher education not from an indigenizing perspective, nor from a postcolonial framework, but rather from a decolonization framework. The goal of decolonializing thinking and doing is to continue re-inscribing, embodying and dignifying those ways of living, thinking and sensing that were violently devalued or demonized by colonial, imperial and interventionist agendas as well as by postmodern and altermodern internal critiques (Baretto 2011 cited in Gaztambide-Fernandez 2012). This approach means that the *structure of engagement must be deconstructed and reconstructed in collaboration with musical communities of practice.* Music education taught within the framework of cultural competence or cultural relevance addresses the bodies who are in the room, but does not address the erased history of the First Peoples of Canada, particularly in areas where there are no students who identify as Indigenous. However, foregrounding the multiple voices of the indigenous experience is a responsibility if we are truly going to redress past actions. Several current initiatives within the Canadian arts scene express an aim to address the historical indigenous experience. An examination within the music teacher education classroom can provide material for discussion, and offer possibilities for deconstructing continuing institutional initiatives to add 'indigeneity' to curriculum in order to inform our own practice.

The National Arts Council of Canada is offering grants for collaborative projects aimed at bringing Indigenous voices to the fore. Collaborators in such projects do not always enjoy a decolonialized experience. Take for example the ballet "Going Home Star", a work commissioned by the Royal Winnipeg Ballet and the Truth and Reconciliation Commission. When asked why TRC would want a project like this in the context of one of the most Western European art forms, TRC commissioner Marie Wilson reportedly replied that the Commission wanted the history to be brought to the people who would attend ballet, who would not hear it otherwise. Likewise, Robinson attests that:

> Music performance [...] has the ability to foster audience identification and empathy with a colonial history that non-Aboriginal Canadians may feel removed from. (2014, p. 299)

To create the score, composer Christos Hatzis collaborated with throat singer Tanya Tagaq and Northern Cree Singers. However, the collaboration was problematic because it faced performance issues such as the indigenous performers not reading traditional notation. Also, to accommodate the strict requirement that ballet music to be subject to the dancers' need for consistency, Hatzis sampled Tagaq's voice, and the Northern Cree drums, and another performer activated those elements in the performance. The perception of erasing the indigenous performers in the actual performance was handled by having them perform solo on stage prior to each act. Further, at each performance, there were counselors, elders and other health care providers to ensure care for indigenous people for whom this performance of their history created trauma. As Robinson reminds us:

> [What inclusionary or collaborative performance] too often assumes is that shared affective, physiological responses (crying, clapping, ovating) signify a common emotion [...] however, such responses may have strikingly different efficacies for Indigenous and settler audience members. Just as it is important not to conflate the social efficacy of collaborative creative processes with the social efficacy of their resultant performances, it is equally essential not to elide differences between audience members' shared affective responses. (2014, p. 280)

There continues to be ongoing discussion about the efficacy of this project.

7 Moving from Cultural Competence to Cultural Humility

One of the popular frames for '[multi]-[inter]-[poly]-[cultural]' music education (the labels we use are a topic for another paper) has been 'cultural competence'. First derived from business contexts, cultural competence often speaks to a set of skills to be learned to aid communication and business negotiations in a culturally respectful way (Tervalon and Murray-Garcia 1998). The connotation of the word 'competence' implies a list of skills that can be learned. Emmanuel (2003), among others, has developed curricula for intercultural competence based on a business model that moved through identifiable stages to evaluate a student's cultural 'development'. Deardorff (2006) examined the definitions of cultural competence to seek a consensus definition. She found that there was not complete agreement on the exact components of the construct, that different populations of professionals, administrators or academics valued different components of a definition. She did, however, propose that cultural competence is a complex, contextually defined construct, and posits a move away from globally defined skills, towards an institutionally specific definition.

Even with this evolving definition of cultural competence, which moves away from observable checklists of skills to be acquired toward valuing less quantifiable affective response and attitudes, I prefer another framework as we decolonialize the music education agenda. I propose that we need to steer away from the discourse of cultural competencies in all musics toward the discourse of 'cultural humility'. While cultural competence emerged from a business model and aimed at culturally ethical interaction, the notion of cultural humility has emerged in the health-care literature owing to the need to assist health care professionals in ethically and compassionately caring for diverse populations (Tervalon and Murray-Garcia 1998). Tervalon and Murray-Garcia speak to the difference between cultural competence and cultural humility, and their work suggests to me the benefits of the latter for music education:

> While cultural competence speaks to abilities and understandings, cultural humility speaks to attitude, inquiry and spirit. Cultural humility is proposed as a more suitable goal in multicultural [medical] education. Cultural humility incorporates a lifelong commitment to self-evaluation and self-critique, to redressing the power imbalances in the [patient-physician] dynamic, and to developing mutually beneficial and nonpaternalistic [clinical] and advocacy partnerships with communities on behalf of individuals and defined populations. (1998, p. 123)

More recently, Deardorff (2015), writing after her decade of research on cultural, and later intercultural competence publication, points toward the promise of the stance of cultural humility as she poses questions about the definitions of intercultural competence. She writes:

> Is it possible to arrive at one universally accepted definition, given the myriad of contexts and perspectives? Or should the focus be not so much on defining ICC but perhaps on cultural humility – of how to approach others with the recognition that ICC is indeed a lifelong developmental process?

This final question is congruent with the goal of nurturing life-long learning in teacher education. As the groups we teach throughout of career are continually changing, the notion that cultural humility provides a model of approaching diverse groups holds promise for teacher education.

8 Teaching for Cultural Humility

Ross posits that cultural humility generally includes three components: knowledge, attitude and skills (2010, p. 315). These components are all critical for teacher education. Culturally situated musical knowledge includes the sociological background of music and music-making within a cultural practice, as well as the historical and political cultural history of the people who make the music. In the case of Canada's indigenous population, this includes the history of colonialism, the suppression of cultural expression, and knowledge about traditional and contemporary music making within First Nations/Inuit/Métis communities. Knowledge must not be constrained to so-called 'museum' music making practices, in which historical practices are frozen in past traditions of performing. I believe that the conversation of reconciliation must not only make an effort to understand and acknowledge the past, but also support and recognize current artists within our classrooms.

The attitude component of cultural humility addresses the issues of how we as practitioners perceive and conceptualize the 'Other'. Drawing on the work of health care educators, Ross gives an excellent summary of the many attitudes that I propose are as relevant to music teacher education as to health care: practitioners' subconscious and conscious bias and stereotyping, recognition of his or her privilege, and understanding about community mistrust that is borne out of historical and institutional practices (Juarez et al. 2006; Kumas-Tan et al. 2007; Tervalon and Murray-Garcia 1998; Wear 2003 in Ross 2010, p. 318). There are two senses in which we need to avoid bias and stereotypical attitudes: those towards the music and those towards groups of learners.

Classical music has been privileged within institutions since the inception of music programs in Canadian universities. Indeed, in many North American universities, admission is based on a skillful classical (or more recently jazz) audition. Incoming students, required to make a long-term commitment to learning a particular genre of music, are being asked to upend their attitude toward classical music as the pinnacle of musical achievement, and their own privileged status as university students to recognize a more inclusive attitude toward music and music makers. This is not a new idea in the discourse on music teacher education, but as long as we keep classical music as the gateway for university music teacher education, it is a discussion we will need to have again, and again.

Finally, the musical and pedagogical skills that embody cultural humility include: new ways of listening; new modes of music teaching that depart from the way most of us were taught; and a willingness to engage in lifelong learning of the multitude ways of making music, actively learning from others, and reinventing our practice as we incorporate new musical voices and expressions in our curriculum. I see echoes of cultural humility in the work of Dion (2007) who uses a "pedagogy of remembrance" to focus on a relationship between pre-service teachers and Indigenous peoples as a basis for decolonizing education. Rather than loading the curriculum with 'indigenous' materials of which the teacher has little or no understanding, she begins by asking teachers to write, draw or reflect on their representation of Indigenous peoples. These are then held up to Indigenous-produced representations to expose gaps in knowledge, any paucity of understanding, and problematic stereotypical images that colonialism has left us with (Dion 2007, p. 331).

In assessing our implicit stereotypes, take, for instance, our notions of Indigenous music. North Americans are fed stereotypes from text-book series, film scores, and other 'indigenous-inspired' compositions. Compare that with works created by Indigenous youth in response to a music education challenge to write a song as a response to Mi'gmaw poet Rita Joe's moving poem, "I lost my talk". Joe's poem is a reflection on the loss of language that resulted from her being taken to residential school. (Videos of the powerful response songs may be found at https://nac-cna.ca/en/ritajoesong). These youth-driven songs demonstrate the complexity of Indigenous music, incorporating traditional drums and country and western guitar, and drawing from hip hop to create their songs. "Gentle Warrior" is a particularly poignant song fusing traditional vocables, pow wow drums and traditional dress with rock-band and casual dress while re-visiting Joe's home and celebrating her awards and accomplishments.

Or consider the work of Chris Derksen, a classically trained Indigenous cellist who moves the orchestra from the foreground of music-making tradition to place the pow wow drum at the center of the musical conversation. In describing her creation of a new genre, Derksen says, "I wanted to take all of my heritage and all of my traditional learnings – that includes Western classical learning – and put them together" (Deerchild 2015).

Ross proposes a framework of experiential learning for social-work students in order to facilitate and promote the learning of an attitude of cultural humility. This framework consists of a seminar that explores the aspects of cultural humility in relation to cultural communities, and fieldwork or experiential learning. While Ross' work is predicated on the actual communities in which her students would engage in professional social work practice, I propose that there is much to be learned from her approach for music education students. Though experiential learning often occurs in the 'field', music teacher education classrooms are rife with opportunities for experiential learning. In the context of developing knowledge of Canadian Indigenous cultures, one project that influences both knowledge and attitude is the 'Blanket project'. This project, designed by Kairos Canada (https://www.kairosblanketexercise.org), was developed to make tangible the brutal experience and effects of colonization on First Peoples in Canada. Participants stand on blankets representing the land of Canada. Some participants are labelled settlers, others indigenous peoples. As the leaders take away land, and declare some participants dead, the precarity of indigenous life and history is brought home. Having spoken with students, community members and family members who have participated in a Blanket Exercise, consensus suggests that no one is left unchanged by the experience. When 1st-year music teacher education students experience a Blanket Exercise in Introduction to Music Education Class, attitudes and expectations are challenged from the beginning of professional learning. Education then becomes a question of: *what knowledge and skills do I need to develop in order to address the responsibility to acknowledge and respond to the inequities and imbalances that I have seen?*

Ross (2010) further stresses the imperative of self-reflection. Self-reflection has become commonplace in the literature, yet it is often without structure. For Ross, self-reflection must be systematic and subject to dialogue with peers and instructors. Not only does self-reflection aid the student in recognizing and verbalizing learning, it offers the opportunity to make decisions about evolving goals based on changing perspectives. As Ross writes:

> Through self-reflection, students and practitioners are encouraged to relinquish the role of expert, work actively to address power imbalance in communication, to create respectful and dynamic partnerships with the community, and ultimately become the student of the community. (2010, p. 318)

Although Ross is reflecting on service learning in the field, setting in place these habits in teacher education can begin with meaningful reflective exercises during in-course experiences of music teacher education.

9 Conclusions

There is a national imperative in Canada to address and engage with issues of reconciliation in all levels of education. Music teacher education can respond to this imperative by framing learning experiences within the discourse of cultural humility. This framing necessitates that the teacher educator actively engages in his/her own development in the three components: knowledge, attitudes and skills. Through sustained engagement and work in communities of music-making practice, the teacher educator not only engages in his/her own professional development, but models the commitment to teaching from a place of cultural humility. Ruben Gaztambide-Fernández suggests,

> educators are called upon to play a central role in constructing the conditions for a different kind of encounter, an encounter that both opposes ongoing colonization and that seeks to heal the social, cultural, and spiritual ravages of colonial history. (2012, p. 42)

I propose that this construction demands an attitude of cultural humility, not simply a checklist of competencies if we are truly going to decolonize the effects of colonial history for Indigenous, Settler and Newcomer populations worldwide. In music this means learning new ways of listening, the inclusion of new voices, and reflecting on our own assumptions and biases. I see these as *imperatives* for music education, and by extension for music teacher education. They change the canon both in content and in methodology, but as Sto'lo scholar Lee Maracle maintains, decolonizing means "doing everything differently" (Maracle 2017).

The conversation continues....

Acknowledgements I am indebted to Ms. Hayley Jane, graduate of the University of Toronto for introducing me to the concept of Cultural Humility.

References

Alorut, R., & Dolloff, L.-A. (2016, October 7–10). *Creating a narrative of reconciliation through the arts: Listening to stories of oppression, responding with stories of engagement.* Paper presented at the Inuit Studies Conference, Memorial University, St. Johns, Newfoundland.

Amagaolik, J. (2012). Reconciliation or conciliation? An Inuit perspective. In *Speaking my truth* (Vol. 1). Ottawa: Aboriginal Healing Foundation.

Baretto, J.-M. (2011). In Commemoration October 12, 1492: Manifesto of Decolonial aesthetics. In *Critical legal thinking*. [Online]. http://criticallegalthinking.com/2011/10/12/in-commemoration-october-12-1492-manifesto-of-decolonial-aesthetics-2/. Accessed 9 June 2017.

Bartleet, B.-L., Bennett, D., Power, A., & Sunderland, N. (Eds.). (2016a). *Engaging first peoples in arts-based service learning*. New York: Springer.

Bartleet, B.-L., Sunderland, N., & Carfoot, G. (2016b). Enhancing intercultural engagement through service learning and music making with indigenous communities in Australia. *Research Studies in Music Education, 38*(2), 173–191.

Blomqvist, R. E. (2016). Decolonization in Europe: Sami musician Sofia Jannok points to Life beyond Colonialism. In *Uneven Earth: Tracking environmental injustice* [Online]. http://unevenearth.org/2016/11/decolonisation-in-europe/. Accessed 25 May 2017.

Deardorff, D. K. (2006). The identification and assessment of intercultural competence as a student outcome of internationalization. *Journal of Studies in International Education, 10*(3), 241–266.

Deardorff, D. (2015). International competence: Mapping the future research agenda. *International Journal of Intercultural Relations, 48*, 3–5.

Deerchild, R. (interviewer). (2015). Cellist Cris Derksen creates new genre with orchestral Pow wow. *Unreserved*. [Online]. http://www.cbc.ca/radio/unreserved. Accessed 14 Feb 2017.

Dion, S. (2007). Disrupting Molded images: Identities, responsibilities and relationships—Teachers and indigenous subject material. *Teaching Education, 18*, 329–342.

Dolloff, L.-A. (2016). A Qallunaaq on Baffin Island: A Canadian experience of decolonizing the teacher. In B.-L. Bartleet, D. Bennett, A. Power, & N. Sunderland (Eds.), *Engaging first peoples in arts-based service learning* (pp. 133–146). New York: Springer.

Emmanuel, D. (2003). An immersion field experience: An undergraduate music education course in intercultural competence. *Journal of Music Teacher Education, 13*(1), 33–41.

Gaztambide-Fernández, R. (2012). Decolonization and the pedagogy of solidarity. *Decolonization: Indigeneity, Education & Society, 1*(1), 41–67.

Going Home Star. (2015). [Online]. http://creativecollaboration.ca/navigating-collaborative-tensions-and-cultural-trauma-in-going-home-star/going-home-star-research-abstract/. Accessed 14 Feb 2017.

Hebert, D. G., & Kertz-Welzel, A. (Eds.). (2012). *Patriotism and nationalism in music education*. Farnham: Ashgate.

Juarez, J. A., Marvel, K., Brezinski, K. L., Glazner, C., Towbin, M. M., & Lawton, S. (2006). Bridging the gap: A curriculum to teach residents cultural humility. *Family Medicine, 38*(2), 97–102.

Kairos Canadian Ecumenical Justice Initiatives. (2017). *What is the blanket exercise? A teaching tool to share the historic and contemporary relationship between indigenous and non-indigenous peoples in Canada* [Online]. https://www.kairosblanketexercise.org. Accessed 15 Jan 2018.

Kallio, A. A., & Partti, H. (2013). Music education for a nation: Teaching patriotic ideas and ideals in global societies. *Action, Criticism, and Theory for Music Education, 12*(3), 5–30.

Kumas-Tan, Z., Beagan, B., Loppie, C., MacLeod, A., & Frank, B. (2007). Measures of cultural competence: Examining hidden assumptions. *Academic Medicine, 82*(6), 548–557.

Madden, B., & McGregor, H. (2013). Ex(er)cising student voice in pedagogy for decolonizing: Exploring complexities through duoethnography. *Review of Education, Pedagogy, and Cultural Studies, 35*(5), 371–391.

Madrid, A. L. (2017). Diversity, tokenism, non-canonical musics, and the crisis of the humanities in U.S. Academia. *Journal of Music History Pedagogy, 7*(2), 124–130.

Maracle, L. (2015). *Memory serves, and other essays*. Edmonton: Newest Press.

Maracle, L. (2017). *Invited lecture to graduate students at the University of Toronto*. Toronto: Edward Johnson Building.

National Arts Centre of Canada. (2015). [Video] *Mighty warrior*. Carter Chiasson, producer [Online]. https://nac-cna.ca/en/ritajoesong/gentle-warrior. Accessed 21 July 2017.

Orner, M. (1992). Interrupting calls for student voice in 'Liberatory' education: A feminist poststructuralist perspective. In C. Luke & J. Gore (Eds.), *Feminisms and critical pedagogy* (pp. 74–89). New York: Routledge.

Robinson, D. (2014). Feeling reconciliation, remaining settled. In E. Hurley (Ed.), *Theatres of affect* (pp. 275–306). Toronto: Playwrights Canada Press.

Robinson, D., & Martin, K. (Eds.). (2016). *Arts of engagement: Taking aesthetic action in and beyond the Truth and Reconciliation Commission of Canada*. Waterloo: Wilfred Laurier Press.

Ross, L. (2010). Notes from the field: Learning cultural humility through critical incidents and central challenges in community-based participatory research. *Journal of Community Practice, 18*, 315–335.

Tervalon, M., & Murray-Garcia, J. (1998). Cultural humility versus cultural competence: A critical distinction in defining physician training outcomes in multicultural education. *Journal of Health Care for the Poor and Underserved, 9*(2), 117–125.

Wear, D. (2003). Insurgent multiculturalism: Rethinking how and why we teach culture in medical education. *Academic Medicine, 78*(6), 549–554.

Wente, J. (2017). *Inclusion over appropriation: Indigenous art and reconciliation*. Keynote presentation, Toronto District School Board Arts Alive Indigenous Focus Day, February 17, 2017, Central Toronto Academy, Toronto, Canada.

11

The Reinvented Music Teacher-Researcher in the Making: Conducting Educational Development Through Intercultural Collaboration

Vilma Timonen, Anna Houmann, and Eva Sæther

Abstract Music educators working in cross-cultural contexts are faced with both challenges and possibilities, often finding themselves in need of multidimensional re-invention. This chapter focuses on teacher-researchers, contextualising them within the frame of institutional change and intercultural music teacher education. Taking an active role in educational development and regenerating usual patterns of action in music-education institutions sets various challenges as well as opportunities for the teacher-researchers involved. In this chapter we reflect on experiences through two intercultural collaborations: (1) *Global Visions Through Mobilizing Networks: Co-Developing Intercultural Music Teacher Education in Finland, Israel and Nepal* (a research sub-project in Nepal), and (2) A collaboration between Malmö Academy of Music and Vietnam National Academy of Music under a project *Supporting Vietnamese Culture for Sustainable Development*. We reflect on these processes through core concepts of affective actions and micropolitics. Our aim is to contribute to knowledge building in the field of sustainable institutional change aiming for globally appropriate music teacher education.

Keywords Institutional development · Micropolitics · Affective action · Teacher education · Music education

---

V. Timonen (✉)
Sibelius Academy, University of the Arts Helsinki, Helsinki, Finland
e-mail: vilma.timonen@uniarts.fi

A. Houmann · E. Sæther
Malmö Academy of Music, Lund University, Malmö, Sweden
e-mail: anna.houmann@mhm.lu.se; eva.saether@mhm.lu.se

1 Introduction

Ultimately, we need to reinvent ourselves (McLaren 1998, 260–261)

The cry to reinvent educators working in multicultural contexts includes academic, institutional, and individual dimensions. Individuals involved in an institutional change often find themselves in the middle of processes that can be emotionally challenging. To successfully conduct their educational work with intercultural qualities, they need to practice epistemological creativity and be ready to work in rapidly changing and unpredictable situations (Hebert and Sæther 2013). This chapter is based on our assumption according to which the painful, yet rewarding and necessary process of reinvention is one of the core characteristics of intercultural and collaborative work. Whilst focusing on teacher–researchers[1] transformative processes, we contextualise their work within the frame of institutional change and intercultural teacher education as it unfolds in two contexts, namely the Academy of Finland funded research project *Global Visions Through Mobilizing Networks: Co-Developing Intercultural Music Teacher Education in Finland, Israel and Nepal,*[2] and the 8-year-long collaboration between the Malmö Academy of Music (MAM) and the Vietnam National Academy of Music (VNAM) in Hanoi.

2 Political and Educational Background

The research is prompted by initiatives that actively aim to change and develop music teacher education to better respond to the demands of current issues, such as immigration, democracy, human rights and freedom of cultural expression(s). Such initiatives, to name a few, include: a teacher education project in Lebanon (Brøske and Storsve 2013); collaborative international master's degree programs, such as the Nordic Master of Global Music (GLOMAS) (Hebert and Sæther 2013); the cultural exchange projects aiming to facilitate student-teachers with intercultural experiences in a 'foreign' culture (Sæther 2003; Westerlund et al. 2015; Kallio and Westerlund in this volume); teacher exchange and curriculum development work (Houmann 2018); research on sustainability in traditional cultures (Schippers and Grant 2016); intercultural music camps, such as Ethno (Ethno 2016); and, finally, global efforts of developing intercultural music teacher education exemplified by the Global Visions research project. All three authors of this chapter are music educators and researchers who have invested multiple years totally immersed in intercultural music education projects in Gambia, Vietnam, Nepal and 'at home' in Finland and Sweden (Houmann 2018; Sæther 2003). This chapter therefore rests on

---

[1] We use the term teacher-researcher to indicate the teachers in the selected cases as 'practitioner –researcher' (Cain 2008).

[2] Later referred as the Global Visions project.

the lived experiences of working with institutional change in global and multicultural contexts. We are not aiming at a comparison between projects carried out in Nepal and Vietnam, rather the focus is on teacher-researcher transformative processes, as experienced in different settings, sharing similar challenges.

We extend McLaren's (1998) concept of the reinvented educator in music teacher-researchers, scrutinize *micropolitics* (see e.g. Hoyle 1982; Pillay 2004), explore challenges, and assess positive *affective actions* (Wetherell 2012) of collaborative activities in two intercultural development projects. We elaborate on these concepts in later sections of the text and strive to grasp the nature of affective actions in the process of educational development, as this dimension contributes to a wider understanding of intercultural educational endeavors. We also reflect how the micropolitical climate of the institutions affected individual work participation.

3 Programme Development in Two Intercultural Cases

Program development in intercultural contexts offers opportunities to explore the nature of the demanding process of reinvention that concerns everyone involved. For the purposes of this chapter, we have selected two cases to examine collaborative transformation processes.

The first case is the Global Visions project's sub-study on collaboration of Finnish and Nepali teacher-researchers in the process of creating a new study program and curriculum for the Nepal Music Center (NMC) in Kathmandu in 2015–2016. The curriculum writing, planning, and programme launch were conducted and led by four teachers at NMC in collaboration with the first author of this chapter, Vilma Timonen. In 2015 a need for establishing more structured ways of conducting music education for advanced level students at NMC was recognized by the teachers and administrative staff. For the future needs of Nepal, demand for pedagogically trained musicians was prominent since music teacher education as such did not yet exist in the country. Building a new programme and its curriculum fit well with the aims of the institutional collaboration between Sibelius Academy and NMC. The collaboration offered a way of learning together and co-constructing knowledge while aiming for a concrete goal. As a result, a new study programme was launched in January 2016 as the first nine students started their studies in the Performance Diploma Programme.

The second case is a sub-project of the Supporting Vietnamese Culture for Sustainable Development programme. We draw on the study (Houmann 2018) on the development of the Music Education Department and music teacher education at the Vietnam National Academy of Music (VNAM) in Hanoi in 2008–2016. Anna Houmann, the researcher in the project and co-author of this chapter, was one of the project leaders within the program *Supporting Vietnamese Culture for Sustainable Development*. The main activities of this project were teacher and student exchanges, training courses in different music subjects both in Vietnam and in Sweden, and cultural exchanges between the two countries. The overall objective, creating conditions for openness and development towards democracy and respect for human rights, was at the core of this project through the implementation of music education. From the point of view that lack of access to cultural forms of expression is a form of poverty, music education could contribute to poverty reduction by strengthening the capacity of those who study music. Poverty reduction in this sense activates what Appadurai (2004) describes as a "capacity to aspire" – a resource for renegotiating positions in society – that could contribute to democracy and the right to cultural diversity by supporting education with different kinds of music. In this project, such processes were in action and the teachers hoped that, in the long-term, the results would reach a large amount of school children through music teacher education, and art in school activities.

Both cases have special characteristics and focus areas. In Vietnam, the overall objective of creating conditions for openness and development towards democracy and respect for human rights was at the core of the subproject. The project had two objectives, namely "to enhance mutual understanding between the two peoples through cultural exchange programs," and "to enhance knowledge and management capacity for people working in the field of culture in Vietnam and Sweden" (Houmann 2018). In Nepal, the focus was on capacity building through enhancing mutual learning by taking account participants' various backgrounds, and bringing local practices into discussion with the global-music education community.

Data examples from Kathmandu, Nepal were generated through reflective group discussions, diaries and written works, where the researcher and the four teachers reflected on their collaborative processes. This data is mirrored with lessons learned from the development activities of intercultural music education in Hanoi, Vietnam. In both contexts, the co-writing of educational documents and establishment of new study programmes required all participants, including the researchers, to expand their horizons from familiar to unfamiliar, to go through a transformational process within themselves, and to re-evaluate cultural and institutional conventions – that is, to go through a process of reinvention.

In the following, we use the data from Kathmandu and experiences from Hanoi to demonstrate: (1) the micropolitical climate of institutions, and (2) the key moments of affective actions in an individual's experiences that shaped the outcome of the intercultural music education work aiming for institutional development in Nepal and Vietnam. We examine the collaborative project work and the ways the role expectations changed along the way. Taking into consideration the flow of activities in the two projects, we discuss the affective actions and micropolitical climate that guide change in intercultural, collaborative educational efforts (such as this Global Visions sub-project and the collaboration between Malmö Academy of Music and Vietnam National Academy of Music). The mutual re-inventions prompted by these collaborative actions in Nepal and Vietnam are used to inform our discussion of intercultural music education. Finally, we discuss the potentials of affective actions for the future of music teacher education.

4 Moments of Affective Action

Following Wetherell (2012), we use the concept of affective action as a pragmatic way to think about affect and emotion and as a way forward for social research, and as it expands on basic terms for emotions (sadness, anger, fear, surprise, disgust and happiness). Further, the concept opens the study of affective performances, affective scenes, and affective events: "Affective practice focuses on the emotional as it appears in social life and tries to follow what participants do. It finds shifting, flexible and often over-determined figurations rather than simple lines of causation, character types and neat emotion categories" (Wetherell 2012, 4). Hence, affective action cannot be reduced to any individual emotion. Rather, it refers to events, moments and experiences that shape the outcome of activities, and, as in the cases presented in this chapter, the developmental aims.

The study of affect is linked to the study of pattern: "Patterns are sometimes imposed, sometimes a matter of actively 'seeing a way through' to what comes next, and sometimes, like a repertoire, simply what is to hand"(Wetherell 2012, 16). Wetherell also argues that affect is about sense as well as sensibility, and that it is practical, communicative, and organised. She states that "affect does display strong pushes for pattern as well as signalling trouble and disturbance in existing patterns" (Wetherell 2012, 13). For instance, in Nepal, the NMC teachers were not used to being given the authorization to take educational leadership by constructing educational policy documents and practices. Thus, this process changed the usual patterns as described by one of the teachers:

> I used to plan my lessons in my head and only later I would write it down in order to submit it to the authorised person, and/or an authorised person would give me the curriculum to be followed. But in this new NMC Performance Diploma this curriculum writing process has been totally different. The curriculum was written by us, a group of teachers who would teach in the program. We planned and wrote down the whole process. Instead of writing a "lesson plan" kind of syllabus, we decided to leave as much room as possible for the teacher to decide on the ways to reach the learning outcomes stated in the curriculum. (Reflective essay, August 2016, Teacher 2)

Affective practices have their own hierarchies, which define how practices, such as classroom activities and writing of educational documents (as in the cases at hand), are grouped and who gets to do what and when. These hierarchies lead to troubling questions regarding what relations an affective practice disrupts or reinforces. Power is crucial to the agenda of affect studies, and consequently Wetherell asks if emotional "capital" (2012, 17) makes sense, as an element of cultural or social capital.

According to Wetherell, affective practices vary in scale. They flourish in the individual, but can be played out on a larger scale, like shared jokes, collective moods and expressions of nationalism (Wetherell 2012). Thus, examination of institutional change from the viewpoint of micropolitical action, that can be described as an interaction shaped by group hierarchies and ideologies (Pillay 2004), is likewise needed. Pillay (2004) also draws our attention to the importance of issues of leadership, organisational goals and objectives. Power is important, as is a sense of being powerless. The power to influence may be exerted in various ways in an institutional hierarchy, which has an impact on those who have less or no power. Therefore, issues of power in micropolitical studies include unanticipated arenas of power, as for example the presence of silence as an expression of micropolitics.

In Kathmandu, the emotional challenges of accepting a leading role in educational change became prominent when the four teachers and Vilma jointly reflected upon the process a couple of months after the implementation of the new programme. Vilma asked the teachers whether they considered themselves as active agents in the process of change, perhaps even activists, since in many ways the new programme differed from the prevailing educational culture. The question remained unanswered as silence took over the discussion. On the following day, the researcher found the team members unsettled, anxious, and upset.

> For me the change and activist word was... its... for me it is something that others determine not the things that we do. But, I think that's ... the things that we are doing is for a change and we are changing things. But for me personally, I think those things are determined by others rather than we ourselves. (Team discussion, March 2016, Teacher 3)

Another teacher continued:

> Actually, yesterday I was thinking about ... those challenges and responsibility in whole. And, actually I think taking [it a] little deeply I found that more complex thing that we were never (...) used to. Listening... being in a role of activist kind of thing. (...) in our context we have not been so used to that kind of role in our society. So, lots of things that we need to discuss among ourselves.... We are not here to make any change (...) [to] the social responsibility and [to] not get to use that voice. Yes, I was thinking about that and get really confused after this discussion. (Team discussion March 2016, Teacher 1)

The quotes themselves do not capture the emotional struggle that was present in the conversation. The word "confused" was used many times in the above conversation (Team discussion March 2016) as in many others, as an expression of unsettled emotions and inner conflict. The teachers were struggling to express their thoughts in words and in a language that is not their mother tongue. Despite this struggle, no one withdrew from the group, but all remained committed to continue the communication, trying to make meaning out of what they were experiencing. The variety of emotions present in this particular conversation could be considered as a manifestation of a high level of affect-based trust that had developed among Vilma and the NMC teachers. This incident also highlights the meaning of silence that took place after the initial question. As it turned out, behind the reaction of silence, there was a world of emotions with significant relevance to the entire process of educational change happening in the institution.

Similar moments of confusion and critical affect-based situations can be detected in the project taking place in Vietnam. For example, the aim of highlighting human rights turned out to be ethically complicated as the Vietnamese teachers feared for sanctions from their institutional and political leaders for talking aloud about these matters. To Anna, this came as an unpleasant surprise. In her Swedish music-education context, human rights belong to the taken-for-granted aims, as do the aims of promoting student rights and musical diversity. The Vietnamese teachers appeared to be quite reluctant to discuss human rights with her from this standpoint. In retrospect, this reluctance turned out to be a result of the local history framing the international collaboration. Thus, in their efforts of implementing a new music teacher education in Vietnam, the participating teachers and researchers experienced a paradoxical situation in which national guidelines (e.g. MOET 2001, 2003, 2015; HERA 2005) pointed towards democratization, placing the teachers in a situation where they were supposed to implement change that no one wanted or dared to discuss.

As exemplified in both cases, in intercultural settings the nature of affective practice can be both an advantage and an obstacle towards creative development. As Wetherell (2012) points out, affective practices can be sometimes moveable, sometimes stubbornly fixed, and sometimes existing beyond talk, words, or texts.

5 Intercultural Twists

Since different cultures have their own 'lexicons' for somatic and affective experiences, it is almost inevitable to feel confused from time to time when working in a foreign culture. As stated by Wetherell, "there are no universal emotion concepts" (2012, 41). Therefore in their intercultural collaboration, participants coming from Finland and Sweden encountered distinct challenges. The obvious ones had to do with the researchers' geographical, educational and societal privilege position. The ongoing re-negotiation of goals and the means for achieving them forced the participants to stay flexible, open, and willing to accept the role of a learner in various ways. Stepping into a new context was anything but easy for the researchers. Vilma's field notes in Nepal reveal both frustration and inspiration:

> I don't have any of my familiar surroundings. I am in a vacuum far from my own life, and have to learn everything from the beginning. I have to challenge all my earlier thoughts, there is no other option. In this intercultural work we are all learning from each other. I just have to keep on challenging my own thinking and keep on learning. (Researcher's diary, March 2016)

During the many years of encountering and collaborating with teachers, students and researchers in Vietnam, the constant need to reflect on provoking, surprising and inspiring moments prompted Anna to unlearn her previous conceptions. For her, the issue of 'copying and pasting' Western educational philosophies and structures became a major issue to deal with:

> On a cautionary note, there is a risk [in] setting up a music teacher education [program] that adopts, somewhat uncritically, models of western education, including western models of music education. This could lead to archetypes of music education more closely aligned with European fine arts and music and less connected with the rich cultural tradition in Vietnam. The formalisation of the education process could undermine local artistic heritage and devalue the inclusion of more local community practices in music. (Houmann 2018)

6 Micropolitics and Trust

The literature on affective actions and micropolitics helps us to examine interpersonal relations and the emotional climate in institutional development work from the point of view of trust and the multiple manifestations and forms play out. Trust is developed at the micropolitical level of educational change (Hoyle 1982). Moreover, trusting and trusted individuals are crucial for organisational ends to be met. In his research McAllister (1995) shows that affective trust, in addition to cognitive-based trust, plays an important role in institutional development. He shows the importance of understanding the affective qualities of work-related relationships. Interestingly, he refers to studies that show how affective trust is difficult to build in cross-cultural and multi-ethnic situations. Trust, and more specifically affective trust, is crucial for the outcome of organisational endeavours. However a path leading towards formation of trust, might be challenging in terms of data collection as it might include silences and sensitive data. Thus, in research this is often a neglected area, maybe because of this sensitive character (Hoyle 1982). However, as Bennet (1999) shows, change does happen when there is a trustful micropolitical climate. Thus, it is possible to understand micropolitics both positively and negatively. In educational developmental work, such as in the cases presented in this chapter, the interplay between the culture of an institution and the micropolitical activities within institutions utterly become a matter of an individual teacher-researcher and his/her capacity to find tools for leading the development process.

The importance of trust was recognized by the participants in both projects for whom the work often felt as emotionally intense. In the process in Nepal, the efforts of overcoming emotional challenges related to change were supported by the strong and positive relations between the team members – relations that grew stronger with time.

> Working in a team and supporting each other has led us to build a strong foundation towards making a community which is motivated in growing music education in our society. (Reflective essay, August 2016, Teacher 1)

The emergence of mutual trust and the practice of sharing and learning from each other contributed to the building of necessary confidence for proceeding with the plans and activities.

> Working in a team with the teachers has been fun and [I have been] getting to learn a lot from everyone. Sharing and communicating has made me learn in many different ways. [Learning] ways to approach while teaching with others' shared ideas has been a lot of help. Achieving the set goal with the collaboration and with the team has been rewarding and is building a sense of collective achievement and progress. Writing, reading and sharing the knowledge has made me learn a lot while doing it with the team and learning to teach in a team has been much easier. (Reflective essay, August 2016, Teacher 3)

In both contexts, the positive personal relationships became essential, requiring, however, enough time spent together, in formal and informal settings. As suggested by Hoyle, one is more likely to talk about the micropolitics of institutional life in settings outside the institution:

> When this aspect of organisational life *is* mooted, for example, on teachers' courses, there is a *frisson* of recognition and although course members have many tales to tell of micropolitical skulduggery, they prefer to tell them in the bar rather than submit them to analysis in the serious context of a course discussion. (1986, 125)

This aspect of the development of trust can be clearly seen in the project in Nepal, where the sense of collegiality was decisively heightened in August 2015, when Vilma and the NMC teachers started to play music together. They organised and performed in a fundraising concert for victims of the earthquakes that had shaken Nepal the previous spring. Practicing and making music together also meant spending more time together, increasingly often outside of the official institution meetings. This provided an invaluable opportunity for deeper discussions that contributed to increased mutual understanding about each other's cultures and backgrounds.

In Vietnam, the use of peer coaching and action research provided job-embedded and ongoing professional support and allowed music teachers to work together professionally, thereby eliminating isolation and developing deep and trusting relationships. It encouraged reflection and analysis of music teaching practice regarding teaching through, in and about traditional musics (Houmann 2018). Moreover, these methods created and built on the sense of trust between the Swedish and Vietnamese participants. A joint presentation of the endeavours at the 2010 ISME conference in Beijing turned out to be a key moment in further enhancing that trust. The design of the project included teacher and student exchange that made it possible for the Vietnamese teachers to spend time at the Swedish institution for lengthy periods. Throughout the project the importance of informal gatherings and meetings, such as dinners, concerts, seminars, excursions and parties, became more and more prominent. In fact, it was during these informal moments when various important discussions took place and many confusions, which had occurred during formal meetings, were solved.

7 Breaking the Familiar

Changing patterns of action against the prevailing educational system was one of the key elements in both cases. The construction of the school curriculum in Vietnam concentrated on child-oriented activities, children's experiences, the importance of play, the process of activities, and individual differences; further it sought to create of a learning environment for children, incorporate theory and practice, and link education with production. Many of these themes were new and perceived as challenges to achieve due to the long tradition of Vietnamese culture having always been adult-oriented (Pham Thi Hong 2010). Whereas the old system focused on the outcome, the new curriculum emphasized the process. Due to the reluctance of institutions to keep up with the change to accommodate the 'reinvented' teacher, curriculum renovation is still ongoing (Houmann 2018).

Questions concerning a student-led approach to teaching was a topic of many discussions in Nepal as well. The hierarchical relationship between teachers and students raised memories as the teachers looked back on their own experiences in school, where a fear of teachers and other authorities had been pervasive. As students, they had had little possibility for making decisions in the classrooms. In their own work as teachers, their aim had been to reduce the power gap between teachers and students and in this way to create a more equal learning environment where students' voices would be present in teaching and learning.

> Another very good thing that has grown in me is that I now have confidence in sharing a lot with them [the students]. Earlier I would hesitate to tell the students that I don't know the answer [to] a question, now I do not hesitate to ask them for help and to find the answer together. I think this will help me being a teacher, and also to promote teaching as a learning process. (Reflective essay, August 2016, Teacher 2)

Navigating between an authoritarian, hierarchical way of teaching, where the teacher is seen as the 'person who knows all,' and a more equal, non-hierarchical relationship, where the teacher could be seen as a co-learner, has not been simple and straight-forward for the Nepali teachers. It required plenty of self-reflection and also openness for the teachers to reflect on their own educational past, including even the painful incidents one would rather not talk about. It is clear, however, that at its best the self-reflection led the teachers to a deep sense of accomplishment and motivation and helped them to stay true to their inner values, emphasizing and working towards equality in their classrooms.

> The three-year performance program [that] was developed in the process where I as a teacher started to provide an environment for both the student and myself to learn together. (Reflective essay, August 2016, Teacher 3)

During the process, the four NMC teachers and the teacher-researchers from Finland formed a study group in which they discussed the literature related to various music education practices around the world in relation to their respective contexts. This provided opportunities to relate their current teaching practices to the wider music-education-research and global-teaching communities, which in turn, gave means for self-reflection.

> Moving forward to another step is being self-aware and creating awareness in a team that has helped us in understanding a broader meaning of music education. This is how I begin exploring different dimensions of my teaching and classroom activities. (Reflective essay, August 2015, Teacher 1)

The reflexivity formed through the increased knowledge and understanding of one's own practices thus acted as a catalyst for taking more responsibility and developing deeper agency in one's everyday work.

> Being a teacher, having freedom to be myself and creative with teaching approaches has been new in the program and a way to motivate oneself. (Reflective essay, August 2016, Teacher 3)

In her researcher diary, Vilma reflects how the process opened up a new understanding of diversity for her. Being exposed to a different environment brought up new angles to teaching practices at her home institution and, through that, a heightened sensibility towards students' diverse backgrounds.

The Reinvented Music Teacher-Researcher in the Making: Conducting...   173

Despite the many challenges along the way, participants in both projects identified many benefits from the intercultural collaborative actions. They placed much emphasis on the reinforcement of their role and the possibilities to use their professional skills as teachers.

> Through this partnership [with the Sibelius Academy] we have definitely gained a lot. We are more confident about our work. This has built a sense of ownership and commitment among teachers which is important for any institution. (Reflective essay, August 2016, Teacher 4)

In Vietnam, music teachers had a sense of determination to overcome difficulties to adapt to the new requirements for the renovation of the school. Most of them grew dedicated to music education for the great cause and the benefit of the Vietnamese nation. One of the music teachers in the project stated that students at primary and secondary schools should be able to access music by sound, and art by color. "Let them feel music and art before forcing them to learn in the rigid way teachers are following the guidelines of the Ministry of Education and Training" (Houmann 2018).

8 Discussion and Conclusion

In this chapter, we have identified and discussed the various challenges that individuals participating in intercultural educational development might face. Taking an active role in educational development and regenerating the usual patterns of action at the institutions in Nepal and Vietnam was emotionally challenging and even painful for the teacher-researchers involved. The concept of affective action (Wetherell 2012) helped us highlight how the participants had to deal with a sense of power as well as being powerless during the process of interaction. Differences between cultures, tradition and values, the difficulties in understanding one another, as well as the recognition of privileged positionings caused unsettled emotions in everyone involved. Through facing many challenges along the way, affective actions such as building trust, collegiality beyond national borders, collaborative knowledge-building, increased agency, and a sense of ownership were identified as driving forces. As discovered in the Global Visions project sub-study in Nepal, the important expansion of teachers' horizons to encompass a wider professional community via intercultural interactions, including collaboration, and discussions about scholarly literature, can indeed act as a springboard to transformative professionalism. Indeed, the collaboration provided new contexts in which teacher-researchers were able to rework and rejuvenate practices as they established and developed them.

The experiences reflected in this chapter highlight the importance of various aspects of micropolitics, as outlined by Hoyle (1982). Overcoming the challenges was possible through strong collegiality and support for each other formed within the team in Nepal. This required plenty of time outside the institution in informal settings talking, eating, and making music together. Also, silence played an important role and required a great deal of contextual sensitivity and understanding. Undoubtedly there are challenges in describing, let alone interpreting, *what is not being said*. However, the relevance of silence was clearly manifested throughout the work. In order to understand the events, the most important question often was: What were the questions that remained unanswered?

This chapter argues for the need to consider emotional and cognitive aspects of change in order for the development efforts to succeed. The importance of developing emotional capital of stakeholders through affective actions can enable educational change. Thus, far from static retrospection, what we have demonstrated here is an analysis which aims to provide ways of re-conceptualizing notions of teacher professionalism in music teacher education. It does so by highlighting the tensions that are shaping the discourses and practices of teacher professionalism. We also envision the importance of music education research as a means for reinventing the professional development of music teachers, and as a strategy for developing the knowledge required for teaching music through affective actions. From our perspective, this contributes to establishing a new type of music teacher professional. We would encourage institutions to support strategies that would help rebuild public trust and interest in the music teaching profession and to mobilize music teachers so that they can be in control of the agenda for reclaiming the terrain of music teacher professionalism. Teacher inquiry and building strong supportive teacher-researcher communities, also across national borders as affective action, are initiatives whereby music teacher professionalism can be developed and reinvented.

Developing new forms of music teacher education stands therefore at the core of developing new forms of professionalism and professional identity among music teachers. The complexity of competing needs and the possibilities for conflict of interest and misunderstandings regarding what is seen to be in the best interest of music teachers and their students all have to be carefully negotiated. Indeed, cooperation between various stakeholders can be a veritable minefield. Developing new forms of music teacher professionalism demands the development of new skills. In order to move beyond old forms of music teacher professionalism, the work of music teaching needs to be redefined and reinvented. This is not only in terms of the skills required in classrooms to ensure effective learning outcomes by students, but also in terms of the needs of music teachers as teacher-researchers.

Hence, systematic development of music teachers as an active part of change has the potential to create a music education culture that engages with diversity, trust and respect both within society as a whole and within its education system in particular. This development includes inspiration and innovation, issues of responsibility and sustainability, and brings together government policy, professional involvement, and public engagement. Successful globally aware music education requires highly confident music teachers who are willing to explore new ideas and approaches. Affective actions should not only be put into curricula but should be recognised as a tool for deep mutual and sustainable development. In other words,

The Reinvented Music Teacher-Researcher in the Making: Conducting... 175

it requires making music education a creative and inspiring site of teaching and learning. A music teacher that acts locally but thinks globally, is changing the world with music education.

This publication has been undertaken as part of the Global Visions through Mobilizing Networks project funded by the Academy of Finland (project no. 286162).

References

Appadurai, A. (2004). The capacity to aspire: Culture and the terms of recognition. In V. Rao & M. Walton (Eds.), *Culture and public action* (pp. 59–84). Stanford: Stanford University Press.

Bennet, J. (1999). Micropolitics in the Tasmanian context of school reform. *School Leadership and Management, 19*(2), 197–101.

Brøske, B. Å., & Storsve, V. (Eds.). (2013). *Løft blikket, gjør en forskjell. Erfaringer og ring-virkninger fra et musikkprosjekt i Libanon.* Oslo: Norges musikkhøgskole.

Cain, T. (2008). The characteristics of action research in music education. *British Journal of Music Education, 25*, 283–313.

Ethno. (2016). http://www.ethno-world.org/. Accessed 4 Nov 2016.

Hebert, D., & Sæther, E. (2013). "Please, give me space": Findings and implications of the GLOMUS intercultural music camp, Ghana 2011. *Music Education Research, 16*(4), 418–435.

Higher Education Reform Agenda (HERA). (2005). *Fundamental and comprehensive reform of higher education in Vietnam 2006–2020.* Resolution no. 14/2005/NQ-CP, dated 2 November 2005.

Houmann, A. (2018). Traditional musics in music education – The sound of (r)evolution. In *Traditional musics in the modern world: Identity, transmission, evolution and challenges,* Leung, B-W (Ed.), *Traditional musics in the modern world: Identity, transmission, evolution and challenges* (pp. 113–128). New York: Springer.

Hoyle, E. (1982). Micropolitics of educational organisations. *Educational Management and Administration, 10*, 87–98.

Hoyle, E. (1986). *The politics of school management.* London: Hodder and Soughton.

McAllister, D. J. (1995). Affect- and cognition-based trust as foundations for interpersonal cooperation in organizations. *Academy of Management Journal, 38*(1), 24–59.

McLaren, P. (1998). *Life in schools. An introduction to critical pedagogy in the foundations of education.* New York: Longman.

Ministry of Education and Training MOET. (2001). *The education development strategic plan for 2001–2010* (Decision no. 201/2001/QD-TTG, 28 December 2001). Hanoi: Ministry of Education and Training MOET.

Ministry of Education and Training MOET. (2003). *Report on the status quo of devolution in Vietnam's educational management and recommendations* (Project in Assistance to the MOET No ala/8-o124). Hanoi: Ministry of Education and Training MOET.

Ministry of Education and Training MOET. (2015). *Viet Nam: Education for all 2015 national review.* [Online]. http://unesdoc.unesco.org/images/0023/002327/232770e.pdf. Accessed 1 May 2018.

Pham Thi Hong, T. (2010). Implementing a student-centered learning approach at Vietnamese Higher Education Institutions. *Journal of Future Studies, 15*(1), 21–38.

Pillay, V. (2004). Towards a broader understanding of the micropolitics of educational change. *Perspectives in Education, 22*(1), 129–138.

Sæther, E. (2003). *The Oral University. Attitudes to music teaching and learning in the Gambia.* Malmö: Malmö Academy of Music, Lund University.

Schippers, H., & Grant, C. (Eds.). (2016). *Sustainable futures for music cultures. An ecological perspective.* New York: Oxford University Press.

Westerlund, H., Partti, H., & Karlsen, S. (2015). Teaching as improvisational experience: Student music teachers' reflections on learning during a bi-cultural exchange project. *Research Studies in Music Education, 37*, 55–75. https://doi.org/10.1177/1321103X15590698.

Wetherell, M. (2012). *Affect and emotion: A new social science understanding.* London: Sage.

12

Bridging Musical Worlds: Musical Collaboration Between Student Musician-Educators and South Sudanese Australian Youth

Kathryn Marsh, Catherine Ingram, and Samantha Dieckmann

Abstract This chapter reports results of an innovative contemporary model of applied urban ethnomusicological research investigating the effects of collaborative musical engagement between students from the Sydney Conservatorium of Music (SCM) and South Sudanese Australian youth in the culturally diverse metropolis of Sydney, Australia. The *Bridging Musical Worlds* project was conducted in 2016 during a period of extraordinary global migration. In Australia, children and young people of South Sudanese heritage occupy a prominent place in emerging communities in many large urban areas but are often subject to discriminatory discourse. The project enabled SCM music education students to engage in reciprocal teaching and learning opportunities relating to South Sudanese music and culture and globalised popular music. In this chapter we outline the major outcomes of the project, including social inclusion through collaborative participatory music making, and explore the impact of these musical activities on the development of cultural competence and intercultural understanding for tertiary students.

Keywords Applied urban ethnomusicology · Cultural competence · Intercultural understanding · Preservice music education · Service learning

1 Introduction

The role of the ethnomusicologist-teacher educator has resulted in particular approaches to the training of music teachers in a number of tertiary institutions internationally. Many university music departments around the world involve students in music ensembles taught by musicians who are experts in particular cultural

---

K. Marsh (✉) · C. Ingram
Sydney Conservatorium of Music, The University of Sydney, Sydney, Australia
e-mail: kathryn.marsh@sydney.edu.au; catherine.ingram@sydney.edu.au

S. Dieckmann
Faculty of Music, University of Oxford, Oxford, UK
e-mail: samantha.dieckmann@music.ox.ac.uk

traditions, or offer service learning opportunities entailing students travelling to remote or overseas locations to interact musically with people living in these areas (e.g. Bartleet et al. 2014, 2016; Broeske-Danielsen 2013; Campbell 2010; Robinson 2005; Westerlund et al. 2015; Wiggins 2005). This chapter outlines the outcomes of an innovative contemporary model for applied urban, musical ethnographic research, involving a conjunction between applied ethnomusicology and service learning of tertiary music students, with particular reference to a case study of a recent collaborative research and teaching project undertaken with undergraduate music teacher-education students at the Sydney Conservatorium of Music (SCM), University of Sydney, Australia.

2 Institutional Context

SCM provides a range of undergraduate and postgraduate programs in performance, composition, musicology and music education. The 4-year undergraduate music education degree program at SCM, the Bachelor of Music (Music Education), aims to train prospective music teachers for future employment, principally in secondary schools. In the state of New South Wales (NSW) in which Sydney is located, the teaching of music is mandated at both primary and secondary levels (for students aged 5–12 years and 12–18 years, respectively),[1] meaning that graduates of the SCM music education program are prepared by course content and in-school practice teaching placements to teach school students from 5 to 18 years of age, with an emphasis on the secondary level.

For many years, the music education degree program at this institution has encompassed a range of learning experiences reflecting the strong disposition of the program's teacher-educators, who are responsible for facilitating the development of students' intercultural understanding. Students' learning experiences are delineated within program content, including specific subjects focused on cultural diversity in music education, Australian Indigenous musics, Balinese gamelan (Dunbar-Hall 2009) and other Asian music ensembles (including the recently established Chinese Music Ensemble), which may be studied as an elective. The majority of these subjects to a greater or lesser degree involve direct interaction with culture-bearers, both inside and beyond the institutional context of SCM, who teach about specific aspects of their music and its sociocultural import. There have been additional opportunities for students to engage further, for example, by participating in overseas modes of delivery of units on Balinese music and dance (Dunbar-Hall 2012; Rowley and Dunbar-Hall 2013).

---

[1] There is a mandatory 100 h of Music tuition for all students in the junior secondary school in NSW, after which students can elect to study Music either up to Year 10, and/or as a senior subject for the Higher School Certificate (HSC). Learning activities include performance, composition, listening and musicological study across a range of musical contexts and styles.

To a large extent such initiatives have been driven by the highly multicultural nature of Australian society. As a nation that has been established and expanded through successive waves of immigration, both voluntary and involuntary, Australia is highly culturally and linguistically diverse, with a population identifying with more than 270 ancestries and speaking more than 260 languages, including those of Australian First Peoples (Department of Immigration and Citizenship 2011).

These initiatives have also developed as a result of the dual identities of the SCM teacher-educators, several of whom are also ethnomusicological researchers. The imperative for inclusion of field research with people representing minority cultures in Australia has underpinned content and assessment in at least one mandatory subject for trainee teachers for nearly two decades (Marsh 2005). Prospects for developing learning experiences of this kind have increasingly been enhanced as strong collaborative partnerships between staff members of SCM with ethnomusicological and pedagogical expertise have continued to emerge.

Impetus has also come from The University of Sydney Strategic Plan, which sees the development of cultural competence – that is, the ability "to work productively, collaboratively and openly in diverse groups and across cultural boundaries" (The University of Sydney 2016, 32) – as inherent to the university educational experience of all students. The university has sought to "Embed cultural competence as a learning outcome in every degree …; provide meaningful learning activities that take advantage of the cultural diversity within the University community, including group projects requiring collaboration skills; [and] ensure that professional programs develop cultural understanding and intercultural capabilities relevant to likely practice" (The University of Sydney 2016, 58). In this chapter we acknowledge that intercultural competence may be defined in multiple ways (Deardorff 2006), but for ease of discussion adopt the university's designation provided above, in conjunction with the more nuanced definition provided by Deardorff: "the ability to communicate effectively and appropriately in intercultural situations based on one's intercultural knowledge, skills, and attitudes" (2006, 247–248).

Just as cultural competence is deemed to be one of the six required "graduate qualities" of students of the University of Sydney, intercultural understanding is one of the planned cross-curricular "general capabilities." These general capabilities are outcomes of the Australian Curriculum, which states that "Intercultural understanding involves students learning about and engaging with diverse cultures in ways that recognise commonalities and differences, create connections with others and cultivate mutual respect" (Australian Curriculum Assessment and Reporting Authority n.d.). Implicit in such definitions is an understanding that the term, 'intercultural' must also acknowledge "the complexity of locations, identities and modes of expression in a global world, and the desire to raise awareness, foster intercultural dialogue and facilitate understanding across and between cultures" (Burnard et al. 2016, 1–2). Thus, general curricular directives both in relation to the training of teaching graduates and their concomitant implementation of school curriculum require the development of cultural competence and intercultural understanding in SCM music education students.

In implementing such directives within an institutional framework, the ongoing practices of the music education program and the specific project discussed in this chapter are in keeping with cross-curricular approaches to intercultural communicative competence found at all levels of education that involve "being able to change perspectives, empathy, openness and willingness to interact in culturally diverse contexts" (Leh et al. 2015, 100). These practices also reflect philosophies of intercultural music education that are articulated by Carson and Westvall, who see the various forms of engagement with "diversified normality" as "transformative aspects of education" (2016, 29). Such engagement is mutually beneficial for students within institutions and the members of the multiple communities with which they engage, in that it creates

> spaces for intercultural dialogues that, rather than promoting assimilation, allow for richer modes of interaction. This happens from all sides. It is not merely that individuals from marginalized communities need to be able to develop the skills necessary to engage with the dominant group's values, but all agents should aim to cultivate a view of society that includes difference and variety as fundamental aspects. (Carson and Westvall 2016, 39)

Carson and Westvall (2016) see that such approaches reduce boundaries between institutions and communities and involve broader and more flexible definitions of what constitutes "community." In addition, recent demographic changes, both within Australia and globally, necessitate more urgent and further enhancement of cultural competence and intercultural understanding in the educators of the future. As Jones argues, music education has particular potential to address the challenges of such cultural diversification since music "serves as a perfect mediating space ... [to] develop a sense of shared identity and intercultural understanding ... [and] teach skills for democratic action such as leading and following, teamwork, debate, [and] compromise" (2010, 295). Despite the long-established advocacy for intercultural music education at all levels (see e.g. Oehrle 1996; O'Flynn 2005), questions remain regarding how music teachers can best be prepared to realize these visions.

3 Constructing Intercultural Music Teacher Education

Although academic coursework and in-school placements are central to music teacher education, research has shown that the development of intercultural understanding requires additional, and intentionally framed, experiences with cultural diversity (Emmanuel 2005). Even where tertiary educators and curricula promote the inclusion of culturally diverse music materials by preservice teachers, the use of such content is rarely modelled for them in primary and secondary placements (Joseph and Southcott 2009). This lack of in situ experience perpetuates the exclusion of multicultural musics from the classroom. However, training preservice music teachers to work with heterogeneous student populations in contexts that may vary greatly from their own educational upbringing moves beyond the inclusion of culturally diverse music content. Teaching in these complex, and for some confronting, situations requires a high level of pedagogical reflexivity informed and enabled by intercultural competence. It involves not only an expansion of notions of legitimate music education materials, but also continued reflection on what music education itself entails (Burton et al. 2012). Exploring the boundaries of music and music education directs attention towards some of the primary goals of intercultural teacher education more broadly: to shift future teachers from ethnocentric to ethnorelative ways of viewing the world, and to develop critical understandings of the "sociocultural dynamic of schooling that is the foundation of culturally-responsive teaching" (Marx and Moss 2011, 36).

Marx and Moss (2011) suggest that conventional domestic in-school placements with culturally diverse student populations do not lend themselves to this sort of perspective transformation, noting that the wider educational system and culture within which most participating schools are encompassed only serve to reinforce the preservice teachers' sense of educational norms. Within such experiences, any 'difference' encountered in the student population can continue to be considered exceptional. Preservice teachers will tend to identify with the school and the teacher, and are not prompted to question the practices in which they have likely been enculturated throughout their own schooling experiences, some of which might negatively affect marginalized students. It is for this reason that tertiary intercultural education often involves immersion experiences, in which "students are put in situations where they have to learn to function within a different cultural context and among members of the host culture who perceive them as cultural others" (Marx and Moss 2011, 42). In the field of intercultural music teacher education, international exchange and cross-institutional collaboration projects have been found to be suitable contexts for such immersion (Broeske-Danielsen 2013; Brøske this volume; Burton et al. 2012; Kallio and Westerlund this volume; Sæther 2013).

The project described in the current chapter took an alternative approach to intercultural immersion. As will be explained, preservice music teachers were situated in a relatively local, community-based setting in which they (and the music education activities they implemented) were seen as culturally Other. Further, the students with whom they worked attended an excursion at the preservice teachers' tertiary institution, inviting reflection on the institute of the Conservatory – and, by extension, classical Western music education – as a 'different' cultural context. By structuring this exchange in its domestic setting, the project was positioned at the intersection of community, cultural diversity and institutionalized music education in the context of Sydney. In line with O'Flynn's argument that, "systems of music education best advance with due regard to the social realities in which that education takes place" (2005, 197), the project aimed to develop intercultural competences and understandings that were directly transferable to the settings of the preservice teachers' future employment.

4 The Bridging Musical Worlds Project

The Bridging Musical Worlds project took place in early 2016, in the context of almost unprecedented global migration flows. Driven by flight from conflict, economic inequity and other factors, refugees and voluntary migrants sought resettlement in Europe, Sub-Saharan Africa, the Middle East, South East Asia, North America and Australia (UNHCR 2016). Among the many migrant groups who have settled in Australia, the South Sudanese Australian community represents a substantial proportion of newly arrived migrants and comprises many people who are refugees who have fled from continuing conflict in South Sudan. Members of this community identify with a diverse range of South Sudanese ethnicities and cultural groups, with South Sudanese Australian children and young people – many of whom were born in Australia or have lived most of their lives outside South Sudan – occupying a prominent place in the communities in many large urban areas, including in Sydney (Cassity and Gow 2006; Dieckmann 2016; Westoby 2009).[2]

Child refugees are frequently viewed as victims of their traumatic circumstances, and psycho-social assistance is seen as a necessary requirement for their resettlement. For refugee and newly arrived immigrant children this often means provision of support by adult members of the dominant society to enhance social inclusion. However, while such support is undeniably valuable, more recent research indicates that children and young people who are refugees or voluntary migrants also function as agentive social actors, and may consciously employ strategies that assist with meeting their own emotional and social needs (Hart 2014). Recent studies point to the role of music in providing collaborative avenues for enhancing social inclusion, identity construction, and self-expression for young refugees and immigrants (Karlsen 2013; Marsh 2012, 2013, 2015, 2017; Marsh and Dieckmann 2016).

The Bridging Musical Worlds project aimed to investigate the effects of collaborative musical engagement between South Sudanese Australian youth and music education students from the Sydney Conservatorium of Music in relation to:

- Children and young people's musical engagement with activities, musical preferences, forms of self-expression and developing musical identities;
- The opportunities for social inclusion of children within participatory musical communities created by musical collaborations; and
- The opportunities for development of cultural competence and intercultural understanding provided by these activities for SCM students.

---

[2] Civil war between the north and south of Sudan has been endemic since Sudan obtained independence from Britain and Egypt in 1956. The initial refugee flows from South Sudan therefore predate 2011 when South Sudan gained independence from Sudan. However, continued conflict both in South Sudan and in southern and western regions of Sudan, including Darfur, South Kordofan and Blue Nile, has resulted in ongoing refugee flows and internal displacement of people from these areas (Cockett 2010; LeRiche and Arnold 2012). Thus, refugees and migrants from both South Sudan and Sudan have entered Australia over the past two decades (Refugee Council of Australia 2016).

The engagement of South Sudanese Australian children and young people with creative music activity, in collaboration with students from the Sydney Conservatorium of Music, occurred under the auspices of the SCM and the Language Discovery (LD)[3] Program in Sydney. The LD Program is a community-based literacy program for children and families of refugee backgrounds. It provides educational assistance and mentoring, and promotes social inclusion and support for children and families through a variety of means including special communal activities involving sport, music, dance and other youth-focused opportunities.

The collaboration came about through SCM ethnomusicologist Catherine Ingram's ongoing research into the music-making of South Sudanese Australians as a cultural minority group in Australia. In her research, Ingram is seeking to better understand how music may influence cultural minorities' engagement with their wider social context. She had also been involved as a volunteer with LD for more than 1 year, and had received an invitation from LD personnel to organize a program of music activities for a group of Sudanese Australian[4] young people. Together with co-author Marsh, Ingram enlisted the services of SCM students in their final year of the music education degree, as part of their compulsory *Cultural Diversity in Music Education* (CDIME) unit of study (coordinated and taught by Marsh). The project subsequently evolved into an interactive, service-learning opportunity for the students to work with Sudanese Australian youth in Sydney. The 34 students enrolled in CDIME were offered the chance either to engage in the service-learning provision or in an alternative set of activities. All students chose to take part in at least the first and third service-learning activities at SCM (outlined below), while seven students volunteered to participate in the full set of service-learning activities at both SCM and LD.

The project involved the development and implementation of a program of creative music activities, focusing on the informal learning methods previously articulated by Green (2008) and Harwood and Marsh (2012), and also promoting active collaboration between the South Sudanese Australian youth and the SCM students. The project had a multifaceted approach, with the following components:

1. A preliminary experiential workshop at SCM provided by a South Sudanese Australian musician, Mary Mamour, to all SCM students in the final-year cohort. The workshop was intended to develop knowledge about South Sudanese music and culture, the ongoing violence that had precipitated the large migratory flows, and the experiences of South Sudanese Australians prior to and post migration to Australia, with the aim of enhancing initial cultural understanding. The workshop included immersive learning of Jieng (or Dinka) songs and dances

---

[3] For ethical reasons, "Language Discovery" and its acronym, "LD" are pseudonyms.

[4] LD aims to fulfil educational needs of young people from both South Sudan and Sudan, though the majority of these young people are from what is now South Sudan or have parents from South Sudan. For this reason, the young people who took part in the LD activities are sometimes designated as South Sudanese Australian and sometimes Sudanese Australian. It should also be noted that not all young people in the program are newly arrived and some have been born in Australia to families who arrived as refugees.

184 Music Teacher Education: Future Perspectives

associated with everyday activities, Christian worship, and social occasions, using culturally relevant pedagogy. The workshop was supplemented by online written and audiovisual materials (provided by Ingram) relating to the above-mentioned relevant cultural and social aspects.

2. A series of three Saturday afternoon workshops were conducted by the seven SCM student volunteers and Marsh with Sudanese Australian youth over a period of 4 weeks in the LD community setting, under the guidance of Ingram. Drawing on Marsh's (2013) prior research with South Sudanese Australian refugee children and Ingram's and Dieckmann's research and experience in the community (Dieckmann 2016; Ingram and Mamour 2016), the initial repertoire choice was designed to accommodate previously observed musical preferences of South Sudanese Australian children for particular genres of popular music, especially as performed by mainstream black artists whose songs are globally disseminated. The workshop sessions consisted of an initial performance by the SCM students of a popular song, as an aural and visual model, followed by predominantly aural learning of the vocal, guitar, ukulele, keyboard, bass and drum parts of the song in small instrument groupings. A separate set of creative activities was simultaneously offered for younger children. At the end of each workshop there was an informal performance of the learnt repertoire to the children's parents and LD coordinators and volunteers.

3. A half-day visit to SCM. This visit occurred in the school holidays during the project period, and the Sudanese Australian children and young people worked with the whole 4th-year Music Education cohort to develop their collaborative musical creations, recreations and performances in conjunction with SCM students. They also had a chance to observe performances of similar musical genres given by the SCM class group. The visit culminated in a performance of a popular song by all SCM students and LD young people, followed by brief stringed-instrument performances by SCM students, and a tour of SCM. In addition to the visit being intended to facilitate development of SCM students' cultural competence, it also enabled the Sudanese Australian young people to augment both their musical skills and experiences and their educational aspirations through collaborative interaction with the SCM students. The capacity for the enhancement of social inclusion through these various activities was increased by the presence of several parents, young siblings (who joined in the early childhood session) and other members of the related South Sudanese Australian community, including Mary Mamour (who led some unplanned, spontaneous singing at one point, as discussed later), in addition to the LD coordinators and volunteers. Forty-six Sudanese Australian participants, from infants to adults, participated in the visit.

Research methods for this project were influenced by the three authors' prior experience as ethnomusicologists employing ethnography as a principal form of research with members of the South Sudanese Australian community, and as music teachers in various educational settings. All acted as participant observers during the project. Data for this ethnographic case study were collected through observations at both LD and SCM, interviews and informal conversations with participating SCM students, and research conversations with Sudanese Australian youth, parents, and other community members. Video recordings were made of Mary Mamour's sessions and the culminating performances of the SCM–LD workshop day, and the student interviews were audio and video recorded for later transcription. All student interviews were conducted on 4 May 2016, soon after the project had been completed. Documents in the form of email and Google Docs communications, preparation materials and written expressions of thanks were also collected as data.

The discussion in this chapter focuses on how the various project activities appeared to affect the SCM students, with the primary data source being the student interviews. The data were analyzed using grounded theory methods (Charmaz 2014; Corbin and Strauss 2008) and findings are outlined chronologically below according to resultant emergent themes.

5 Understanding Participatory Music Making

The broader results of the research, as outlined below, indicate that outcomes reported by preservice music teachers may not always align with those for which intercultural service learning programs are primarily designed: namely, the development of intercultural competence and understanding towards establishing reflexive and culturally-responsive teaching skills. Although developing SCM students' intercultural competence was one of the core aims of Bridging Musical Worlds, SCM student interviews revealed that, for the students, the practicalities and pedagogies involved in teaching music in a relatively unstructured community context were also very significant. The forms of cultural immersion and information provided by the initial parts of the project did not prepare the SCM students for the disjunct between the teaching and learning experiences that they had previously encountered in schools, and the more chaotic environment of a community setting, even though they had been briefed about its fluid nature and the students' need for flexibility:

> Hailey: I knew that it wasn't going to be a really formal setting, from what they'd said. I think I expected to have a little more control, so it was a bit, it was a bit interesting going in and sort of, I think the first thing we saw was kids just running around this room screaming. And like, we'd put instruments down, they'd come run, pick up the instrument, run off with it and go outside. We're like, "No! That's really expensive!" …. Kids that were coming over with their lunch and using the djembes as a table for their pizza, and we're like, "Oh okay, alright. Well you know what, fine." So, you sort of had to let go of the, "This is what I want exactly to happen." And you've just got to be like, "Let's see what we can teach them in the time we've got, and just make it fun and enjoyable." So, once I'd accepted that, it was really great.
>
> Sam: Letting go….
>
> Hailey: Quite cathartic actually.

Learning to 'let go' and act in a more facilitative role involved a change in orientation from focusing on a careful teaching sequence (for example, to develop a particular musical product or specific skill), to focusing on encouraging and engaging the students in musical participation. This change of orientation presented a considerable challenge that all of the students working in the LD setting articulated as their initial primary concern. It required an inclusive approach, as exemplified by Toby's reframing of his guitar activities with the LD young people:

> by that stage it was more like, "Have a go. We can all have a go at the different guitars, and play around on the amps. I'll teach you some stuff but I think it's being able to get the instruments in your hands and being able to have a play at it" which was the main target, I think.

The adoption of this mode of action is in keeping with the tenets of community music practice, as outlined by Higgins, including the utilization of "flexible facilitation modes" and commitment to "multiple participant/facilitator relationships and processes" (Higgins 2012, 5). However, in the students' comments, there is also a developing acknowledgement of another characteristic of music-making in community settings – the recognition that "participants' social and personal growths are as important as their musical growth" (Higgins 2012, 5).

The social dimensions of musical participation have also been a primary concern in ethnomusicology in recent decades, as reflected in the title of Turino's (2008) seminal *Music as Social Life: The Politics of Participation*. Higgins's "multiple participant/facilitator relationships and processes" (2012, 5) resonate with what Turino terms "participatory performance," in which there are "only participants and potential participants performing different roles, and the primary goal is to involve the maximum number of people in some performance role" (2008, 26). Although Higgins is focusing on a pedagogical role, and Turino on a performative one, in reality, these both merge within the context of a participatory musical community. Participatory music making is described by Turino as an activity in which "stylized sound and motion are conceptualized most importantly as heightened social interaction. In participatory music making one's primary attention is on the activity, on the doing and on the other participants, rather than on an end product resulting from the activity" (2008, 28). Turino associates this form of music making with the development of "social synchrony" (2008, 41), entailing "a crucial underpinning of feelings of social comfort, belonging and identity" (2008, 44), to which this discussion returns below with a further examination of student responses to and outcomes of the project.

The tension between students' nascent awareness of music as integral to the social benefit of community and their developing intercultural understanding emerged when students were asked to explicitly address the intercultural aspects of the service learning program. They discussed both the pedagogical implications of the everyday music practices of the Sudanese Australian youth, and the ways that cultural and behavioral differences affected the interpersonal and relational dimensions of their teaching.

6 Understanding Music in the Lives of South Sudanese Australians: Pedagogical Implications

For many years, the CDIME subject has, as a matter of course, encompassed the involvement of musicians who are a part of the culturally diverse Sydney environment. The rationale for this has been to enable students to understand that skilled musicians who can share their authentic knowledge of culturally contextualized music live within the local community and are not part of an exoticized Other. Students are encouraged to consider the benefits of involving musicians who may be seen as 'culture-bearers' within music education programs in schools to dispel stereotypical notions of music and culture and to experience the variability of 'authentic' musical experiences which may be related to folk, classical, popular, jazz, or fusion forms of musical and kinesthetic expression (Marsh 2005). However, the rationale for Mary Mamour's session as a form of preparation for the LD activities was not immediately apparent to some of the students.

> Joseph: I'd say that Kathy wouldn't have brought in somebody from South Sudan to teach us, and, you know, spend a whole session on South Sudanese music without the intent of us getting something out of it. So, I knew we'd be getting something out of it, and I had absolutely, you know, I knew we would. I just couldn't see directly how it would relate to … the LD project.

Partially, this lack of immediate perception of relevance was due to the seeming disjunct between the contemporary, mainstream popular music from the USA that was taught by SCM students (and favored by the young people from LD) and the kinds of repertoire performed and taught by Mary, which were in the Jieng language and ranged from traditional songs to newly composed Christian praise songs.

> Julia: it was much more traditional music or religious music, whereas LD – we were told – they love hip hop, they're young.... So that's what we stuck to.

The inclusion of contemporary popular music in the teaching repertoire was directed by the LD children themselves, following an informal survey of their musical preferences. However, research shows that while popular music from the UK and USA is significant in culturally and linguistically diverse students' lives, in private settings they also listen to international popular music connected to their families' languages and countries of origin, though sometimes in unpredictable ways (Carson and Westvall 2016; Karlsen 2013; Marsh 2012, 2013). Therefore, intercultural music education cannot solely involve content influenced by globalized media, which in itself establishes a type of "normative 'comfort zone'" (Carson and Westvall 2016, 45), and must also include sustained engagement with a range of vernacular music practices (O'Flynn 2005).

The importance of understanding the broader implications of culture in a learning context was evident to some of the students following Mary's workshop.

Julia: She [Mary] said a lot about her cultural context, I suppose. Like some of the lecture was just, her explaining about culture, about making baby handbags and stuff. Which was really interesting, we were, "Oh wow, we didn't expect this." Because we were expecting just music, but you can't put them in two categories. It's not mutually exclusive, like music and culture, like it is the same thing. So, I suppose in that way it made us realize, yeah, it's really important to them....

Jenny: I think it's always good to have background knowledge on the culture that you're going in, before. Yeah, sort of interacting with them and everything, just so that you can be culturally sensitive to what they may have experienced or what their parents have experienced.

Julia also discussed the information that Mary provided on the ongoing dislocation and trauma experienced by refugee families in the resettlement process, and the need to develop sensitivity to possible behavioral manifestations in the music-learning context:

And she mentioned that some of them are, they're from broken homes, or their siblings have died.... Yeah and so we had to be quite sensitive to that. And sometimes [we] had kids crying because they couldn't play a drum, but part of you is like, "It's so much more than that. Their whole experience goes beyond that."

As the project developed, the students also began to recognize certain culturally congruent aspects of pedagogy utilized in Mary's workshop and their possible application in the LD setting. This was most evident in relation to imitative ways of learning, which were often structurally reinforced by call and response elements in the Jieng songs that were taught. Although learning by imitation was certainly practiced within some SCM music education subjects (especially in relation to forms of oral/aural musical teaching typical of informal learning), there was still a natural inclination for some students to rely on the more formal approaches that characterized Western classical music training in other areas of the SCM curriculum. Julia described her initial struggle to learn music with unfamiliar structures in this way:

Well she [Mary] taught us very differently.... She'd teach you vocally a melody or a rhythm, and ... it was really hard to let go. Let go of those formulated structures you're trying to find, and just kind of copy her and let it settle.... So, it was really different because it was all just about copying her, not about trying to analyze it, or whatever.

These methods of oral transmission, once accepted, were easily deployed for teaching song melodies, drum rhythms or guitar riffs to the young people from LD, as described by Toby:

Yeah, so the way Mary taught us to do, to sing and to do the songs that she was teaching us, I think was something we implemented in LD a little bit. Probably more the singers than me on the guitars, but at least with, like when we performed the songs it was very much just get everyone included because she would sing the line, and we'd sing it back, that kind of thing. And I think that would work very well with the LD group, because then you can jump straight into music without having to learn guitar or learn ukulele straight away. And with adding the percussion, I think that worked very well.

Other SCM students working with the LD young people on a range of musical activities found the methods of teaching that they observed in Mary's session to be equally applicable throughout.

> Hailey: Yeah, oh there was just little behavioral things. And she showed us videos of celebrations like weddings, and it was, I found that really interesting because it.... The learning experience, like... they'd shown us one video ... but it was, like they were all doing a dance together, and there was one person in the middle of them all that was leading the dance. And everyone just copied. She didn't say, "This is what you need to do, step, step, step, do it." It was just, she'd just do it and they'd play with it. So then I noticed, we did a similar thing with the drumming. We were just like, she'd just sing through the song and they'd copy us. And they'd respond to that much better than, "Play this rhythm," that would've just went over their head.

SCM students' perceptions of cultural behavioral norms, and the ways that they affected teacher-student interaction in the service-learning program, resonated with broader discussions about the rationale for and implementation of intercultural music education in tertiary settings.

7 Music as Lived Experience: The Interpersonal/Relational Dimension

The social dimensions of music making, as signifiers of varying aspects of culture and of lived experience, were conveyed to many students through the immersive experience of Mary's workshop, and had quite a profound effect on their understandings of culturally inclusive music education.

> Ella: I thought it was a turning point for me. With this cultural diversity, I was like, "Well why are we doing this?" Like it didn't really click. "Why are we at this subject?" Until Kathy said, "It's really important that we explore different cultures." "Yes, yes." But then when Mary came in, it was like, "Oh! Okay that's why." Because you're actually getting someone from a different culture and it's really, I thought that was just a turning point.
>
> Luke: It energizes you though, as well. To see someone live it.

It was especially interesting that Ella, who was bicultural, and who persuaded her Vietnamese mother to teach her to play the Dàn Tranh (a Vietnamese zither) for her presentation on her fieldwork project relating to music in her mother's life, had not initially recognized the need for cultural diversity in music education. Similarly, for Clea, one of the few interviewed students who had experienced a culturally diverse approach to music education in her secondary schooling, the personal engagement with Mary created an additional meaningful dimension to the experience.

> Clea: It just gives you a bit more context, because a lot of the time – especially in high school – it felt like you were just ticking off the dot points.
>
> Luke: Yeah, yeah. "Let's play African music."
>
> Clea: You'd come to music and it'd be, "That's right, we have to do African music." And your Anglo-Saxon teacher will teach you it. It's not – like it's wonderful that it exists in the curriculum and that sort of thing, but it's not....

190 Music Teacher Education: Future Perspectives

Ella: And they're giving it a go.

Clea: Oh yeah, that's wonderful, they're trying their hardest, but it gave a little bit of something more when some, a South Sudanese lady, Mary, actually came in and talked to us herself.

This immersive experience extended to the social interactions with South Sudanese Australian children and other members of the community on the day of the LD workshops at SCM. The main music education teaching room was packed with children, parents and other members of the community (including Mary Mamour) for the initial performances by the SCM students and the final combined performances. Following the small-group learning activities (held in various suitable locations outside the main music-education room), everyone returned to the main room for refreshments. The large number of people occupying the room created a certain level of apparent chaos that was unnerving for some students, but also provided an opportunity for interaction and engagement and further learning for others. In the very crowded and noisy space, Mary initiated some short impromptu performances of drumming, singing and dance, in which both children and parents, as well as some SCM students, participated sporadically at will, thereby extending upon previously established musical connections. During these activities, there was lively talking within and between the various groups. Julia, who participated in the weekend LD workshops, found this experience of holistic community engagement enlightening:

It was, I suppose that whole community aspect came into it a lot stronger because you have mums at the back making tea, at the back. And grandma's watching, and kids crying and it was so funny because they're so used to it, this is music for them. It's not meant to be on a stage, lights on, audience in darkness. Yeah, it's just the way they do it.

While these perceptions of engagement with culture were, perhaps, still somewhat essentialist in nature, it represented another example of Julia's significant realization of the non-dichotomous nature of music and culture, and the personal investment of members of the community in the multiple activities, mores and relationships that constitute culture. Hailey stated:

It was really nice ... even just seeing the way they interact with each other, and their parents, and seeing the way their parents interacted with each other, I sort of really enjoyed that aspect.

Jenny also commented on these interactions, but also on the relationships that were evidently developing between the SCM students and the Sudanese Australian young people as a result of the LD musical activities, even in the space of these few relatively short encounters. She noted:

Well I thought... it was just really interesting to see how they all engaged with each other, and to see... I mean, even after just one session, they were even pretty close to the people that went to LD.... And they were like, you could tell that they knew who they were, and that they were kind of more inclined to go towards them. But other than that, I think it was, it was great having them in this room.... It felt very community in here.

This "community" encompassed multiple communities, including young and adult members of the Sudanese Australian community and SCM students, brought together by mutual engagement in participatory music-making. As Julia had noticed, this music-making had "no artist audience distinctions" (Turino 2008, 26). The success of this mutual engagement was clearly demonstrated by the excitement of the Sudanese Australian children and young people who, in the new surroundings, with multiple tutors to assist their learning and much greater availability of instruments and equipment than in the LD setting, "were just having a blast" (Julia). It was evident from the interviewed students that they, too, found the experience exciting and fulfilling, as expressed by Julia and Luke.

> Julia: It was really rewarding I guess, because… there's nothing like teaching kids that want to learn, I guess that's the main thing. They were all very, very interested and engaged, and you love that.

> Luke: I was right in my element, I think. Just jamming, playing, doing things right there, thinking on my feet…. And it was great, they all reacted really positively and I felt pretty comfortable with everything we were doing so I felt right in my, right in my shell. This is what I'm here to do. This is what I've been put on this earth to do.

These accounts of the participatory musical experience resonate with Turino's description of "a kind of heightened, immediate social intercourse" in participatory performance:

> when the performance is going well, differences among participants melt away as attention is focused on the seamlessness of sound and motion. At such moments, moving together and sounding together in a group creates a direct sense of *being* together and of deeply felt similarity… among participants. (Turino 2008, 43)

The rewards for all participants were evident in an exuberant performance of "Count on Me" (Mars et al. 2010, track 9) by Sudanese Australian youth and SCM students at the end of the day at SCM, which was enthusiastically received by the adult audience and followed by plaudits from the LD organizers. This performance (and those in following workshops) was not, however, seen as an endpoint by many of the students.

> Joanne: Well you know, you've only just started, you start to see some personalities coming out in kids and you're like, "Oh man." You know, you just see things and you're like, I really want to…

> Luke: Continue.

> Ella: Watch it grow.

> Joanne: Yeah watch it grow.

Such experiences represent what Carson and Westvall constitute as "the beginning of the conversation" (2016, 39), which may ultimately result in real changes in cultural responsiveness. Marotta notes that:

to adopt an intercultural mode of interpretation is to acknowledge that the other is not an end but a means with which to enlarge our understanding and knowledge of ourselves and others. The intercultural mode of understanding would also appreciate that understanding is never complete and final. (2009, 270)

The need for continued participatory musical experiences to enable evolving development of intercultural understanding was articulated by Clea.

Clea: Even… just being in the moment, immersing yourself within a culture rather than just… like the lectures here are wonderful about different cultures, but it's totally different actually teaching these kids, talking to the kids, there's a definite. We should definitely do it next year, it's very important because, yeah, you can have this many lectures about how cultural diversity is important, blah, blah, blah, but actually being there and you know, chatting, experiencing it yourself….

Luke: Totally different thing.

8 Conclusion

In discussing the now-integral ethnomusicological practice of developing knowledge about music through musical participation, Russell and Ingram summarize the many outcomes of musical participation (as simultaneously observed and experienced by ethnomusicological researchers) as including not only the acquisition of knowledge, but the advancement of social connection and the power to "unite diverse individuals in particular contexts of time and space" (2013, 1). Through participating musically with Sudanese Australian young people and community members, the SCM students' development of social connectedness appears to have set them on a pathway to cultural connectedness and understanding. Collaborative engagement in such intercultural practices enables members of the receiving society to increase their capacity to "participate in the emotional and aesthetic experiences of cultural strangers, and the resourcefulness with which to make appropriate behavioral adjustments to specific situations and to manage them effectively and creatively" (Kim 2015, 6), thus increasing their cultural competence.

The data presented in this chapter offer only the perspectives of the SCM students and represent only one aspect of a project which had multi-faceted outcomes. Participating in a spatially, physically, sonically and culturally varied community context provided pedagogical challenges for the students which meant that learning about flexibility, teamwork and "going with the flow" was equally important to them. The challenges entailed remind us that the dichotomy between cultures may be institutional and situational, as well as ethnocultural, and such forms of 'cultural dissonance' may be equally unsettling for students but also lead to their ultimate growth of self-knowledge and pedagogical flexibility. The project took place over a relatively short period of time, and therefore, could not be expected to result in a complete change of intercultural understanding or values. There was a level of essentialism that remained which, in following iterations of the project, could be addressed by additional levels of mandatory, guided reflection (Marx and Moss 2011). At the same time, there was a marked recognition on the part of some students that difference was not only cultural but also individual, and that there was a need for ongoing experiences and interactions of this kind to further their understandings.

Leh et al. emphasize the importance of developing intercultural competence in teacher education "because teachers are mediators and facilitators of their students' intercultural learning processes and must be not only familiar with factors that are essential in successful intercultural communication but they also have to be intercultural learners themselves" (2015, 7). The Bridging Musical Worlds project provided students with opportunities for: developing cultural understandings through meaningful interactions with people; understanding the lived experience of people from refugee backgrounds; understanding cultural mores and their relational and pedagogical implications; and understanding the need for cultural authenticity in repertoire or teaching/learning practices. In so doing, the project offered a vision of approaches that combine applied ethnomusicology and service learning in ways that will be mutually beneficial for teacher-education students and young members of culturally diverse communities in their continued evolution towards intercultural personhood.

Acknowledgements We wish to acknowledge the generosity of Mary Mamour in sharing her musical and cultural expertise with the SCM students, and the LD coordinators and members of the Sudanese Australian LD community for facilitating this project. Financial support was provided by a 2016 Sydney Conservatorium of Music Research Project Grant.

References

Australian Curriculum, Assessment and Reporting Authority (ACARA). (n.d.). Intercultural understanding. *The Australian Curriculum* [Online]. http://www.australiancurriculum.edu.au/generalcapabilities/intercultural-understanding/introduction/introduction. Accessed 20 Nov 2016.

Bartleet, B.-L., Bennett, D., Power, A., Marsh, K., Sunderland, N. (2014). Reconciliation and transformation through mutual learning: Outlining a framework for arts-based service learning with Indigenous communities in Australia. *International Journal of Education and the Arts, 15*(8) [Online]. http://www.ijea.org/v15n8/. Accessed 21 Nov 2016.

Bartleet, B.-L., Sunderland, N., & Carfoot, G. (2016). Enhancing intercultural engagement through service learning and music making with indigenous communities in Australia. *Research Studies in Music Education, 38*(2), 173–191.

Broeske-Danielsen, B. A. (2013). Community music activity in a refugee camp – Student music teachers' practicum experiences. *Music Education Research, 15*(3), 304–316.

Burnard, P., Mackinlay, E., & Powell, K. (2016). Introduction and overview. In P. Burnard, E. Mackinlay, & K. Powell (Eds.), *The Routledge international handbook of intercultural arts research* (pp. 1–9). New York: Routledge.

Burton, S. L., Westvall, M., & Karlsson, S. (2012). Stepping aside from myself: Intercultural perspectives on music teacher education. *Journal of Music Teacher Education, 23*(1), 92–105.

Campbell, P. S. (2010). Music alive! In the Yakima Valley. *International Journal of Community Music, 3*(2), 303–308. https://doi.org/10.1386/ijcm.3.2.303_7.

Carson, C., & Westvall, M. (2016). Intercultural approaches and "diversified normality" in music teacher education: Reflections from two angles. *Action, Criticism, and Theory for Music Education, 15*(3), 37–52. [Online]. act.maydaygroup.org/articles/CarsonWestvall15_3.pdf. Accessed 15 Jan 2018.

Cassity, E., & Gow, G. (2006). *Making up for lost time: Young African refugees in Western Sydney high schools.* Sydney: Centre for Cultural Research, University of Western Sydney.

Charmaz, K. (2014). *Constructing grounded theory* (2nd ed.). London: Sage.

Cockett, R. (2010). *Sudan: Darfur and the failure of an African state.* New Haven: Yale University Press.

Corbin, J., & Strauss, A. (2008). *Basics of qualitative research: Techniques and procedures for developing grounded theory* (3rd ed.). Thousand Oaks: Sage.

Deardorff, D. K. (2006). Identification and assessment of intercultural competence as a student outcome of internationalization. *Journal of Studies in International Education, 10*(3), 241–266.

Department of Immigration and Citizenship. (2011). *The people of Australia: Australia's multicultural policy.* Canberra: DIAC, Australian Government. [Online]. https://www.runnyme-detrust.org/uploads/events/people-of-australia-multicultural-policy-booklet.pdf. Accessed 13 Aug 2019.

Dieckmann, S. (2016). *Exploring musical acculturation: The musical lives of South Sudanese Australians, Filipino Australians and White Australians in Blacktown.* Unpublished doctoral thesis. University of Sydney, Australia [Online]. http://hdl.handle.net/2123/14956. Accessed 20 Nov 2016.

Dunbar-Hall, P. (2009). Ethnopedagogy: Culturally contextualised learning and teaching as an agent of change. *Action, Criticism, and Theory for Music Education 8*(2): 60–78 [Online]. http://act.maydaygroup.org/articles/Dunbar-Hall8_2.pdf. Accessed 23 Nov 2016.

Dunbar-Hall, P. (2012). Engaging with learning: Shaping pre-service music education students' understandings of pedagogy through international fieldwork. In I. Solomonides, A. Reid, & P. Petocz (Eds.), *Engaging with learning in higher education* (pp. 319–332). Faringdon: Libri Publishing.

Emmanuel, D. T. (2005). The effects of a music education immersion internship in a culturally diverse setting on the beliefs and attitudes of pre-service music teachers. *International Journal of Music Education, 23*(1), 49–62.

Green, L. (2008). *Music, informal learning and the school: A new classroom pedagogy.* Aldershot: Ashgate.

Hart, J. (2014). Children and forced migration. In E. Fiddian-Qasmiyeh, G. Loescher, K. Long, & N. Sigona (Eds.), *The Oxford handbook of refugee and forced migration studies* (pp. 383–393). Oxford: Oxford University Press.

Harwood, E., & Marsh, K. (2012). Children's ways of learning inside and outside the classroom. In G. E. McPherson & G. F. Welch (Eds.), *The Oxford handbook of music education* (pp. 322–340). New York: Oxford University Press.

Higgins, L. (2012). *Community music in theory and practice.* New York: Oxford University Press.

Ingram, C., & Mamour, M. (2016). Bulls, *Balabel*, Beyoncé: The musical aesthetics of South Sudanese Australians. Paper presented at the Musicological Society of Australia Annual Conference, University of Adelaide.

Jones, P. M. (2010). Developing social capital: A role for music education and community music in fostering civic engagement and intercultural understanding. *International Journal of Community Music, 3*(2), 291–302.

Joseph, D., & Southcott, J. (2009). 'Opening the doors to multiculturalism': Australian pre-service music teacher education students' understandings of cultural diversity. *Music Education Research, 11*(4), 457–472.

Karlsen, S. (2013). Immigrant students and the "homeland music": Meanings, negotiations and implications. *Research Studies in Music Education, 35*(2), 161–177.

Kim, Y. Y. (2015). Finding a "home" beyond culture: The emergence of intercultural personhood in the globalizing world. *International Journal of Intercultural Relations, 46*, 3–12.

Leh, J. M., Grau, M., & Guiseppe, J. A. (2015). Navigating the development of pre-service teachers' intercultural competence and understanding of diversity: The benefits of facilitating online intercultural exchange. *Journal for Multicultural Education, 9*(2), 98–110. https://doi.org/10.1108/JME-12-2014-0042.

LeRiche, M., & Arnold, M. (2012). *South Sudan: From revolution to Independence*. London: Hurst.

Marotta, V. (2009). Intercultural hermeneutics and the cross-cultural subject. *Journal of Intercultural Studies, 30*(3), 267–284.

Mars, B., Lawrence, P., & Levine, A. (2010). *Count on me. On Doo-Wops & Hooligans [CD]*. Los Angeles: Larrabee Recording Studios and Levcon Studios.

Marsh, K. (2005). Going behind the doors: The role of fieldwork in changing tertiary students' attitudes to world music education. In P. S. Campbell, J. Drummond, P. Dunbar-Hall, K. Howard, H. Schippers, & T. Wiggins (Eds.), *Cultural diversity in music education: Directions and challenges for the 21st century* (pp. 37–47). Brisbane: Australian Academic Press.

Marsh, K. (2012). "The beat will make you be courage": The role of a secondary school music program in supporting young refugees and newly arrived immigrants in Australia. *Research Studies in Music Education, 34*(2), 93–111.

Marsh, K. (2013). Music in the lives of refugee and newly arrived immigrant children in Sydney, Australia. In P. S. Campbell & T. Wiggins (Eds.), *The Oxford handbook of children's musical cultures* (pp. 492–509). New York: Oxford University Press.

Marsh, K. (2015). Music, social justice, and social inclusion: The role of collaborative music activities in supporting young refugees and newly arrived immigrants in Australia. In C. Benedict, P. Schmidt, G. Spruce, & P. Woodford (Eds.), *The Oxford handbook of social justice in music education* (pp. 173–189). New York: Oxford University Press.

Marsh, K. (2017). Creating bridges: Music, play and wellbeing in the lives of refugee and immigrant children and young people. *Music Education Research, 19*(1), 60–73. https://doi.org/10.1080/14613808.2016.1189525.

Marsh, K., & Dieckmann, S. (2016). Interculturality in the playground and playgroup: Music as shared space for young immigrant children and their mothers. In P. Burnard, E. Mackinlay, & K. Powell (Eds.), *The Routledge international handbook of intercultural arts research* (pp. 358–368). Abingdon: Routledge.

Marx, H., & Moss, D. M. (2011). Please mind the culture gap: Intercultural development during a teacher education study abroad program. *Journal of Teacher Education, 62*(1), 35–47.

O'Flynn, J. (2005). Re-appraising ideas of musicality in intercultural contexts of music education. *International Journal of Music Education, 23*(3), 191–203.

Oehrle, E. (1996). Intercultural education through music: Towards a culture of tolerance. *British Journal of Music Education, 13*, 95–100.

Refugee Council of Australia. (2016). *Key facts on the conflict in South Sudan* [Online]. http://www.refugeecouncil.org.au/getfacts/international/south-sudan/. Accessed 25 Nov 2016.

Robinson, K. (2005). Professional development in the diamond fields of South Africa: Musical and personal transformations. In P. S. Campbell, J. Drummond, P. Dunbar-Hall, K. Howard, H. Schippers, & T. Wiggins (Eds.), *Cultural diversity in music education: Directions and challenges for the 21st century* (pp. 171–179). Brisbane: Australian Academic Press.

Rowley, J., & Dunbar-Hall, P. (2013). Cultural diversity in music learning: Developing identity as a music teacher and learner. *Pacific-Asian Education, 25*(2), 41–50.

Russell, I., & Ingram, C. (2013). Introduction. In I. Russell, & C. Ingram (Eds.), *Taking part in music: Case studies in ethnomusicology* (pp. 1–13). Aberdeen: Aberdeen University Press and European Seminar in Ethnomusicology.

Sæther, E. (2013). The art of stepping outside comfort zones: Intercultural collaborative learning in the international GLOMUS camp. In H. Gaunt & H. Westerlund (Eds.), *Collaborative learning in higher music education: Why, what and how?* (pp. 37–48). London: Routledge.

The University of Sydney. (2016). *The University of Sydney 2016–20 strategic plan* [Online]. https://sydney.edu.au/dam/intranet/documents/strategy-and-planning/strategic-plan-2016-20.pdf. Accessed 20 Nov 2016.

Turino, T. (2008). *Music as social life: The politics of participation.* Chicago: University of Chicago Press.

UNHCR. (2016). *Global trends: Forced displacement in 2015.* United Nations High Commissioner for Refugees [Online]. http://www.unhcr.org/statistics/country/576408cd7/unhcr-global-trends-2015.html. Accessed 24 Nov 2016.

Westerlund, H., Partti, H., & Karlsen, S. (2015). Teaching as improvisational experience: Student music teachers' reflections on learning during an intercultural project. *Research Studies in Music Education, 37*(1), 55–75.

Westoby, P. (2009). *The sociality of refugee healing: In dialogue with Southern Sudanese refugees resettling in Australia.* Altona: Common Ground Publishing.

Wiggins, T. (2005). Cultivating shadows in the field?: Challenges for traditions in institutional contexts. In P. S. Campbell, J. Drummond, P. Dunbar-Hall, K. Howard, H. Schippers, & T. Wiggins (Eds.), *Cultural diversity in music education: Directions and challenges for the 21st century* (pp. 13–21). Brisbane: Australian Academic Press.

Permissions

All chapters in this book were first published by Springer; hereby published with permission under the Creative Commons Attribution License or equivalent. Every chapter published in this book has been scrutinized by our experts. Their significance has been extensively debated. The topics covered herein carry significant findings which will fuel the growth of the discipline. They may even be implemented as practical applications or may be referred to as a beginning point for another development.

The contributors of this book come from diverse backgrounds, making this book a truly international effort. This book will bring forth new frontiers with its revolutionizing research information and detailed analysis of the nascent developments around the world.

We would like to thank all the contributing authors for lending their expertise to make the book truly unique. They have played a crucial role in the development of this book. Without their invaluable contributions this book wouldn't have been possible. They have made vital efforts to compile up to date information on the varied aspects of this subject to make this book a valuable addition to the collection of many professionals and students.

This book was conceptualized with the vision of imparting up-to-date information and advanced data in this field. To ensure the same, a matchless editorial board was set up. Every individual on the board went through rigorous rounds of assessment to prove their worth. After which they invested a large part of their time researching and compiling the most relevant data for our readers.

The editorial board has been involved in producing this book since its inception. They have spent rigorous hours researching and exploring the diverse topics which have resulted in the successful publishing of this book. They have passed on their knowledge of decades through this book. To expedite this challenging task, the publisher supported the team at every step. A small team of assistant editors was also appointed to further simplify the editing procedure and attain best results for the readers.

Apart from the editorial board, the designing team has also invested a significant amount of their time in understanding the subject and creating the most relevant covers. They scrutinized every image to scout for the most suitable representation of the subject and create an appropriate cover for the book.

The publishing team has been an ardent support to the editorial, designing and production team. Their endless efforts to recruit the best for this project, has resulted in the accomplishment of this book. They are a veteran in the field of academics and their pool of knowledge is as vast as their experience in printing. Their expertise and guidance has proved useful at every step. Their uncompromising quality standards have made this book an exceptional effort. Their encouragement from time to time has been an inspiration for everyone.

The publisher and the editorial board hope that this book will prove to be a valuable piece of knowledge for researchers, students, practitioners and scholars across the globe.

List of Contributors

Eva Sæther
Malmö Academy of Music, Lund University, Malmö, Sweden

Amira Ehrlich
Faculty of Music Education, Levinsky College of Education, Tel Aviv, Israel

Belal Badarne
Department of Education, Sakhnin College for Teacher Education, Sakhnin, Israel

Danielle Shannon Treacy
Sibelius Academy, University of the Arts Helsinki, Helsinki, Finland

Patrick Schmidt
Don Wright Faculty of Music, Western University, London, ON, Canada

Joseph Abramo
Neag School of Education, University of Connecticut, Mansfield, CT, USA

Albi Odendaal
MASARA, North-West University, Potchefstroom, South Africa

Alexis A. Kallio and Heidi Westerlund
Sibelius Academy, University of the Arts Helsinki, Helsinki, Finland

Sapna Thapa
Early Childhood Teacher Education, University of Wisconsin-Stout, Menomonie, WI, USA

Brit Ågot Brøske
Music Education and Music Therapy Department, Norwegian Academy of Music, Oslo, Norway

Laura Miettinen
Sibelius Academy, University of the Arts Helsinki, Helsinki, Finland

Claudia Gluschankof
Faculty of Music Education, Levinsky College of Education, Tel Aviv, Israel

Lori-Anne Dolloff
Faculty of Music, University of Toronto, Toronto, ON, Canada.

Vilma Timonen
Sibelius Academy, University of the Arts Helsinki, Helsinki, Finland

Anna Houmann
Malmö Academy of Music, Lund University, Malmö, Sweden

Kathryn Marsh and Catherine Ingram
Sydney Conservatorium of Music, The University of Sydney, Sydney, Australia

Samantha Dieckmann
Faculty of Music, University of Oxford, Oxford, UK

Index

A
Aesthetic Learning, 104
Appreciative Inquiry, 36, 38, 40-41, 44, 52, 54-55, 132, 137, 146, 148
Arts Education, 35, 55, 71, 84, 86, 92
Audio Recordings, 42, 46, 90-91

B
Blanket Exercise, 160, 162

C
Caring Pedagogy, 102, 106, 111
Civic Learning, 104
Classroom Activities, 167, 172
Collaborative Learning, 8, 36, 100, 130, 147, 195
Cross-cultural Context, 106, 113
Cultural Background, 102
Cultural Boundaries, 179
Cultural Diversity, 5, 7, 16, 18, 20, 24, 26, 34-35, 74, 99, 103, 129, 133-134, 138, 140, 142-143, 145-146, 166, 178-181, 183, 189, 192, 194-196
Cultural Historical Activity, 74, 130
Cultural Humility, 149-150, 157-162
Culturally Responsive Teaching, 20, 32, 35, 113, 133, 147
Culture Bearers, 77

D
Data Analysis, 107, 139
Decision-making, 59-60, 88
Democratic Participation, 40

E
Educational Documents, 166-167
Educational Environment, 59, 62
Educational Settings, 59, 64, 152, 184

Ethical Reflexivity, 133
Ethnocentrism, 37-38, 40-41, 54, 105
Ethnomusicology, 83, 177-178, 186, 193, 195
Expansive Learning, 74, 82-83, 115-116, 118-119, 121-130

F
Forced Migration, 59, 194
Foundational Strategy, 101
Future Employment, 178, 181

G
Global Mobility, 133-134
Glocal Phenomenon, 1-2, 4, 15

H
Habitus Crises, 1, 4, 10, 14-16
Higher Education Institutions, 132, 145, 175
Human Dignity, 103
Human Rights, 19, 76, 83, 117, 164, 166, 168-169

I
Immigrant Children, 13, 15, 182, 195
Indigenous Communities, 153, 161, 193
Indigenous Issues, 149, 153
Indigenous Music, 150, 154-155, 159
Institutional Development, 163, 166, 170
Intercultural Collaboration, 163, 169
Intercultural Communication, 3-4, 35, 101-102, 105-106, 112, 193
Intercultural Competence, 1, 3, 9, 92-93, 95-97, 99, 101-103, 105, 112, 115, 122, 124, 127-129, 134, 147, 157, 161, 179, 181, 185, 193-195

Index

Intercultural Experience, 112, 146

Intercultural Sensitivity, 4, 101-107, 111, 113, 146

Interreligious Dialogue, 20-22, 34-35

K

Knowledge Building, 38, 135, 163

M

Majority World, 36-37, 39, 52, 54

Methodological Framework, 83, 132

Micropolitics, 70, 163, 165, 168, 170, 173, 175

Mono-culturalism, 111

Multicultural Social Action, 133

Multicultural Society, 3

Multiculturalism, 21, 67-68, 73, 75-76, 83, 98-100, 127, 133, 140, 148, 162, 194

Music Curriculum, 25, 29, 32, 136, 153

Music Education Programs, 32, 135, 187

Music Education Students, 31, 33-34, 88, 159, 177, 179, 182, 194

Music Teacher Education, 1-2, 4, 15-16, 20-23, 26, 73-74, 77, 81-83, 85-88, 158-161, 163-166, 169, 174, 177, 180-181, 193-194

Musical Experience, 191

O

Organizational Change, 83, 132, 135, 146-147

P

Pedagogical Implications, 186-187, 193

Peer Assessment, 8

Poor Minority Children, 102, 111

Pre-service Teachers, 23, 101-104, 106, 111-112, 130, 147, 159, 195

Professional Placement, 115-117, 120, 122, 124-125, 128

R

Radical Constructivism, 111

Refugee Camp, 115-119, 123, 125, 129-130, 193

S

Self-awareness, 96, 107

Self-reflection, 104, 160, 172

Service Learning, 160-161, 177-178, 185-186, 193

Social Justice, 54, 69, 71, 103, 133-134, 146-148, 195

Social Learning, 104, 146

Sustainable Development, 163, 165, 174

T

Teacher Educators, 21, 23, 26, 33-34, 37, 53-54, 56-58, 60-61, 63, 65-69, 73-75, 77-83, 126, 132-135, 137-145

Teacher Professionalism, 174

Theoretical Awareness, 2, 15

Trained Teachers, 101, 103, 106

Transformative Possibility, 91-92

V

Voluntary Migrants, 182

Printed in the USA
CPSIA information can be obtained
at www.ICGtesting.com
LVHW022132041023
760082LV00002B/27